Sand Dunes

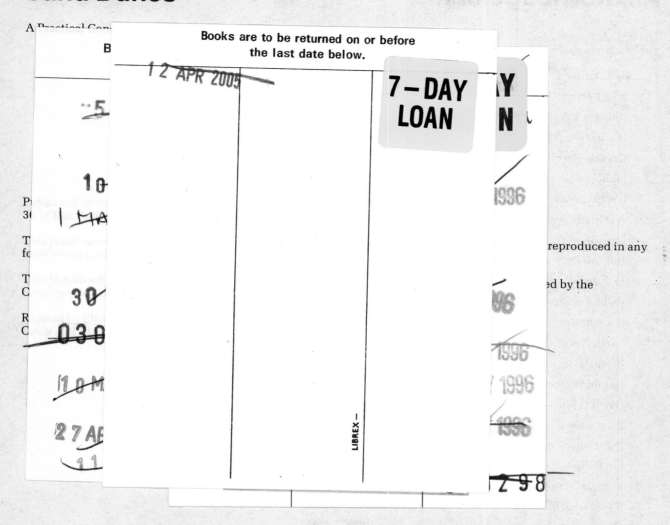

... reproduced in any

... ed by the

ISBN 0 9501643 6 4

Published July 1979
First Revision November 1986
Reprinted October 1991
Typeset by Katerprint Typesetting Services, Oxford

Printed by The Eastern Press Ltd., Reading, on 80g/m² recycled paper.

Acknowledgements

The British Trust for Conservation Volunteers acknowledges with thanks the help it has received in producing this publication from the following individuals:

R W Arthur

John Bacon

William T Band

Alistair Barclay

Graham Barrow

I R Bonner

L A Boorman

A D Bradshaw

John Breeds

Duncan Brown

Jo Burgon

Ralph Calvert

Bob Chestney

J Rees Cox

Peter Davis

Harold Dollman

David O Elias

Peter Evans

Pete Fordham

Ian Fullerton

Martyn Garbett

David Henshilwood

D G Hewett

John Houston

J C W Howden

Mike Hughes

D J Jefferies

Charles Johnson

Pete Johnson

Inigo Jones

Penny Jones

Dave Lewis

Archie Mathieson

J McCarthy

Frank Metson

R Mitchell

Martin Musgrave

David O'Connor

Bob Owen

Keith Payne

Brian Pickess

Eric Pithers

Jennifer Pizzey

Jeff Redgrave

Iorwerth Rees

W Ritchie

N A Robinson

Mike Stagg

Roland Tarr

F P Tindall

James P F Venner

Andrew Warren

David Wheeler

Barry Wilkinson

The other individuals with an interest in coastal conservation who were consulted

The staff and volunteers of the BTCV who have contributed their advice and experience

Contents

Introduction

This is a Handbook of sand dune management. It is intended to be used by conservation volunteers and all others interested in maintaining or improving valuable natural habitats through manual work.

Like many coastal habitats, sand dunes are extremely fragile, attuned to natural changes but not to those caused by man. Pollution, ill-planned development and overuse have already degraded great stretches of coastline and threaten to engulf others. Solutions, in many cases, must be legal and political and require integrated planning techniques which are beyond the scope of this Handbook. What *is* covered are problems which volunteer conservation groups can successfully attack, and the tools, organisation and methods which they can use on their tasks.

This Handbook first describes sand dune formation and the ecological and management principles of their conservation. It then goes into detail on why and how to protect and restore them and their wildlife. An understanding of dune ecology, accretion and erosion provides the key to sensitive handling of visitor problems which threaten to degrade even the most scenic and scientifically important dune systems. Reasons for stabilising dunes, appropriate strategies and methods of contouring, fencing and planting sand-trapping grasses and shrubs are given in detail. Access management and the siting and surfacing of pathways are described as a necessary part of dune protection. Further topics in vegetation management include control of sea buckthorn and other scrub as

well as management by grazing and mowing. Important aspects of animal management are treated briefly, including the protection of two rare and declining coastal species, the natterjack toad and the sand lizard.

Coastlands, particularly in Britain, have a diversity of physical form and of plant and animal life perhaps unequalled anywhere else. And despite the dangers which they now face, they remain among the areas least modified by man. How long this will hold true is open to doubt. What is certain is that conservation management is increasingly important. Volunteers can supply the necessary work force for many coastal protection tasks. And with luck they may even get a tan at the same time.

Throughout the text, points which it is desired to stress and lists of items of equipment etc are set out in a, b, c order. Sequential operations and procedures are given in 1, 2, 3 order. Scientific terms and words used in a technical sense are defined in the Glossary. References to written source material are incorporated in the text and give the author first, followed by publishing date. Full listings of these and other useful works are given in the Bibliography.

Measurements are given first in metric units, followed in brackets by the imperial equivalent approximated to the accuracy required. Occasionally a dimension, and more often a product specification, is given in one unit only, according to current manufacturers' listings.

1 A Look at Sand Dunes

Sand dunes can form anywhere that the essential requirements of a supply of dry sand and the wind to move it exist together. In Britain, these conditions are confined to the coast, but in other parts of the world they occur inland as well. The basic process that forms coastal sand dunes and desert sand dunes is similar, although the resulting dunes are different in shape, because of the way that coastal vegetation modifies the effect of the wind.

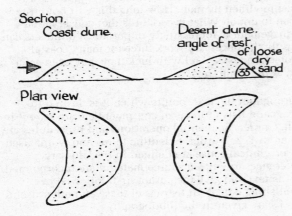

Once waves have built up a beach of sand on the coastline, of a height that is only reached by exceptional tides or storms, sand dunes may form. Formation is triggered by obstacles to the wind, such as tidal litter, shingle or vegetation, which slow the wind and cause deposition of sand. Of these, vegetation is the most important, as it is able to keep growing upwards through the accumulating sand. Other obstacles, once buried, cease to be of importance unless they are re-exposed. As will be detailed later, this pioneer vegetation is perfectly adapted to its role in sand trapping. It forms the crucial first stage which gives rise to the succession of communities that make up a sand dune system.

The youngest stages of this system, the foredunes, are not only the most susceptible to natural erosion from storms and high tides, but they are also the most attractive for recreation. Unfortunately, the foredune vegetation, which is so well adapted to coping with conditions of sand, drought and maritime exposure, is the least suited to withstand the effects of trampling. Most conservation work is thus concentrated on these vulnerable foredunes. Work may include protecting the dunes that still remain, and recreating denuded dunes by trapping wind-blown sand using fencing, brushwood and transplanted vegetation. As visitor pressure is usually the most important agent in the destruction of sand dunes, this factor must be tackled first by providing suitable access routes to the beach.

Other important sand dune work involves management of the fixed or back-dune vegetation, both to maintain particular communities of plants and animals, and to conserve individual species of importance.

The plant life of British dunes in general is extremely rich. Altogether more than 1,000 species of flowering plants and ferns may be found (Coastal Ecology Research Station, 1973). Many of these are introduced species which have been spread by man, often in the course of afforestation within the last century, or by birds. In addition to the vascular plants, several hundred species of lichens, bryophytes, fungi and algae occur in the dune systems.

The reason for this immense richness, in striking contrast to the relative simplicity of salt marsh flora, is the highly variable conditions within the dune environment. This creates a complex mosaic of habitats according to climate, substrate, water table, soil chemistry, exposure and other factors which are discussed further in the next section. This mosaic is further diversified by the plants themselves, particularly as they modify wind scour, protect the soil surface, increase its organic content and water-retaining capacity and form a sheltered platform for the colonisation of other species. Near the landward edge of the dunes, grazing may further modify the flora towards increasing diversity.

The invertebrate life of dunes and slacks is as diverse as the plant life. Common and conspicuous insects include grasshoppers, earwigs, and many species of beetles, butterflies and moths. Sand-burrowing hunting wasps and bees are abundant on open dunes, while several species of bumble-bee inhabit older dunes. Crane-flies hover in mating swarms in late spring; later in the year their leather-jacket grubs destroy many young shoots of marram grass. Large flies include the robber and horse flies. Spiders are notable, especially wolf and jumping spiders. In the pools and marshes of wet slacks, dragonflies, mayflies and caddis flies live out most of their lives as aquatic larvae before developing as free-flying adults, while pond skaters, water boatmen and whirligig beetles remain always in or on the water. The common banded snail (*Cepaea nemoralis*) and garden snail (*Helix aspersa*) are also frequently found.

Among the vertebrates, certain dune systems are notable for their colonies of natterjack toads and sand lizards, two species which are rare and declining in this country mainly due to loss of habitat (p94). Shore-nesting birds include terns on beaches and embryo dunes and shelduck in old rabbit burrows on fixed dunes. Hawks, owls and other birds of prey hunt the dunes and slacks while birds of passage such as fieldfares and redwings sometimes winter in vast flocks among extensive sea buckthorn thickets where they feed on the plentiful berries. On fixed dunes and dune heaths and grasslands, species such as skylark and meadow pipit are typical. The mammals include several species of voles and mice, and, more importantly for their effect on dune vegetation and therefore on stability, rabbits. Where man allows it, sheep and less frequently cattle and horses graze the dunes and dune grasslands, with effects which are discussed on page 88. Foxes are major predators of small mammals and shore-nesting birds, while, in Wales, polecats destroy many rabbits. Man himself, although seldom an inhabitant of dunes, exercises more influence than any other species through his use or misuse of this environment.

Sand dunes are not only fascinating places of study for the botanist or zoologist, but also for those interested in ecology, geomorphology, hydrology or the development of soils. This interest stems not only from the form of the dunes and the wildlife contained at any one time, but in the way the dune system changes and develops over time, changes which are more rapid than in any other type of landform. These changes may be induced by man or by natural causes, and vary from the slow development of a plant community, to the transformation of a foredune by an overnight storm. Development over the years can be seen in the successive dune ridges and slacks, and in historical changes including alteration of the coastline, and the covering of farmland and dwellings by the movement of sand. As will be seen in chapter 2, management decisions are not easy to make in a system which is inherently unstable.

Formation and Distribution of Dune Systems

Dunes form where there is an expanse of sand exposed at low tide, the surface of which dries in the sun and wind, so allowing sand to be blown by the wind. The shape and size of the dunes will depend on the volume of sand supply, the wind regime and the profile of the shore.

Volume of sand

The immediate sand supply is provided by the beach. Sand is moved from the lower part of the beach by wave action in calm weather, and where the sand dries out between tides, may be blown by the wind.

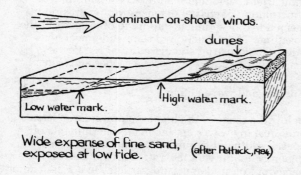

dominant on-shore winds.

dunes

High water mark.

Low water mark.

Wide expanse of fine sand, exposed at low tide. (after Pethick, 1984)

The most important part of the beach for supplying the dunes is the backshore, the zone above mean high water mark, which is only covered 2–3 days a month by exceptionally high tides or storms. Where dominant sand-moving winds are oblique to the shore, a long narrow backshore may provide as much sand as a shorter broader one (Ranwell and Boar, 1986).

Wind regime

Dunes on the west coast of Britain are formed by the dominant and prevailing on-shore south-westerly winds, and usually form as multiple-ridge systems, with the ridges at right angles to the prevailing wind. Examples of these large systems include Braunton Burrows in North Devon, Whiteford on the Gower Peninsula, Newborough Warren on Anglesey, and Formby and Ainsdale sand dunes, Merseyside.

On the east coast, the dominant dune-building easterlies, blowing over the beach, are balanced by the prevailing south-westerlies. The sand behind the main foredune stabilises rapidly, creating a narrow

dune system. These are characteristic of the Northumberland coast, for example at Druridge Bay, and the east coast of Scotland, notably in East Lothian.

Shoreline

Dunes cannot form where the beach backs on cliffs, but only where the shore rises gently. In some places the sand may be blown up over rock outcrops or scree, making 'climbing dunes', which are often irregular in form and may have an unusually steep angle of rest. Examples include Penhale, Cornwall, St. Cyrus and Eoligarry on the island of Barra, and at Sandwood Bay and Bettyhill in Sutherland. Where dunes form over adjacent ridges of plateaux they may reach over 91m (300') O.D., as at Druim Chuibhe, Strathnaver, Sutherland.

The biggest dune system in Britain is Culbin Sands, Morayshire, at 3,100 hectares (7,600 acres). Altogether there are six systems over 1,200 hectares (3,000 acres), twenty between 400 and 1,200 hectares (1,000–3,000 acres) and just over 100 between 40 and 400 hectares (100–1,000 acres), with many more smaller isolated sites (North Berwick Study Group, 1970). The Nature Conservancy Council considers about 15,000 hectares (36,000 acres) to be of outstanding scientific interest (Natural Environment Research Council, 1973).

According to their relationship to the shoreline, dune systems can be classified into two main categories, frontshore and hindshore systems (Ranwell, 1972,

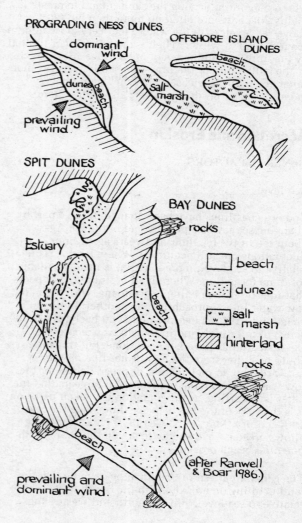

PROGRADING NESS DUNES.

dominant wind

OFFSHORE ISLAND DUNES

beach

dunes beach

salt marsh

prevailing wind

SPIT DUNES

BAY DUNES

rocks

Estuary

beach

□ beach

⋮ dunes

salt marsh

▨ hinterland

rocks

beach

prevailing and dominant wind.

(after Ranwell & Boar 1986.)

pp35–9). The frontshore systems project seawards, and are generally prograding ie developing farther along or into the open water. They are more characteristic of sheltered shores, including those where the prevailing and dominant winds are in opposition, as on the east coast of Britain. Features which form include offshore islands, spits and nesses.

Hindshore systems include bay dunes, hindshore dunes with slacks, and hindshore plains, also known as 'links', 'dune pastures' or, in north-west Scotland where they are characteristic, 'machairs'. Hindshore systems are progressively more terrestrial in position, although their point of origin is the shoreline itself.

Bay dunes are common on the indented coastline of north and west Scotland, where they often form a narrow strip at the head of the bay with some extension, where conditions allow, onto the land behind. Small bay systems on cliffed coasts are much influenced by the shelter of the surrounding land which greatly modifies winds, causing extensive variations in systems only a few miles apart.

Sand plains or machairs are an extreme type of hindshore system and are much like the fixed pastures of unenclosed hindshore dunes. Machairs are typical of the wet and windy northwest coast of Scotland, covering some 10% of the land area of the Uists for example. They develop under conditions of extreme exposure, where full Atlantic gales sweep the low island and offshore sandbanks free of any dunes which may form, driving the sand inland to create low plains. Machairs are often no more than 6m (20′) above sea level, with the water table very close to or at ground level in winter. Their growth is further limited by the universal influence of open-range sheep grazing or the cultivation of the lime-rich sandy soils. At their inner edge, calcareous sand overlies lime-poor moorland peat, producing a very diversified flora.

Accretion and Erosion

GENERAL FACTORS

Sea levels

Today's coastlines have been shaped in large part by changing sea levels since the end of the Ice Ages, about ten or twelve thousand years ago. Minor fluctuations are still occurring. Where land is rising relative to sea level, more material is made available for dune formation. Where land is sinking, it appears that intertidal steepening is occurring, with high and low water line approaching one another. In the 30 years up to 1911, a net loss of 19,000 hectares (47,000 acres) of intertidal land in Britain was recorded. Detailed studies have not been done, but this loss could be either from the high water line moving outwards due to reclamation or progradation, or the low water line moving landwards. It appears that the latter is occurring, as progradation has taken place on less than 7% of the English coastline since the late 19th century (May, in NCC, 1985). This steepening allows greater wave energy to act on the shore, with potential beach erosion.

The general pattern in Britain appears to be that the land is tilting on an axis, with the South East sinking relative to sea level, and the north and west rising.

Trends in sea levels are difficult to record, but past developments can sometimes be deduced from topographical features and stratigraphy. For example, dunes which are homogenous in cross-section suggest relatively rapid development in the past, while shingle horizons preserved in dunes (as opposed to existing basement shingles underlying homogenous dunes) indicate cycles of development and erosion during the dunes' history.

Sources of sediment

Supplies of sediment for the formation of sand and shingle banks and sand dunes may come from eroding land surfaces, the coastline itself or the sea bed mainly during high winds and rains. 'Young' rivers, or those flowing through existing dunes and beaches, bring down suspended sand and provide material for beach and dune growth. Most rivers in Britain are relatively 'mature' and transport finer materials which go towards the construction of mud banks. Eroding cliffs also supply beach and dune sediments, not always for deposition nearby. Where neither river nor cliff erosion seems responsible for a particular coastal feature, Ritchie (1972, p29) argues the strong probability of glacial origin, ie reworked clays, sands and gravels laid down by glaciers when sea levels were lower. Submarine glacial deposits seem to be the prime source of material, for example, for the banks and bars of the north Norfolk Coast.

The amount of sediment available is affected by changes elsewhere on the coastline. Urban and industrial development on the coast, and the construction of coastal defences to stop erosion may mean a loss of sediment supply to other parts of the coastline. The extraction of sand and gravel for building, industrial and agricultural use can also decrease the supply to nearby beaches and dunes.

Current and wave action

Below the range of the highest storm tides, currents and breaking waves are the main determinants of coastal sediment features. The effect of currents depends not only on their strength but also on the behaviour of mud and sand particles in a mass and on the formation of eddies which can locally increase current speed. The effects of breaking waves are rather more easily generalised. The diagram below shows how waves which approach a shoreline obliquely push material along the beach with the swash and pull it down with the backwash.

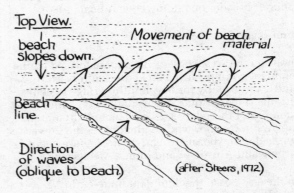

The overall direction of drift depends on the orientation of the beach relative to the prevailing winds. For example, drift is eastward along the Sussex Coast, due to the prevailing westerlies, but southward along the Suffolk coast, which receives the full force of northeasterly storms.

The interaction of storms and swells, 'destructive' and 'constructive' waves, is complex. Storm waves are 'destructive' in the sense that they break steeply and have a relatively powerful backwash, but they may in fact cause most beach accumulation by moving large stones and shingle far up the beach.

Wave action only rarely reaches the sand dunes backing the beach, but when it does it can be disastrous, biting away yards of foredune at a time. Any measures aimed at protecting dunes from the sea must be based on exceptional rather than typical wave conditions.

Wind action

Wind is the main agent of sand dune formation. A wind speed as low as 5 metres per second (about 16km/hr, 10mph) can lift sand grains from a bare surface and start them moving. However, the grains are not merely carried in the wind and deposited as wind speeds slow, but move along by a process called 'saltation', described below.

The rough surface of the sand grains on a beach slows the wind by surface drag, and creates a zone of still air immediately above the surface. This zone is $\frac{1}{30}$th of the average grain diameter of the sand, for example 0.03mm for 1mm diameter sand grains. When a wind of 5 metres a second or more blows across the surface, those grains which protrude above the zone of still air will roll or slide forward until they meet larger immobile grains. The impact flicks the smaller grain up into the air. The grain moves forward in the pattern shown below, ploughing back down into the sand surface, and exploding more grains into the air. This domino effect causes the beach downwind of the original grain to be alive with moving sand grains in a 'saltating cloud'.

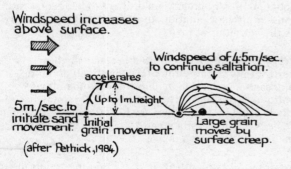

(after Pethick, 1984)

Larger sand grains, up to six times the diameter of the saltating grain, are jerked forward by the descending grains in a process called 'surface creep'. This causes sorting of the grains, the saltating grains moving further downwind than those moved by surface creep. Very fine grains remain in the zone of still air, and are only lifted by the action of vehicles or feet on the sand surface. These fine grains, once disturbed, may become suspended or blown away from the dunes, or they may collect on the top of the higher dunes.

The amount of sand transported depends on the cube of the wind velocity. For example, on a stormy day

with a wind velocity of 50km/hour, 0.5 tonne of sand may be moved per metre width of beach per hour (Pethick, 1984). An increase in wind speed by 16% to 58km/hour, will increase the amount of sand transported by 100%, to 1.0 tonne per metre width per hour. Sand movement is therefore very responsive to wind speed. The occasional very high wind will influence dune alignment and position more than steady prevailing winds, if these are different.

During saltation, there is a balance between energy losses and gains, according to the type of surface. Softer surfaces absorb more energy and result in less transport. A saltating cloud passing over a soft sandy surface will lose energy, causing a decrease in transport rate and increased deposition. An area of shingle or concrete will cause an increase in transport rate and the hard surface will be swept clean.

The effect of the foredune vegetation on the saltating cloud is dramatic. Firstly, the vegetation intercepts the descending saltating grains, and being a soft and springy surface, absorbs much of their energy. Secondly, a zone of still air is created very much greater than that on a sandy surface. This zone can be as high as 180mm (8") depending on the species and density of vegetation. As the saltating cloud reaches the vegetation saltation is greatly reduced, as few grains are propelled up out of the zone of still air. Saltation cannot be initiated within the vegetation, because of the zero wind velocity at the surface.

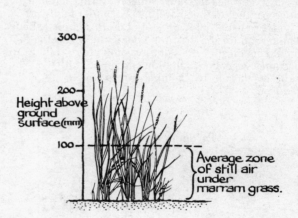

These two effects cause rapid deposition, which can range from 0.3m to 1m (1–3') per year. As will be described on page 70, the physiology of the dune grasses has to be able to cope with this inundation.

The overall height of a dune is determined partly by average wind speed in the area, and partly by the fact that surface speeds increase with the height of the dune. Eventually the dune becomes so high that accretion and erosion, even from a vegetated surface, balance out.

Most sand which blows on to a dune is deposited on the windward face (Trew, 1973), but on this side the wind speed and saltation effects are also greater. The result is that sand moves over the top and settles on the lee side. Deposition in the further lee zone is limited, as the sand load has already been dropped. As wind speeds again approach the ground, they carve down as far as the non-erodable damp sand (in the absence of vegetation), creating a slack. As shown below, the result is a steepening of the windward slope, and a flattening of the lee slope, so that the whole dune gradually 'rolls over', and advances in the direction of the dominant wind, sometimes by as much as 7m (22½') a year.

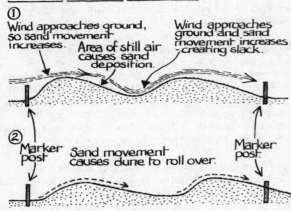

Movement of dunes to windward.

① Wind approaches ground, so sand movement increases. Area of still air causes sand deposition. Wind approaches ground and sand movement increases - creating slack.

② Marker Post. Sand movement causes dune to roll over. Marker Post.

SAND DUNE DYNAMICS

Dune system development

The youngest dune, nearest the beach, is usually the highest, and has the most coherent form, that of a ridge parallel to the shoreline. The older landward dunes are usually lower, and of more complex shapes. The reason for the first dune being the highest is that it collects most of the saltating sand grains, and as it becomes vegetated, saltation cannot be initiated. Thus supplies of sand to the inner dunes are greatly reduced.

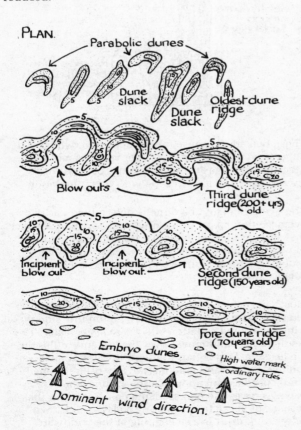

PLAN.

Parabolic dunes

Dune slack

Oldest dune ridge

Dune slack

Blow outs

Third dune ridge (200+ yrs) old

Incipient blow out

Incipient blow out

Second dune ridge (150 years old)

Fore dune ridge (70 years old)

Embryo dunes

High water mark - ordinary tides

Dominant wind direction.

The parallel formation is broken when trampling or other agents initiate erosion in the ridge, creating a blowout. Large quantities of sand are blown over to the lee slope, making a bulge which moves downwind. The sides remain vegetated, creating a U shape, until the 'arms' eventually break away leaving an isolated 'U shaped' or 'parabolic' dune. The oldest dunes are dominated by the orientation of the arms, which is related to the dominant wind direction.

Where sand supplies are available, a new ridge may form at the mouth of the blowout.

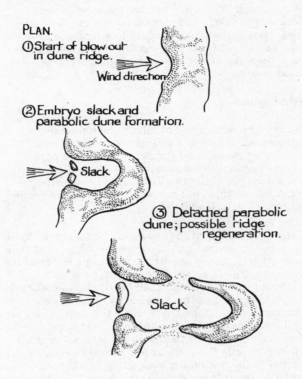

PLAN.

① Start of blow out in dune ridge.

Wind direction

② Embryo slack and parabolic dune formation.

Slack

③ Detached parabolic dune; possible ridge regeneration.

Slack

Prograding or eroding systems

The classic formation of a dune system, as described above, will vary greatly according to factors of wind, sand supply, orientation and local topography, as well as the activities of man.

Where sand supply is limited because the beach is narrow, any dunes which form are likely to erode unless the feeder zone is long, and winds blow oblique to the shore. Dunes in small bays may become stable at a low level, then erode and recycle. An open coast with an abundant sand supply is most likely to take the form shown above.

Where sand is plentiful, so that foredunes continue to grow rather than becoming stabilised in place at an early stage, one of two things may happen. Where the high-level backshore is broad and onshore winds are moderate, new foredunes may form to seaward of the first ones in a 'prograding' or 'fixed' system. Or, where the backshore is narrow and prevailing and dominant winds are onshore, the foredunes may grow to a certain height and then start to erode and move landward, forming an 'eroding' or 'plastic' system.

In prograding systems the seaward growth of dunes is limited by the height of storm tides which undercut them and form near-vertical seaward faces. The eroded sand may form offshore bars to supply material for renewed dune formation, provided there is no offshore dredging. Behind this seaward ridge, the dunes in a prograding system are often quite stable.

Where prevailing winds are directly onshore, as is the case on many west-coast sites, the highest dunes are usually some way inland where wind speeds are slightly reduced. Where prevailing winds are offshore, as at Strathbeg, Aberdeen and on the east coast generally, the highest dunes are likely to be the coast dunes themselves which grade directly into dune pastures.

An understanding of wind effects shows why a system such as Ynyslas Dunes (Dyfi NNR), Dyfed, is particularly vulnerable to visitor pressure. This system projects out into the mouth of the Dyfi estuary and is subject to both prevailing westerlies and storm easterlies. It is so narrow that strong winds from either direction coupled with high tides tend to disperse the dunes rather than build them up, although there is adequate offshore sand for their renewal after erosion.

Local instability

Any area of dry sand, whether vegetated or not, forms a potential instability zone. In many dune systems, local erosion followed by regeneration of new foredunes proceeds naturally in what Ritchie (1972) emphasises is a state of dynamic equilibrium. Factors influencing erosion include: the direction and strength of the prevailing and storm winds; the incidence of gales; the reach of the tides and their coincidence with strong winds; the removal of sand (eg by quarrying or by passive interference in natural beach drift from coastal protection devices); biotic factors such as grazing (especially by rabbits), fires, tree removal, wear and tear by people (which causes problems of wind funnel along paths and the death of sand-trapping and stabilising grasses); and structures which cause scour such as large concrete barriers or Second World War defences. As new embryo dunes build up, the sand supply to existing dunes is cut off and they become more subject to visitor damage. This has occurred for example at Gibraltar Point, Lincolnshire, bringing serious dune erosion problems to what had been a fairly stable system.

Erosion normally occurs as blowouts in the dune ridge. Blowout formation is extremely varied and depends on local winds and topography and on associated flat erosional surfaces where the blowout reaches the water table, buried organic horizons, layers of shingle or anything else which stops it deepening. Associated with blowouts are redepositional hillocks. These are normally amorphous or conical, at least in Scotland under variable wind conditions, and their location is related to the direction of the excavating wind. Where dune ridges lie in roughly parallel series, blowout sand may be deposited on the next ridge downwind.

Where blowouts develop in coastal dunes or where storm tides erode a dune ridge, new embryo dunes are established mainly through the rerooting of rhizome fragments from toppled clumps of marram (*Ammophila arenaria*). This is a sort of natural equivalent to the transplantation techniques discussed in the chapter, 'Vegetation Establishment'. This natural regeneration is prevented at places such as Holkham,

Norfolk, where the seaward dunes have been afforested and the marram shaded out, with serious consequences where the dunes act as a wall to protect low-lying land behind.

In large, deep dune systems such as Newborough Warren, natural erosion may be followed by renewed accretion in the blowout base. This cycling is inexact and the overall picture is very complex, since blowouts in different parts of the system may evolve at different rates, but it must be taken into account if management efforts are not to be wasted in a misguided attempt to fix the dunes. Changes are both geomorphological and vegetational. A typical cycle is shown schematically below (after Ranwell, 1960, p130).

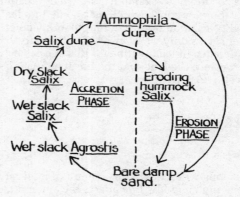

Machairs, although they appear at first glance to be relatively unchanging, do undergo a slow but continuous cycle of growth and erosion. Grass grows up through accumulating layers of blown sand until the ground level becomes too high and dry for the turf to repair itself after some minor damage such as rabbit burrowing. This opens up an erosion face which eats back through the machair, stripping it down to a wet sand level which eventually revegetates. The whole cycle may take many centuries on most machairs but it can be much quicker in exposed cliff-top machairs such as at Sangomore, Sutherland. Machairs which suffer from visitor pressure are vulnerable mainly in the revegetation phase, when trampling of the 'naturally' eroded surface prevents the re-establishment of a closed turf (Countryside Commission for Scotland, 1977).

Ecology

CLIMATE

The sea has a major influence on the climate of adjacent coasts. In particular, it reduces annual temperature fluctuations so that many frost-tender plants, especially annuals and biennials, can survive where inland conditions are too harsh. Because of this, small climatic changes which appear to have little effect inland may produce striking changes in the coastal flora. Perring (1974) notes that many of the recent changes (mostly declines) in our seashore flora are probably attributable to climatic trends rather than to human impact, even though the latter is often assumed to be the cause.

Although the less hardy strandline and dune annuals are summer-growing and winter-dormant, many dune plants grow during the cooler, moister months and pass the hot summer as seed, germinating the next autumn for winter growth. Such species are especially typical of open dunes and areas of short turf subject to moderate grazing or trampling. Because of this, these areas are most sensitive to pressure during the summer, just when it is likely to be greatest.

Coastal microclimate is important mainly as it affects plant zonation (p13). In general, there is a simple climatic gradient from more to less marine in a direction away from the sea (whether inland or, in the case of cliffs, upward). Dunes and slacks are exceptional in that they show many microclimatic variations depending on factors such as aspect, slope, wind effects and the water table. This helps produce a complex mosaic pattern of vegetation and prevents simple zonation. An example is shown by creeping willow (*Salix repens*), which may come into leaf a fortnight earlier on hot dry dunes than in cooler, damper slacks only yards away. This is equivalent to the difference in leafing time for this species between south-western England and the north of Scotland (Ranwell, 1970, p10).

WATER

Tides

As previously described, the amount of tidal range between high and low tide affects the amount of beach exposed, and thus the sand supply to dunes. This tidal range is determined by the depth of the ocean, and the coastal configuration, thus shallow estuarine waters experience the greatest tidal range. The highest tides, called spring tides, occur when the sun and moon are in line with the earth, creating the greatest gravitational pull. This occurs every $29\frac{1}{2}$ days. The combination of the highest spring tides, at the spring and autumn equinoxes, and storm winds or low atmospheric pressure can produce conditions in which damage and erosion is likely to occur to frontal dunes. If damage occurs to sand-trap or access control fencing on the backshore, any repair that is possible should be done as soon as possible. Otherwise the next high tide is likely to completely destroy the damaged fencing.

Tides have a vital role to play in the formation of embryo dunes, by depositing tidal litter. This may be brought to shore in large amounts when autumn and winter storms tear seaweed from intertidal and subtidal surfaces. The litter is piled up on the backshore by the high tides of the spring equinox, and helps trap sand and provide nutrients for colonising strandline plants.

Soil water

Soil water is of great importance on beaches and dunes. Pure shingle holds very little water between the stones, but with even a slight admixture of sand the 'field capacity' (ability to retain water) increases. This may mean the difference between unvegetated shingle and areas where plants find a roothold. With a 'mulch' of surface shingle or of organic material the field capacity rises further, making it much easier for plants to germinate and survive (Fuller, 1975).

In dune systems, the soil water level is the main determinant of the pattern of plant cover. Ranwell (1972) divides dune habitats into four categories based on this factor:

a Semiaquatic, with the water table never more than 500m ($1\frac{1}{2}'$) below the soil surface. Autumn-spring floods and frequent water-logging make this habitat favourable to aquatic and marsh plants such as shoreweed (*Littorella uniflora*), amphibious bistort (*Polygonum amphibium*) and common water crowfoot (*Ranunculus aquatilis*).

b Wet slack, with the water table never more than 1m (3') below the surface. Moisture is always adequate. Bryophytes (mosses and liverworts) are common and the flora is characterised by species with intermediate water requirements, with few grasses.

c Dry slack, with the water table between 1–2m (3–6') below the surface at all seasons. In this habitat shallower-rooted species are uninfluenced by the water table but deeper-rooted plants can benefit from it in drought. Plants with deep tap-roots and grasses are especially abundant and lichens may be locally abundant where there is rabbit grazing.

d Dune, with the water table never nearer than 2m (6') from the surface. Most plant growth is independent of ground water and dependent on seasonal rainfall. Plants with low water requirements are common and vegetative cover tends to stay open.

Minor slack habitats include wet flushes, man-made pools and turf or peat cuttings, low hummocks, mole and ant hills and rabbit-disturbed ground. In wet slacks, banded communities often develop at slightly different levels according to the local water table and the intensity of wind erosion at the time of formation. In dry slacks, water relations are less important and community boundaries are most often determined by biological factors such as beetle attack or rabbit burrowing.

Many dune systems face a lowering of their water tables, due to the extraction of ground water for public use. This can mean the end of damp slack communities which may have developed over many years – perhaps up to a century. In Britain, manipulation of dune water regimes for conservation purposes has been limited to the digging of breeding pools for natterjack toads (p94), but in the Netherlands there have been a number of experiments in damp slack creation and maintenance. Boorman (1977) summarises the main conclusions:

a Ground water lost to extraction can be replaced by infiltration. The infiltration water should be as mineral-poor as possible (especially in nitrogen and phosphorus) and it should be cleaned of fine sediments, otherwise it is likely to enrich dune soils with a resultant decrease in floristic diversity. Average water levels should be kept as constant as possible but with regular fluctuations in each year. Vegetation should be mown regularly in autumn and the cuttings removed to help keep the habitat mineral-poor.

b If the water table cannot be restored to its original level, damp slacks can be created by excavation or by allowing blowouts to develop naturally. The use of controlled blowouts has several advantages. The wind excavates the sand automatically to the correct depth (the ground water level). Fluctuations in this level produce local erosion and redeposition which increases natural microrelief and habitat diversity. Blowouts develop over a considerable period so that habitats of different ages result. Blowouts also increase the diversity of adjoining dry areas due to the juxtaposition of stable and unstable habitats.

c   Where natural blowouts are unlikely to develop or where instability cannot be tolerated, dune slacks can be excavated by hand or machine. For botanical diversity, most of the surface should be between the average summer groundwater level and a level 700–800mm (27–31″) above the winter water level. Slopes should be very gentle (between 1:30 and 1:80) in the area up to 250mm (10″) above winter water level. Areas higher than this should have steeper slopes (1:3 to 1:5). A number of small, irregular slacks is better than a few large ones, since isolation tends to produce diversity. In a large slack, isolation can be achieved by creating low dune ridges within the slack.

Beach and dune soils tend to hold increasing amounts of moisture as they mature through the gradual buildup of humus and more extensive plant cover. But even in well-vegetated backdune communities, seedlings are very dependent on rainfall since the top inch or so of soil quickly heats up and dries out in hot weather. This poses great problems on mobile dunes and can severely limit the success of artificial seeding programmes unless mulching is included in the treatment.

SOILS

Dune soils are based on sand blown inshore. Their chemical makeup depends on the material from which the sand is derived. At the extremes are the 'white' sands of mainly shell origin and the 'yellow' sands formed almost entirely of quartz grains more or less coloured by iron salts. White sands are characteristic of the rocky coasts of the west of Britain, since these provide good shellfish habitats. Shell sands can build up into steeper dunes than quartz sands, having a maximum angle of rest of about 42° as compared to 25° (Ritchie, 1972, p22). With a good growth of marram (*Ammophila arenaria*) the slope can be held at over 45° whatever the sand type (Nature Conservancy, 1969), although this may not be advisable from a management viewpoint.

On dunes, salts are quickly washed out of the soil. The situation is one of general mineral deficiency except on shell sands which are highly calcareous in origin and where calcium levels may remain high. Yellow sands are mineral deficient to begin with, and intermixed sands, which occur in every grade, tend to become deficient quite early in their development.

The nutritional impact of salt spray is clearly visible at the strandline and foredunes or where, as on the Isles of Scilly, low cliffs of acid soil develop an acid heath vegetation except in the spray zone where a narrow band of grassland predominates.

Beach soils may also be salty, but it is the lack of humus rather than salinity which causes real problems. At first the only organic matter consists of sea drift, mainly seaweeds thrown up by storm tides. Once plants establish themselves, their dead remains help build up the soil's organic content. In places favoured by terns or other socially ground-nesting birds, their excrement, waste food and dead chicks provide the nutrients for a more luxuriant vegetation.

Beaches and dunes are low in productivity. This is true even where the soil is calcareous, since base-rich soils are not necessarily nutrient rich, and nutrients essential for plant growth are easily leached out of dune soils. Nutrient poverty in dunes favours a great diversity of plant species since it restricts the growth of coarse, tall plants and allows many smaller species to flourish.

The general low level of nutrients in dune soils does not, on the whole, affect management. But it does seem that calcareous dune vegetation is rather more resistant to trampling than that of acid dunes. In some cases it may help to mulch and fertilise dune soils to raise nutrient levels and improve water retention and texture (p79). This process occurs naturally as the soil ages, although the buildup of organic material tends to be restricted to the soil litter layer, below which leaching continues. Where old dunes weather, the nutrient-rich surface breaks down and is mixed with the subsurface sand to counteract, locally, the progression towards more impoverished conditions.

One important side-effect of artificially fertilising dune soils is that it may lead to the dominance of those plant species which can best respond to higher nutrient levels, so that the diversity of species decreases. In addition, local nutrient variations, which are important for species and habitat diversity, are evened out by any overall increase in soil fertility (Boorman, 1977, pp171–2).

Nutrients which leach from the dunes tend to collect in the intervening slacks. Where the slack soil is well aerated, plants can make use of the nutrients but where waterlogging occurs, peat builds up and acid bog vegetation takes over. If the dune then erodes to dry slack level, you may find a mixed situation in which shallow-rooted plants of acid soil grow side by side with deep-rooted plants tapping the more base-rich soil below (Ranwell, 1972, p162).

SUCCESSION

Ecological succession is the process by which plant communities tend to create conditions which eventually allow new species to invade. The dynamic nature of a sand dune system means that many if not all the stages of the succession can be seen at any one time, and changes can be seen to take place in only a few years.

Succession on dunes is mainly the result of the buildup of soil humus under increasingly sheltered conditions, combined with leaching of nutrients. Dune succession has such important effects on dune physiography, and on management, that it is worth describing in some detail.

Dune succession may be initiated by strandline plants which trap small amounts of sand during the growing season.

Strandline plants may include sea rocket (*Cakile maritima*), common orache (*Atriplex patula*) and prickly saltwort (*Salsola kali*). But such tiny dunelets are usually overswept and destroyed by winter storms. The formation of dunes which are relatively long lived and capable of growth and extension depends on the invasion of the strandline flora by one of the perennial grasses capable of trapping wind-blown sand and of growing vigorously through it.

Sand couchgrass (*Elymus farctus* syn. *Agropyron junceiforme*) usually initiates foredunes or 'embryo' dunes. It is well fitted for its pioneer role because it withstands short immersions in salt water and can thus grow within reach of high spring tides. Sea sandwort (*Honkenya peploides*) is often associated and sometimes produces miniature dunes by itself.

Sand couch dunes tend to remain low and flat-topped. Once the sand is raised above the reach of even the highest tides, marram grass (*Ammophila arenaria*) usually invades and becomes the most important dune-forming species. Its dunes tend to be high and dome-shaped. Where sand couch is absent, marram may form the foredunes as well as main dune ridges. Where marram is absent, as in some of the sandy bays of the west coast of Ireland, sand couch continues to dominate and the dunes remain low.

Sea lyme grass (*Leymus arenarius* syn. *Elymus arenarius*), the third British dune-building species, is important in the North. All three species may be used in dune stabilisation programmes, although marram is most versatile and usually most common. These plants are described further on page 69.

Once marram or, more rarely, sea lyme grass initiates main dune formation, other species begin to colonise the loose dry sand between grass clumps. The community remains open, however, and as the grasses do little to fix the sand surface the dune remains unstable if exposed to strong winds. The dunes are known as 'yellow' or 'white' dunes, from the colour of the unvegetated areas of sand. Typical species of these mobile dunes include sand sedge (*Carex arenaria*), ragwort (*Senecio jacobaea*), hawkweed (*Hieracium umbellatum*), creeping thistle (*Cirsium arvense*), sand fescue (*Festuca rubra* var *arenaria*), sea holly (*Eryngium maritimum*) and sea bindweed (*Calystegia soldanella*).

Where new dunes form in front of an existing dune, it becomes less subject to wind erosion. At this stage sand-fixing as opposed to sand-trapping plants invade and cover the surface in a vegetative mat which resists further disruption by the wind. Mosses and lichens raise the humus content of the soil and create a carpet through which sand is unable to escape. It is the *Cladonia* lichens which give fixed dunes their characteristic grey appearance, and the name of 'grey' dunes. Sand sedge often replaces marram as the dominant species, since marram loses its vigour and degenerates once it is cut off from fresh supplies of blown sand. Sand sedge may grow thickly enough to form a loose turf, accompanied by such species as sand fescue, wild thyme (*Thymus serpyllum*) and

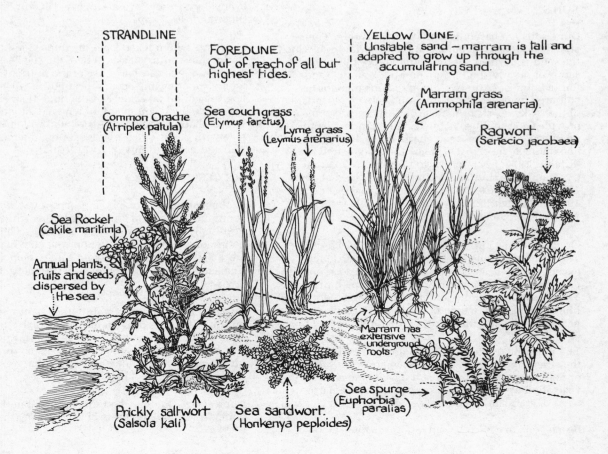

STRANDLINE

FOREDUNE
Out of reach of all but highest tides.

YELLOW DUNE.
Unstable sand – marram is tall and adapted to grow up through the accumulating sand.

Common Orache (Atriplex patula)

Sea couch grass. (Elymus farctus)

Lyme grass (Leymus arenarius)

Marram grass (Ammophila arenaria).

Ragwort (Senecio jacobaea)

Sea Rocket (Cakile maritima)

Annual plants, fruits and seeds dispersed by the sea.

Marram has extensive underground roots.

Prickly saltwort (Salsola kali)

Sea sandwort (Honkenya peploides)

Sea spurge (Euphorbia paralias)

birdsfoot trefoil (*Lotus corniculatus*). In the very wet climate of the west of Ireland, where the main dune-builders are often absent, any creeping plant which roots at the nodes can fix sand on a limited scale to help form a sand plain. Under these conditions, creeping buttercup (*Ranunculus repens*), creeping thistle and silverweed (*Potentilla anserina*) are among the most prevalent sand binders.

Additional plants then colonise, depending largely on the dune's soil chemistry. Sand comprised mainly of sea-shell fragments and other calcareous material tends to result in a species-rich grassland, similar to that on chalk or limestone. Species may include restharrow (*Ononis repens*) and viper's bugloss (*Echium vulgare*), with marsh helleborine (*Epipactis palustris*), wintergreen (*Pyrola rotundifolia*) and creeping willow (*Salix repens*) in the damper dune slacks.

In contrast, sand dunes made of silica sand, or very old dunes where the lime has been leached from the surface, result in acidic conditions, with heather (*Calluna vulgaris*) often dominant.

Where dunes are fairly stable, ranker grasses and eventually scrub species may seed in, shading out much of the interesting low-growing vegetation. Some of the invading scrub species, notably sea buckthorn (*Hippophae rhamnoides*), are capable of fixing nitrogen in their roots so that they leave a much-enriched soil if they are later cut down. This means that nitrogen-demanding plants such as nettle (*Urtica*

dioica) and elder (*Sambucus nigra*) may spring up in the clearings instead of the earlier more diverse dune communities.

At the landward edge of the dunes, succession is determined as much by management practices as by changes in soil composition. Where grazing predominates, dune grassland may persist. Where the soil is very acid, dune heath develops, often dominated by heather. Orchids are an interesting feature of backdune areas. Scrub or woodland is typical where the climate is not too wet and where grazing does not prevent the establishment of seedlings. The effects of wind and salt spray may remain noticeable, especially on trees which may show extreme wind pruning.

This picture of dune succession may be affected at any time by the renewal of erosion and the exposure of bare sand. On some dune systems, cyclic alternations of erosion and accretion may effectively prevent unbroken succession for a very long time (p11).

The presence of slacks between dune ridges further complicates matters since in these areas succession is determined largely by whether or not the soil remains waterlogged and develops increasing acidity. If it does, then rushes (*Juncus* spp) and bog-moss (*Sphagnum* spp) are liable to dominate and acid bog conditions will result. Where the water table is lower and the soil remains at least seasonally aerated, shrubs such as creeping willow are likely to seed in, often

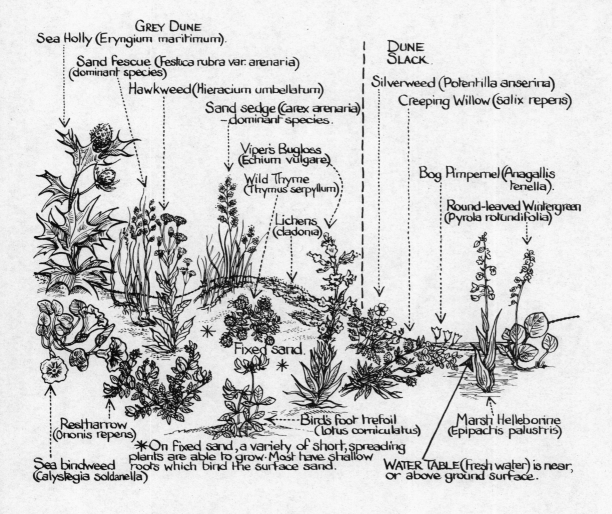

GREY DUNE
Sea Holly (*Eryngium maritimum*).
Sand Fescue (*Festuca rubra var. arenaria*) (dominant species)
Hawkweed (*Hieracium umbellatum*)
Sand sedge (*Carex arenaria*) – dominant species.
Viper's Bugloss (*Echium vulgare*)
Wild Thyme (*Thymus serpyllum*)
Lichens (cladonia)
Fixed sand.
Restharrow (*Ononis repens*)
Sea bindweed (*Calystegia soldanella*)
Bird's foot trefoil (*Lotus corniculatus*)
✳On fixed sand, a variety of short, spreading plants are able to grow. Most have shallow roots which bind the surface sand.

DUNE SLACK.
Silverweed (*Potentilla anserina*)
Creeping Willow (*Salix repens*)
Bog Pimpernel (*Anagallis tenella*).
Round-leaved Wintergreen (*Pyrola rotundifolia*)
Marsh Helleborine (*Epipactis palustris*)
WATER TABLE (fresh water) is near, or above ground surface.

spreading to surrounding dunes where they grow up through moderate amounts of blown sand.

At the early stage in the development of vegetation on the foredunes, animal species are not noticeably abundant, though butterflies, hoverflies and moths may be seen feeding on the nectar of flowers. Spiders and insects are the dominant animal species, and many are highly mobile and roam over large areas. Characteristic species include the sandwasp (*Ammophila*) which prey on caterpillars with which to stock their 'larder', a hole dug in the sand. Grasshoppers may be heard chirping in the tall marram grass, with shield bugs on the open sandy south facing slopes. Away from the foredunes, the number of species increases greatly. Dragonflies and damselflies may be found in the damp slacks, and earwigs live in the leaf litter of the mature dunes. Beetles are abundant, including the 'click' beetles, which can be found in June and July on the mature dunes. The 'click' is the sound made as they fling themselves in the air as a protective device to escape from predators. Sometimes dunes are subject to plagues of insects which have migrated or been blown over large stretches of water.

Although dunes are too open and unstable to provide food, shelter or nest sites for many birds, in the summer months skylarks, meadow pipits, linnets and stonechats may be abundant. Likewise, mammals are restricted by the lack of cover, although the soft sandy soils and short turf are suited to rabbits. Although they can cause damage by burrowing, their grazing is an important factor in maintaining the short turf and consequent diversity of plant species. Their populations vary from year to year and place to place according to the mortality from myxomatosis, the disease introduced in 1954 to control their population. Where rabbits exist, predators such as foxes, weasels and stoats may be attracted onto the dunes.

In wooded dunes, grey or red squirrels may be resident, with voles, woodmice, house mice and common shrews where there is suitable cover. The soils are mostly too thin and dry for earthworms, so moles are not abundant.

Sand dunes are nationally important sites for reptiles, notably sand lizards and natterjack toads, for which special management may be required. These species are described on page 94.

2 Management Planning

Many stretches of Britain's coasts retain much scientific, scenic and recreational interest. This is obvious when compared, for example, with some of the grossly over-used coastlands of southern Europe, as Steers (1970) points out. Yet threats to the coasts of this country, as others, are bafflingly diverse, so that while protection is achieved on some fronts, deterioration accelerates on others.

Unlike hard rocky shores, sand dunes and salt marshes contain a large hinterland which is inherently coastal, and found nowhere else. These are fragile areas, built up over thousands of years, and containing their own unique assemblage of topography, soils, plants and animals, influenced by local climate and water table. This fragility means that apparently small changes induced by man or natural causes can have a great effect on this coastal environment. The ease with which it can be manipulated has resulted in sand dunes being affected by many different factors over the years. These are detailed below.

Threats and Opportunities

Afforestation

Of the total area of about 56,000 hectares (138,000 acres) of sand dune in Great Britain, it is estimated that about 4,048 hectares (10,000 acres) were planted in Britain from 1922 to 1952. These conifer plantations have many effects. Firstly, the shelter effect may extend in their lee over a distance equivalent to up to 25 times their height (Ranwell and Boar, 1986). Such shelter can allow the spread of scrub and trees which would be scorched in unprotected areas. Mature conifers of 25–30 years old provide a prolific seed source, seeding into slacks within the plantations as well as the open areas beyond. Trees lower the water table by their transpiration of soil water. Within the plantations, any remaining ground cover is shaded out, and the decaying needles acidify the soil, possibly destroying any seed bank of native dune species contained within it. When felled, there is little dormant vegetation in the way of seeds or rhizomes to cover the bare ground, so leaving it open to erosion. Measures to clear the forest and restore the nutrient-poor duneland vegetation can be expensive, as all tree stumps must be removed to prevent them rotting and enriching the nitrogen status of the soil.

There may also be a dilemma where the plantations have themselves developed a few interesting dependent plant or animal species, or where the trees are an accepted part of the local scenery, which people enjoy. Many dune forests were planted to reduce sand-blow inland, and this also may be seen as a possible threat if clearance is done.

Grazing

Grazing by rabbits, sheep and cattle has over the centuries been an important influence in the creation and maintenance of short-sward dune turf. In the past, it is likely that grazing was kept at sustainable levels by the knowledge of local people, and by the absence of machinery, fertilisers, wire fencing, piped water supplies and cheap winter feed. These modern changes permit over-grazing, often only for the benefit of short-term gain. In the past, rabbit populations were also managed by being enclosed in warrens, and by culling. This is in contrast to the greatly fluctuating rabbit populations in the decades since the introduction of myxomatosis.

Close grazing by sheep reduces the sand trapping ability of the dune grasses. Trampling and over-grazing leads to destruction of the sward and erosion of the thin soils and underlying sand. The areas where stock habitually rest become badly eroded.

Lack of grazing can be equally damaging as it allows rough grasses and scrub to invade. Experimental work has been done in recent years to investigate various grazing regimes and techniques suitable for managing sand dune reserves. Grazing is further discussed in the chapter on Vegetation Management.

Cultivation

The extent of cultivation is most serious in the shallow lee slopes of dunes in Scotland, called the machair. Cultivation is traditional, but recent use of fertiliser in place of seaweed has meant a loss of organic matter in these light and fragile soils. Elsewhere, cultivation is done on the landward margins of dune systems, which are mostly long altered from their natural state.

Housing

Housing and caravan development on sand dunes brings a host of problems. As well as the actual loss of sand dune area, there is increased recreational pressure on the remainder, both in total numbers and in out-of-season use. Associated development of roads and services means disturbance of the topography, soils, vegetation, natural drainage and water table. Plant species are introduced from gardens and garden rubbish, and the existence of homes in an unstable environment means increased pressure to undertake coastal defences, which in the long term disturb the natural cycle of coastal erosion and deposition (see p19).

Industry

This brings many of the problems described above, with the added risk of major pollution, alteration of water table and the necessity for large-scale interference with natural processes to allow industry to function in an unstable environment. Fortunately, in Britain most sand dune areas are now protected against further housing or industrial development.

Military use

Emergency need, the perception of dunes as 'waste' land, and their coastal location has meant they have been heavily used by the military over many years. Some areas were just used in wartime, and have since been returned to public use. In some, such as Braunton Burrows, military use continues alongside management for nature conservation and public access. In others, particularly where airfields have been constructed, the military use is retained to the exclusion of others. Much military use involves large and heavy machinery which can greatly alter the dune habitat. Long-abandoned debris can still cause problems for dune managers by damaging mowing machinery and causing localised wind erosion. Military roads, now in public use, have resulted in the layout of access being haphazard rather than planned, and exacerbating management problems. Airstrips involve a major alteration to the topography and vegetation of a large area of duneland.

Recreation

This is possibly the most serious current threat to sand dunes, and the one most often tackled by conservation authorities and volunteers. The problems mainly arise from increased trampling destroying the dune vegetation, particularly on the foredunes, and the associated problems of car-parking, vandalism, camping, increased fire-risk, and direct damage to dune wildlife. Erosion is a natural process of dune systems, but that caused by public pressure greatly accelerates blowout formation in precisely those dunes where it can be tolerated least.

Examples are plentiful of sites where dune erosion requires public access control and stabilisation work. They range from intensively used nature reserves such as Ynyslas Dunes in Dyfed, Studland Heath in Dorset and Oxwich on the Gower Peninsula, where the damage is to important natural or semi-natural communities of plants and animals, to developed holiday areas such as Camber Sands, East Sussex, where damage to dunes is less significant than that caused by sand blow on poorly sited houses just back of the dunes. Each situation demands a different response, from severe access restrictions on the one hand to virtual remodelling of the dunes and their vegetation on the other.

An important concept in coastal management is that of 'zonal use' (McCarthy, 1970, p17). Fragile ecosystems such as dunes may be graded according to environmental qualities with associated appropriate usage levels. This suggests encouraging intensive recreation in areas which are already severely modified, such as Camber, which can be managed specifically for this, while prohibiting it as much as possible in relatively natural dune systems such as Ainsdale Sand Dunes, Merseyside. Large systems may be able to tolerate multiple-use zoning in space or time. For example, dunes which are beginning to erode can be temporarily fenced to let them recover while pressure is diverted to either side. Pony trekkers can be restricted to specially designed tracks, as at Oxwich, and 'nests' can be created to attract picnickers away from sensitive foredunes, as has been done at Gullane and elsewhere on the East Lothian coast. Access routes can be controlled across back-dune pastures, especially if these are used for golf courses, and car park spaces can be designed to limit peak-period use. Large systems, such as Studland, which already have high recreational use but which retain much wildlife interest, can be devoted to education along with recreation and conservation. Small, remote dune systems with climatically distinctive communities, as at Invernaver, Sutherland, are best left completely undeveloped for recreation if possible.

To successfully zone activities or intensities of use, one must know the 'carrying capacity' of an area. This can be defined as the level of use 'just before the point where the species least resistant to trampling is degraded beyond its capacity to recover' (Trew, 1973, p43). Carrying capacity is difficult to evaluate for dunes and is likely to vary according to local climate and exposure and the pattern of visitor use, but experience at one site on the west coast of Scotland (McCarthy, 1970, p16) suggests that vegetation cover, even in the rear dunes, is significantly damaged where a single track or footpath is used by more than two or three thousand people during the summer season. Dr William Band reports similar findings for established machair vegetation at Achmelvich, Sutherland. At Gibraltar Point, Lincolnshire, 7,500 people passing over the yellow dunes in a summer (Trew, 1973, p44) and 3,500–4,500 over the grey dunes (Schofield, 1967, p110) caused local exposure of soil and sand. Even where, as on the latter site, the dunes are little subject to wind erosion the habitat destruction can be considerable, especially for the invertebrate fauna which is often more severely affected than the dune plants themselves. Within dune systems, short turf areas are much more resistant to trampling than are dune heaths, which are in turn more resistant than the open marram or sea lyme dunes. But, according to Boorman and Fuller (1977), people tend to prefer these grassy areas in inverse ratio to their ability to withstand pressure. At Ynyslas NNR, pedestrian counters on the site have recorded a **daily** passage of 3,500 people during periods of July and August. Here, clearly, artificial path surfacing is essential to prevent serious erosion and habitat damage.

Golf courses

The light sandy soils, undulating terrain and coastal location have made sand dunes a favoured location for golf courses, and nearly every sand dune system has its quota. Indeed, the word 'links', a Scottish word for undulating sandy ground near the coast has become synonymous with golf courses. This recreational use may be seen as a mixed blessing. The restricted access means that trampling damage and erosion is controlled, and the management of roughs and fairways prevent scrub encroachment. The greens and fairways are largely altered by fertilising and re-seeding, but many of the roughs maintain a valuable duneland vegetation. It is ironic that some nature reserves are struggling with the problems of maintaining a short sward turf, whilst adjacent golf courses have no shortage of resources for this type of management.

A problem noted in Ranwell and Board (ITE, 1986) is that the siting of greens, tees and fairways near to the shore can restrict the options for coast management, for example by forcing protection of areas which are naturally eroding. On the other hand, the influential voice of the golfing fraternity can be the catalyst for action by local authorities and other agencies, for example to restore and replant eroded dunes where the sand is blowing onto adjacent greens. As in all situations where many agencies are involved in managing different sections of an integrated habitat, it is vital that there are good relations and co-operation between the various parties. In a recent example, a golf course management unwittingly destroyed a sand lizard colony by spraying a herbicide and replanting the site with introduced shrubs. However, it later co-operated with volunteers to try and recreate the habitat by transplanting turves of duneland vegetation back onto the site (see p96).

Wave erosion

Soft coasts are amongst the most naturally unstable environments in the world, and are constantly changing. In recent years, parts of the Merseyside sand dune system have eroded up to 9m (30′) in a single overnight storm, while parts of Studland dunes in Dorset are accreting at the rate of 3m (10′) every year. These changes are not of course a new phenomenon, but have been happening for thousands of years. What is new, and is increasing every year, is the length of coastline protected against erosion by groynes and sea walls, erected mostly to protect areas of housing and industrial development. This is reducing the capacity of the coast to erode and deposit, so that material which would previously have been eroded from one place and then washed up to replenish another is 'locked up' behind sea defences. Dredging offshore for sand and other sand winning operations have further decreased the natural 'bank' of sediments.

Thus not only has the area of sand dunes reduced from its extent say a century ago, but its capacity to restore and replenish itself has been lessened. This is an ever-decreasing cycle, as sand dunes themselves are the best form of coastal defence, being a wide natural buffer zone against flooding that has its own system of self-repair from revegetation. Thus loss means a greater need for man-made defences.

This all adds up to a great dilemma for sand dune managers, as in the natural state, erosion by the sea would be accepted as a process which keeps the whole system developing and changing. By stopping erosion and the formation of blowouts one is trying to fossilise a system which needs to be dynamic. On the other hand, the actual area of sand dune is so precious, and under threat from other factors, that it is difficult to stand by and not take action. The situation can resolve itself however, when sea erosion proves too powerful for any wave barriers which can be built. The recent publication by the Institute of Terrestrial Ecology (Ranwell and Boar, 1986), is aimed at giving guidance to engineers on the formation of dunes and their role in coastal defence. It advocates small-scale activities such as revegetating, access control fencing and so on as being more appropriate than massive engineering solutions.

SAND AND SHINGLE BEACHES

Beaches are often tempting sources of sand and gravel for local construction projects. Yet sand and gravel 'winning' almost always severely damages not only the beach itself but the higher land or dunes which back it. Quarrying of beach material lowers its level, allowing storm tides and waves to surge against the land behind. Dunes and soft coasts erode rapidly. Even relatively stable hard-rock coasts can be reactivated in this way, especially where beach material is taken from areas where natural replenishment is slow or absent. Steers (1969, p28) points out that in Scotland serious erosion is seldom a natural condition but is almost always the result of indiscriminate mining of beaches.

Where mining takes place not on the beach itself but on the land behind, restitution is often possible

although prohibition is better. In East Lothian the council has required that operators cut away and roll up turf from the area to be mined, for reuse later, that they grade the excavated surface to resist wind erosion and that they replace the turf on the graded surface. This does nothing, of course, to preserve any particularly interesting plants which may grow in the quarried area. In the Shetlands, for example, entire populations of the oyster plant (*Mertensia maritima*) have been destroyed by mining.

A positive side of gravel winning is seen at Snettisham, Norfolk, where extensive shingle deposits were mined behind a narrow shoreline strand. Quarrying ceased when the great flood of 1953 overwhelmed this defence. Since then the Royal Society for the Protection of Birds has acquired the flooded pits and turned the area into an important freshwater wildfowl reserve.

Many beaches and dunes were used for military training during the Second World War, with effects which persisted for many years. Braunton Burrows National Nature Reserve, Devon, required extensive dune rehabilitation for this reason as well as because of increasing public pressure. The central part of the Burrows is still a military training area, but these days the MoD co-operates closely with the Nature Conservancy Council to minimise damage. Other legacies of the war are concrete anti-tank blocks and other beach defences. In places such as Gullane Dunes, East Lothian, these initiated severe local wind erosion before being removed. Simply burying them in place did no good because it further disrupted the beach and prevented the growth of vegetation where the tops lay just below the sand. At one stage, almost all the beaches in east Scotland had such defences. On the Suffolk coast they are still numerous, and range from metal 'impalers' to slowly disintegrating concrete pill-boxes. In some cases, it may be best to leave the major installations intact or to mound them over and provide interpretive signs so that their historical interest is not lost. Elsewhere destruction and removal is the only answer.

Pollution is particularly visible on recreational beaches and abatement efforts are often concentrated there even though adjacent sections of coastline may suffer just as much. In places, raw sewage is still pumped from poorly sited outfalls, causing widespread pollution for instance on the Glamorgan coast (Vale of Glamorgan Borough Council et al, 1975, p16). Oil is the chief pollutant, drifting in from spills to settle on beaches in sheets or tarry lumps. The actual damage caused by oil is probably more significant offshore, where it may cause disastrous bird kills (see page 97 for coping with oiled birds), and on intertidal flats where it suffocates and poisons invertebrates when it settles to the bottom. But aesthetically it is beached oil which is most objectionable. An important side effect of strandline pollution, especially from oil, is that it tends to shift public pressure away from beaches to the sensitive foredunes, increasing the likelihood of serious erosion.

Once ashore, oil can be removed by burning, absorption into a wicking material such as straw, covering with powder, mechanical collection or dispersal by detergents. All of these are labour intensive and may require specially adapted equipment. For this reason and because oil removal (especially by detergents) may cause more damage than the oil itself, Warren Spring Laboratory (1972) recommends that oil be left in place in mud flats and salt marshes. On recreational beaches, lumps of oil can be drawn into rows by hand or preferably by tractor-drawn horticultural rakes, where it can be loaded into lorries for removal. Where the oil is in a film it is necessary to use detergent, but damage to the beach may be extensive so that only small sections should be cleaned for bathing and recreation. Elsewhere notices should be posted to warn the public of the pollution. Shingle beaches are particularly difficult to clean, and since to a great extent they are slowly self-cleaning due to wave action it is almost always best not to attempt to remove the oil.

Litter is a type of pollution which is more subject to abatement by volunteers. Not much can be done about rubbish dumped at sea, of course, other than to attempt to educate captains of ships using local ports, as is being done on the Glamorgan Heritage Coast (Vale of Glamorgan Borough Council et al, 1975, p16). Litter has its virtues: on the strandline it may help sand to accumulate by providing obstacles, and it has even been used to fill blowouts prior to reshaping of the sand surface. But in general it is best to keep litter under control. Many countryside managers feel that an area clear of litter encourages people to take their litter home, while an area which is badly littered acts as a magnet for yet more litter. Wardens and volunteers should, if possible, pick it up routinely rather than wait for the occasional litter drive which only has a temporary effect. Bins, if provided, must be emptied frequently so that they do not become overfull. Otherwise the wind just scatters the contents. Bins in exposed locations should have heavy, waterproof and wind-resistant lids. Where disposable bags are used, they often need to be fenced or clad against gulls or foxes which can rip them open.

Where litter drives are necessary, they are best done just before and again part-way through the holiday season, eg around Easter and in July. This way, you clear away the worst of the mess left by winter storms and keep the accumulation under control. Post-season drives do little good since the autumn gales are likely to bring in fresh supplies from the sea or elsewhere on the coast.

Litter drives, whatever their amenity effect, are a good way to involve local people, especially children, in practical conservation. Initially, it may be best to go through schools or scout groups for recruits, but in the long run a corps of willing workers who can be called on when necessary will get more accomplished. Children often work better if they have an incentive. Pay them by the sackful, or at least give them something at the end of the season. Try a sponsored drive: you might even make a profit!

Vegetated shingle beaches are easily disturbed by trampling. Although people avoid walking on shingle when possible, they may have to cross it to reach the sea. Hewett (1973, p53) describes the impact of people on the vegetation of Chesil Beach, Dorset. Where there is easy access, there is little vegetation. Where access is restricted to a few distinct trackways, these stand out clearly as bare strips in the general mat of plant life. Where the beach is closed to the public, the vegetation is well developed, especially where it is manured by birds flying over the bank to reach the sanctuary of the Swannery.

Unvegetated beaches are relatively immune to direct recreational damage. But they do suffer from the increasing complexity of conflicting demands such as swimming, skin diving, spear fishing, boating and sand yachting. One solution is to zone beaches either in space or in time so that all interests may be catered for. This does not mean, of course, that all sites should admit jetties, hamburger stands, portaloos and amusement arcades. As public pressure increases, wardening becomes more vital. On nature reserves and heritage coasts where wardens are already hard pressed, volunteers can perform an important service during busier times of year. Newborough Warren, Ainsdale Sand Dunes and Winterton Dunes are among the National Nature Reserves where volunteer wardens are used. Besides general policing, volunteer wardens can mount the sort of intensive seasonal watch necessary, for example, for the protection of terns on many of their shoreline nesting sites. Local volunteers can often get the conservation message across to visitors as effectively as professional wardens, provided they are suitably trained in the art of gentle persuasion.

Management Problems and Principles

'To manage' means to direct or to control. So, while it may be perfectly valid to choose a policy of strict non-intervention on a particular site, this would hardly qualify as management in the sense used here. Conservation management means interference, either to produce desired changes or to prevent others which may be undesirable. Management may require massive alterations to a site, with or without continuous or long-term follow-up, or it may consist of no more than fencing, screening, signposting or policing to protect the site from further interference. In every case, the aims, requirements and likely effects of the programme must be evaluated before it is begun.

'Conservation management' means as many things to people as does conservation itself. A list of possible aims may help land managers and volunteer workers evaluate their own views.

Aims include:

a   To limit human impact in a natural area.

b   To maintain geomorphological interest. This is of primary importance on many coastal nature reserves, eg Ynyslas, Dyfed.

c   To affect ecological succession in order to preserve or increase a site's scientific interest. In this case management may accelerate, maintain or retard the rate of succession depending on the perceived effects of succession on wildlife.

d   To save species endangered on a local, national or global level, by providing for their habitat requirements, or, further, by creating sanctuaries for their protection.

e   To create, protect or maintain 'unofficial nature reserves' which act as supply areas for official reserves without which the latter may lose certain species which cannot be maintained by the official reserves alone.

'Linear reserves', eg roadside verges, hedgerows, shelterbelts, streams and ditches, are particularly important and may act as vital links between sanctuaries.

f   To serve people, usually by protecting a resource 'for the use of the most people for the longest period of time'. Amenity, recreation and resource utilisation may be accepted as legitimate in this view, although each use may be valued differently by different interests.

On the coast, perhaps more than anywhere else, land managers must seek to reconcile the demands of recreation and amenity with those of nature conservation. The goal is to combine these uses in a balance which is appropriate to the individual site. With careful planning and clearly stated priorities, such a balance can usually be achieved.

SITE SURVEY AND ANALYSIS

On the coast, geophysical, biotic and human factors interact with great complexity. Separating these factors, and assessing which ones can or should be controlled by management, requires ecological and historical surveys of trends and patterns of site development. Such work is beyond the scope of conservation volunteers although they can help with certain aspects such as mapping and vegetation studies. Ritchie (1972) shows the value of the geomorphological approach for sand dune systems. Boorman (1977, pp176–80) describes a variety of dune survey approaches and gives references for those who want details.

Surveys ideally should include the following:

a   Vegetation survey and map. This is usually the best single index of environmental conditions and pinpoints areas of deterioration or evident imbalance.

b   Geomorphological survey. This should relate the management site to the larger physiographic system so that management problems can be put in the context of overall physical dynamics of the coastal area.

c   Large-scale gridded topographical survey of the site. This forms a reference document against which all management work can be noted, to avoid ambiguity in carrying out work and to provide a baseline against which progress can be measured.

Aerial reconnaissance is almost essential when dealing with large systems and intertidal areas. Air photo surveys should be repeated at regular intervals if possible. Their frequency will depend on the speed of change of site features and the importance of monitoring processes of erosion and deposition in each case.

d   Historical research, to discover as much as possible about past changes in site topography and use. Without this it is difficult to estimate the degree to which today's changes are an extension of past trends or are due to new factors. Old maps and local records may be useful along with interviews with long-time residents who know the area well.

e   Current use survey. Depending on the importance of various types of use, this might include such things as visitor questionnaires, monitoring of footpath traffic and assessment of grazing and other agricultural pressures.

IS MANAGEMENT REQUIRED?

Once preliminary analysis and site surveys have been made, the following questions should be asked to clarify management requirements:

a   Is there a need for direct habitat management? This means, most often, control of ecological succession and diversification of existing habitats. Which plant species are dominant? Should they be controlled? Or are additional plantings needed? If so, which species would best adapt to the site without becoming too invasive? Coastal habitats can usually be left to themselves, but certain invasive species such as sea buckthorn (Hippophae rhamnoides) and other scrub species on dunes, may threaten to choke out certain localised plant communities or radically alter successional development. The decision whether or not to control invasive species depends on the scale of the problem, the significance of the threatened community and whether or not the species involved is native to the site.

Certain rare and declining species, particularly animals such as little terns, sand lizards and natterjack toads, may require specific habitat protection or improvement, eg of nesting or spawning sites, for their survival. Because these species are now limited to a very few sites in Britain and cannot readily colonise or adapt to new ones, measures to protect them even at the expense of other species are justified. In other cases it is usually more worthwhile to provide general habitat diversity than to attempt to cater for particular species.

b   Is there a need to manage human uses of the site? What can be done to counteract damaging development in the vicinity? What is the carrying capacity for desired uses?

Human misuse of coastal habitats almost always provides the main cause of their deterioration. Access facilities should be planned as carefully as possible before their installation, since damage afterwards may be hard to correct. Cars and caravans should be strictly regulated or excluded from dune systems. Foot and horse traffic may be harder to limit but it can often be regulated and its impact minimised by suitable fencing and trackway development, as explained in the chapter, 'Access Management'. It is almost impossible to prevent boats from landing on offshore islands and bars which may be important bird nesting and roosting sites. The best approach here is personal persuasion and information.

c   Does the area surrounding the site need management as well? Many threats to coastal habitats come from industrial, recreational, agricultural or housing developments outside the immediate vicinity. A site may lose much of its wildlife interest if surrounding land is improperly developed. Pollution and alteration of the surrounding environment are often manageable but in many cases only through political and legal procedures outside the scope of this Handbook.

d Is management needed to protect existing site uses or surrounding developments, which cannot themselves readily be changed? Even where dune erosion, for example, is naturally caused it may be necessary to stabilise the dunes to protect housing or roads. This interference with the natural dynamics of the dune environment should only be considered as a last resort.

e Does the site have management priority over others? Does it really need interference or can it go its own way for some time without losing value? Given the limited resources available for any management work, are there other sites more in need of immediate attention? On coastal sites it is especially important to distinguish natural from man-caused or accelerated disturbances, and where possible to limit management to the latter.

f Can less be attempted than is tempting? The sensitivity of some habitats to interference means that there may be a danger of trying too much too soon, with unexpected and unwanted repercussions. This is especially the case with coastal installations which affect patterns of sedimentation or wind deposition. On wild, remote sites such as some of the beaches of northwest Scotland, almost any management, no matter how discrete, may seem an intrusion which is worse than the problem it attempts to correct. Management work should be phased, if possible, so that it can be checked early before making a commitment to the entire programme and so that unavoidable damage is localised and minimised. If a programme requires completion in order to be successful, it should be started only when there is certainty of carrying it through.

g How long will improvements due to the work remain? Will they wear off and conditions be the same or possibly worse as a result? Put another way, will the site require continued surveillance and management? If so, this must be included as part of the work programme.

This is especially important to consider where management is aimed at rehabilitating overused sites, especially dunes which remain subject to renewed erosion if access exceeds carrying capacity. Carrying capacity of foredunes, especially, cannot be increased by stabilisation work alone but is only restored to the natural level. If public pressure returns to prework levels, additional stabilisation will prove necessary.

CHOOSING A METHOD

If management work is judged necessary, each available work method should be evaluated by asking if it will:

a Achieve the desired results

b Minimise disturbance to wildlife due to habitat destruction. Coastal soils are particularly fragile and management must be carried out so as to minimise the inevitable disruption.

c Minimise disturbance to wildlife due to interference at crucial times, eg flowering or nesting seasons

d Involve risk to humans, non-target wildlife or agricultural crops and livestock

e Risk damage to equipment or physical installations on site

f Risk damage to other people's property

g Require legal permission from government authorities or landowners. Often a tactful, low-key approach to the people concerned will clear up any misunderstandings which might otherwise cause problems

h Be possible given available labour

i Be possible given available funds for capital and operating costs

j Be possible given site topography and problems of access

On coastal sites, management is seldom once-and-for-all. Areas must be fenced and planted in rotation, paths must be realigned and duckboards lifted and so on. It is usually most sensible, and cheapest in the long run, to choose techniques which require a continuing but low-level management input rather than to attempt more permanent but expensive and inflexible measures.

PROBLEMS OF ANIMAL MANAGEMENT

Expert knowledge is essential for the management of any species, plant or animal, but for most invertebrates and many of the higher animals this knowledge is as yet unavailable or scattered. Even the concept of 'habitat', by which botanists define a site in terms of distinct areas characterised by dominant and associated species, is difficult to apply to animals. Nevertheless, the obvious richness of coastal habitats for animals, especially invertebrates, means that more study is imperative so that animals can be more fully accounted for in management programmes.

'Take care of the plants and the animals will look after themselves'. This approach is at present the best rule where the aim is general wildlife protection. The creation and maintenance of floristic diversity is usually the key to animal conservation since all animal food webs are based on plants and because the greater the variety of plant life the better the chance of providing the needed habitat for most animals. Certain species of animals, limited to known specialised habitats, can be provided for as a conscious management aim where their declining status demands it. On coastal sites the natterjack toad, sand lizard and some shore-nesting birds come within this category. Measures to encourage these species are outlined later in the chapter on Dune Wildlife.

INTRODUCTIONS

New species of plants or animals may be introduced to a site for several reasons: to propagate species under threat elsewhere, to add diversity and interest to a site, to attract other species not yet present on a site, or to stabilise an unbalanced ecosystem, by bringing in predators for example. On the coast, there is a further reason for plant introductions. This is to help stabilise eroding soils or to trap mud, silt or sand to raise the soil level. The question of whether or not introductions are justifiable in any particular case is complex. The following safeguards are basic to ensure that harmful introductions can be avoided and all introductions are properly recorded:

a   Draw up a list of species considered acceptable for introduction to the site. Indicate in which management areas within the site introduction is acceptable or unacceptable

b   Having consulted the landowner, consult and invite the participation of the local county naturalists' trust, the Biological Records Centre and the Nature Conservancy Council in any large-scale introductions or those involving rare species

c   Notify either the local county naturalists' trust or the Biological Records Centre of all introductions. In this way future scientific study of the area can take introduced species into account

Principles of Dune Stabilisation

Unstable dune surfaces are subject to erosion and provide a source of sand which may blow and smother adjacent areas. Stabilisation may be needed to:

a   Prevent the loss or deterioration of valuable natural habitat

b   Maintain dune ridges which act as coastal protection for low-lying hinterland

c   Protect backdunes development of agricultural or recreational dune grasslands

d   Allow maintained or increased levels of public use (but see 'General principles' point d, below)

e   Allow the afforestation of backdunes and stabilised dune ridges

GENERAL PRINCIPLES

a   Be sure that instability is occurring on a scale and with effects which are destructive enough to warrant stabilisation.

b   Where instability is due to natural factors unaffected by public or grazing pressure, it is often impractical and even undesirable to correct it unless valuable hinterland is threatened.

c   Measures designed to protect pioneer strandline and foredune communities differ from those aimed at restoring stable backdune or dune grassland conditions. The choice of stabilisation strategy also depends on whether the dune system as a whole is eroding, accreting or stable, and on local wind and water regimes, access problems etc. Examples are given under 'Strategies', below and on page 53.

d   Dune restoration and stabilisation does little to increase the carrying capacity of the system. For this, you need to establish plants which resist trampling better than those which occur naturally. In most cases, erosion starts again if public or grazing pressure returns to the levels which prevailed prior to stabilisation.

Along access routes, carrying capacity can be increased by suitably sited and designed trackways. See the chapter on Access Management.

e   Fencing is usually necessary to keep people and grazing animals off the dunes while stabilisation is in progress. This focuses pressure on the dunes just outside the fence line. Choose boundaries to the work area where adjacent erosion will not cause problems, or be prepared to expand the area as fresh erosion occurs at the boundaries.

On heavily used sites, rotational management may be necessary. Areas can be fenced and restored or 'rested' while adjacent areas are subjected to increased pressure. Fences can then be shifted to re-open the restored areas and enclose the previously open areas before these erode too badly.

f   Allow time for dune plants to establish themselves and to spread. Maintain protection for at least this period even where biotic pressures are low. Although turf may form within a few months of sowing and fertilising, it may take several years for the vegetation to reach optimum density. Experience at Oxwich National Nature Reserve, Gower, suggests that revegetated dunes achieve their greatest diversity only after at least a decade of protection.

g   Review dune restoration programmes each autumn, where seasonal public pressure is heavy, so that you can plan autumn and winter maintenance according to the situation at hand, within an overall long-term strategy.

METHODS

There are three ways of stabilising dunes: trapping sand, preventing sand blow and developing erosion-resistant landforms. These methods are rarely mutually exclusive. Usually, two or even all three must be used, concurrently or consecutively, in a complete stabilisation programme. In particular, it is seldom worth trying to create erosion-resistant landforms unless the other methods are also applied.

a   Sand may be trapped by the use of solid or porous barriers or by vegetation. Solid barriers seldom work well against wind-blown sand because they often cause scour.

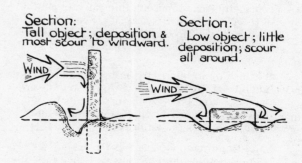

Section:
Tall object; deposition & most scour to windward.

Section:
Low object; little deposition; scour all around.

They may however be useful in preventing wave erosion or in trapping water-borne sediments. Porous barriers (such as fences, p39) and vegetation (p69) allow the wind to pass through but slow it so that it drops some of its load of sand.

Sections:

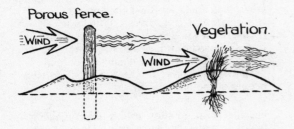

b   Start trapping or fixing wind-blown sand as near as possible to the source, ie at the strandline or the windward edge of a blowout, and work downwind. Otherwise, newly planted areas may be buried in drifting sand from untreated areas upwind.

This sequence may vary in detail when you build up a new dune ridge (p41) or where you need to rebuild a large blowout and do not want to cut off the sand supply to the back of the blowout until it is well filled with sand.

c   Leave natural and relatively permanent slacks unfenced and unplanted. These wind-scour-areas are unlikely either to supply much sand or to receive significant buildup.

d   Choose sand-trapping measures according to the amount of blown sand. If this is relatively small, plant or sow sand-trapping grasses (or in some cases shrubs) and encourage them as necessary with fertilisers (p79) and protective fencing. If more than about 1m (3′) of sand comes into the system each year, all vegetation is likely to be smothered and fences are required instead. Fencing and thatching (p.81) are also useful to supplement planting. Where there is insufficient blown sand to support sand-trapping grasses, the best approach is to sow meadow grasses (p78) and to fertilise and bind the sand surface (p84) as necessary.

e   Normally the best way to stabilise an area of sand blow is to plant marram (*Ammophila arenaria*) or one of the other sand-trapping grasses. Planting alone may be insufficient and may cause problems of secondary erosion unless combined with contouring. This is especially true of marram dunes which tend to develop a steep windward face. Seedlings or offsets may fail to survive unless protected by fencing.

It is also important to try and plant marram on a broad front, if possible covering the whole area in one season. Piecemeal work results in uneven dune growth which gives rise to new, unforeseen erosion patterns.

f   Sand-trapping plants, especially the grasses of open foredune communities, do little to fix the sand surface. Fixation is, in general, only possible on secondary dune ridges or in relatively stable systems where there is enough shelter for other plants to seed in or to be introduced artificially. You can encourage new

or existing stands of vegetation by fertilising, mulching and binding. But this may not be justifiable in nature conservation areas since it increases soil productivity and may allow uncharacteristic species to invade. Wherever possible, use seed mixtures containing only native species which are adaptable to the site.

g   Steep sand faces, particularly on the windward sides of dunes, are prime erosion sites. You can make these more erosion resistant by thatching and planting or by contouring them to a gradually sloping, aerodynamically stable profile (p37).

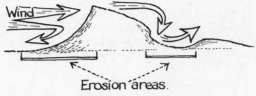

Section: Over-steepened dune.

Erosion areas.

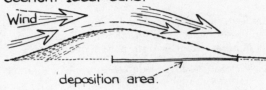

Section: "Ideal" dune.

deposition area.

Combine contouring with other measures, since it does nothing in itself to trap sand or fix the surface. Usually planting and fencing are both required in addition to contouring.

h   Surface roughness increases wind turbulence and erosion. Make dune profiles as smooth as possible. Blowouts, gullies, notches and holes cause the wind to funnel and concentrate its scouring action. Fill these in by contouring, planting, fencing and thatching.

i   When stabilising a slope, start at the top and proceed downhill. Finish treating the section from top to bottom as soon as possible – within a few weeks at most. Otherwise the bottom edge will erode and threaten the work which has been done above.

STRATEGIES

Eroding systems

Eroding systems may be in a state of overall dynamic equilibrium (p11) or they may be suffering from the lessening of sand supplies which in earlier times balanced the losses caused by natural erosion. Most often, though, they receive enough sand to make up for natural erosion but not enough for the extra erosion caused by increased biotic pressure. Strategies for eroding systems apply also to blowouts within otherwise accreting or stable systems.

At Ainsdale NNR, Merseyside, trampling along a popular footpath had created a blowout through the foredunes, with the sand being blown through onto an area of slack beyond. The dunes are eroding quite severely at this point, so it was felt that action had to be taken. The gully through the foredunes was fenced with a series of parallel sand trap fences, of either chestnut paling or 'Enkamat' (see p49), leaving a fenced footpath through to the beach. This followed a dog-leg route, to prevent creating a wind tunnel. As the fences fill with sand, more will be built on top, until the former gully has reached a sufficient height and stability for replanting with marram.

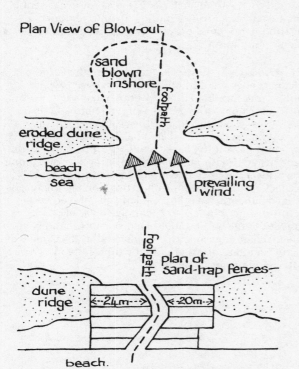

At the same time, the most severely eroding foredune face was 'thatched' with a synthetic material (see p83), through which marram was planted. A major fencing programme was carried out to fence all along the front of the foredunes, so forcing people to use the designated route, which joins to a boardwalk on the landward edge of the foredune.

A similar but more serious situation at Hayle, Cornwall was tackled by first using a bulldozer to contour the eroded area, followed by access control and sand trap fencing and then replanting of the entire area with marram. This is described on page 42.

Accreting systems

In accreting or prograding dune systems, the supply of fresh sand is greater than that of the sand lost, at least under natural conditions. Normally this sort of system needs no stabilisation unless public pressure is such that embryo dunes are literally trampled flat and the vegetation of existing foredunes is largely killed off. Even then there is little danger to coastal defences and the major effect, aside from loss of dune habitat, is increased sand-blow inland.

Camber, East Sussex, is an example of a system where the quantities of sand liberated by passing feet can be considerable. Dune stabilisation has been required mainly to reduce damage to poorly sited roads and housing just back of the dunes. Pizzey (1975) describes the piecemeal methods which were tried

without success from 1945 until 1967 as well as the coordinated approach which eventually brought the problem under control. This began with contouring the dunes, which had become oversteepened at their inland side where they had shifted back towards the road.

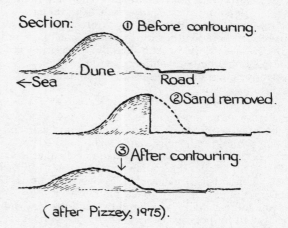

(after Pizzey, 1975).

Because the problem was one of too much sand, excess material could safely be removed from the inland edge of the dunes and was taken away for use in building the Dungeness Power Station. The dune ridge was then reshaped to the more stable profile shown above.

Plants have trouble seeding into loose sand, so at Camber it was essential to stabilise the graded surface by hydraulically seeding and mulching the bare areas. This was accompanied by a bitumen spray to bind the straw mulch and sand in place and to improve germination of the grasses. The straw was disk harrowed to partly bury it and improve its stabilising effect. Fences were then erected around the entire work site, including the sides of such paths as were needed to channel people to and from the beach. The fences at the seaward side were positioned along the strandline to help form new embryo dunes and prevent smothering of the grassy slopes behind. Further steps are to plant marram grass and native shrub species to develop a more natural vegetation. Marram on its own would be inadequate because the need is to fix the sand surface rather than simply trap more sand.

Stable systems

In stable dune systems, little sand goes into or is lost from the system. Many east-coast dunes, such as those in East Lothian and Lincolnshire, have a very slow accretion rate and can be considered more or less stable.

Gibraltar Point, Lincolnshire, shows the interesting situation of a system which was until recently gradually accreting but which has had its sand supply virtually cut off by foreshore salt marsh development. A new dune ridge may eventually arise to seaward of the marsh, causing it to become brackish or fresh, but in any case the present dune system is essentially static.

Wilcock and Carter (1975 and undated) emphasize that with the stable system at Portrush, County Antrim, Northern Ireland, 'traditional' restoration methods of planting and fencing could not succeed alone because the sand supply was inadequate and the eroded slopes too steep. Nor was it necessarily desirable to initiate new dune formation had this been possible. Contouring provided the key. Regraded, smoothly sloping dune faces formed a much better rooting medium for marram, at least when supplied with additional nutrients and mulch. Marram may gradually decline on this site but it only needs to last long enough here to allow other plants to colonise and fix the surface. More difficult than the contouring and planting, but equally essential, was the erection of relatively vandal-proof fences to keep people out of the restored area.

Dune grasslands, especially in their extreme form of machair plains, illustrate flat, virtually unbroken sand systems which can be considered stable in the short run even though they may go through cyclical erosion and deposition over the course of decades or centuries (p87). Machair is easily disturbed by overstocking of grazing animals or poorly timed ploughing, or by caravan and car tracks which cut through the turf and create wind funnels, especially where the vehicles park and turn. Unlike dunes, machairs often end at a rather steep cliff at the beach edge. This area is particularly sensitive to erosion where people clamber down, creating gullies which then eat farther into the plain behind.

Seaton (1968) describes various attempts at restoring a large-scale blowout on machair at Bornish, South Uist, caused primarily by agricultural mismanagement. The most successful measures involved beginning restoration at the point of scour and increasing the fertility and stability of the soil through heavy applications of organic mulches. Mulching with dung also introduced many quick-growing weeds which helped fix the sand surface. Other measures, essential to prevent a recurrence of the blowout, included restricting the numbers of sheep and controlling the rabbit population.

At Achmelvich, Sutherland, and on the Isle of Mull, machair-edge restoration became necessary where public pressure increased without adequate restrictions on parking or the provision of suitable pathways to the beach. Stabilisation has focussed on the cliff edge itself. This area has been fenced with post and wire at the back, against people and grazing animals, and with post and rail plus brushwood along the seaward edge to encourage sand buildup and protect against wave erosion. After fencing, the face is graded and returfed (p76), seeded and sprayed with fertilisers and binders to encourage a variety of grasses. Large gullies are treated as continuations of the machair edge and are 'toughened' in the same way, while smaller gullies are filled with sand and brushwood prior to seeding.

3 Coastlands and the Law

Coastal law, particularly as it relates to ownership and usage, is extremely complex. There is no area defined as the coastal zone which is treated by law as an integrated whole. Regulatory controls, many of which are recent in origin, have developed fragmentarily under the pressure of different and competing interests and public bodies. A detailed treatment is outside the scope of this Handbook. For further information, see 'Legislation and the Coastal Zone' from 'Nature Conservation and the Marine Environment' (Nature Conservancy Council/Natural Environment Research Council, 1979), which has formed the basis for much of this chapter. Professional legal advice, and direct reference to the relevant Act or authority, should be sought in any ambiguous or disputed case.

Ownership

a   The sea and sea bed, from the mean low water mark to the three mile limit of territorial waters, is vested in the Crown.

b   The foreshore, meaning the area between low and high water marks of ordinary tides (LWMOT and HWMOT) in England and Wales, and between low and high water marks of ordinary spring tides (LWMOST and HWMOST) in Scotland, as well as the bed of arms and estuaries of the sea and tidal rivers, is vested in the Crown except where the ownership has passed to a subject by charter, grant, prescription or possessory title. Today, much of the coastline is owned by local authorities, private individuals and lords of the manor, or by the National Trust.

c   Land above the foreshore is presumed to belong to the adjoining owners, but there is no legal presumption that the foreshore between high and low water marks belongs to the owners of the adjacent property.

Rights of Usage

Access

a   The public are legally entitled to have access to the foreshore in the exercise of their rights of navigation and fishery (see below). Public access for any other purpose must be by permission of the owner. Access across lands above the foreshore must be along permitted routes.

b   An owner or occupier of the land adjacent to the sea has a right of access to the sea, whether the tide is in or across the uncovered foreshore.

c   Inhabitants of a village or local fishermen may have a right over the adjacent foreshore acquired by immemorial custom.

Fishing

a   There is a common law right to fish 'in the tidal reaches of all rivers and estuaries and in the sea and arms of the sea within the limits of the territorial waters of the kingdom except where the Crown or some subject has acquired a proprietary (ie ownership) exclusive of the public right or where Parliament has restricted the common law rights of the public' (Natural Environment Research Council, 1973, p18).

b   The public do not have the right to dig bait on the foreshore and in some areas this activity is controlled by byelaws (this interpretation is currently being challenged by angling organisations).

c   Fishing may be by means of lines, draw nets and other 'ordinary modes', and includes taking of shellfish, but does not include use of weirs and other 'engines fixed in the soil' since this involves use of the soil which is in possession of the Crown or a private owner. Local byelaws may make further restrictions on permitted methods, net sizes etc.

d   There is no statutory closed season for sea fish other than those stated in local byelaws. The Sea Fisheries Committee specifies closed seasons on shellfish. Size limits for various species of sea fish are laid down in orders made by the Minister of Agriculture. Salmon and migratory trout are dealt with in the Salmon and Freshwater Fisheries Act 1965. For details see 'Angling and the Law' by Michael Gregory (Charles Knight, 1976).

Shooting

a   Under the Firearms Act 1968 S20 (2), it is illegal to enter upon land as a trespasser with a firearm without reasonable excuse. 'Land' includes land covered by water.

b   The Protection of Birds Act 1954 outlines restrictions on shooting of wildfowl and game birds. The following shorebirds are among the species protected at all times: all swans, brent goose, shelduck, eider duck, snew, green plover (lapwing), dunlin, knot, common sandpiper, little stint and turnstone. Species for which there is general but not full protection include the barnacle goose (limited shooting on certain islands off the West of Scotland), merganser and goosander (may be taken in Scotland) and oystercatcher (may be taken in limited areas of north Norfolk, Wales and Morecambe Bay). For a full listing of scheduled species, shooting restrictions and close seasons, see the RSPB booklet, 'Wild Birds and the Law'.

Navigation

The public have a right to navigate over the whole space in which the tide flows, and this right is not suspended when the tide is out or too low for vessels to float. This right can be extinguished by Act of Parliament or, within water authority areas or internal drainage districts, by the Ministry of Agriculture, Fisheries and Food. The master of a vessel must exercise this right reasonably, eg he will be held liable if by improper navigation he damages an oyster bed.

Coast defences and mining

a   Coast protection authorities and water authorities are empowered to carry out works to protect land against erosion and encroachment by the sea and by tidal water. Anyone responsible for a sea wall is entitled to an injunction to restrain other persons from removing a natural shingle bank if this forms a sea defence.

b   Highway departments are empowered to take away gravel, sand, stone and other materials to repair highways, so long as this does not expose the land to erosion or inundation. The general public have no right to remove such materials from the foreshore unless granted a licence by the owner of the foreshore. A right to take sea sand may exist under statute. Dredging for 'aggregate' for the building industry is licensed by the Crown Estate Commissioners under consultation with, among others, the Department of the Environment and the Ministry of Agriculture, Fisheries and Food.

Pollution

Control of pollution of the coastal zone is too complex to summarise briefly. The main acts which govern it are the Control of Pollution Act 1974, the Dumping at Sea Act 1974 and the Prevention of Oil Pollution Act 1971. Various other acts deal with estuarial and river pollution. A legal right to pollute water within defined limits may be acquired by statute, prescription, custom or grant.

Protected Species

In addition to the species mentioned under 'Shooting' (above), the Wild Creatures and Wild Plants Act 1975 gives complete protection to the natterjack toad and the sand lizard. Other animals (and plants) covered by the Act are described in a pamphlet, 'Wildlife, the Law and You', published by the Department of Public Services, British Museum (Natural History).

Wreck

a   'Wreck' ie property cast ashore after shipwreck or found in or on the shores of any tidal water, may be either owned or unclaimed. In either case the 'salvor' must inform the Receiver of Wreck (usually HM Coastguard) so that he may register it as necessary. Wreck includes 'derelict' articles, ie property abandoned without hope of recovery.

b   With owned wreck the salvor may claim salvage rights under agreement with the owner (The Receiver arbitrates any disputes).

c   With unclaimed wreck, the property reverts to the Crown after one year with the salvor usually receiving one third of the proceeds (this is not a legal requirement and varies from case to case).

d   Articles not classed as wreck are treated as lost property, including deck cargo washed overboard (except fishing gear, which is treated in this case as wreck) and anything found within a harbour or above mean high water mark spring tides. Lost property should be handed in to the police. Its theft constitutes common larceny.

e   It is an offence to board a wrecked vessel without consent of the owner or the Receiver.

f   Certain wrecks may be of archaeological interest. These should be left undisturbed and, after the Receiver has been notified, should be reported to the Council for Nautical Archaeology, c/o the National Maritime Museum, Romney Road, Greenwich, London SE10 9NF.

g   Beached cetaceans (whales, porpoises and dolphins) must by law be reported to the British Museum (Natural History). In England and Wales, the procedure is to contact the local coastguard who will pass on the information immediately. In Scotland, the coastguard are not required to report specimens of the smaller species, so it is best to contact the Museum directly (telephone 01 589 6323).

4 Safety, Equipment and Organisation

Volunteer tasks which are specifically coastal, such as marram planting, are on the whole simple and undemanding and require little equipment. Generalised volunteer tasks such as footpath construction, fencing and scrub and tree clearance, on the other hand, require much more care and a considerable variety of tools. The points which follow are basic and, for the latter type of work, cover minimum needs only. Machine work also demands protective clothing and safety equipment additional to that which is listed below. The leaflets of the Forestry Safety Council (c/o the Forestry Commission) give codes of practice for most of the power tools likely to be used by volunteers.

Materials needed for constructing features such as footpaths and fences are described where appropriate in the text.

Safety Precautions

For recreational safety on the coast see page 100. The following points cover work precautions.

a   Have a suitable first aid kit on hand at the work site (see p31).

b   All volunteers should be immunized against tetanus.

c   Coastal work sites are usually very exposed. Conditions may be deceiving, so take care to avoid sunburn, heat exhaustion and wind chill. Use lotion before the first signs of burning. If you start to feel dizzy, rest in the shade with a drink. A hot drink, which cools the body by increasing perspiration and evaporative heat loss, refreshes more than a cold drink. Wear a hat. Take a change of clothing if working in wet conditions. In cold weather, have lunch and tea breaks in the lee of a dune or belt of scrub to get out of the wind.

d   Tools are hazardous when used in water or in slippery, muddy conditions. Keep a safe distance from other people, even when working in a team. Avoid using edged tools in wet conditions, particularly where visibility is limited by tall vegetation.

e   Your back and knees are under great stress in all heavy clearance work. Sand is deceptively heavy, especially when wet, so be very careful when shovelling and lifting. Do all heavy lifting with the back as straight as possible, bending from the knees to take the strain on the leg muscles. When shifting a pile of earth or sand, shovel from the bottom of the pile.

When carrying a heavy shovel load, swing it around to the hip as shown below. This reduces strain on the back and allows you to empty the load with a turn of the wrist.

f   Wear adequate foot gear: mud and sand disguise glass, rusty tins, shell fragments and thorny plants even on the cleanest coastlines.

g   Take care when crossing mud or sand flats and salt marshes. Try to avoid drainage channels and other depressions. Always travel with at least one other person unless you know the area intimately. Deep mud is the usual hazard. Quicksand is rare but does occur in certain areas. If you stumble into it, try to fall onto your back with your limbs outstretched and 'swim' to safety.

h   Do not drive a vehicle onto the foreshore or tidal flats unless you are certain it is safe. Cars are easily trapped when they try to cross 'fulls' (raised undulations) on otherwise firm beaches, where they may sink up to their hubs. Crests of

Right.

Wrong.

Right.

Wrong

fulls are best crossed where they are cut by shallow channels. Always seek expert local advice before venturing out into silty or muddy areas, even with a four-wheel-drive vehicle. Never drive into dune areas except on hardened tracks. Not only are you likely to get stuck, you may severely damage the soil and vegetation as well.

When driving a Land Rover across the foreshore or an area of blown sand, select the appropriate gear before venturing onto the soft terrain. Second gear in low ratio is often right. Drive at a steady speed and moderate revs (you may stall at low revs and spin if they are too high). Do not stop until you are across the area, since if you do the wheels may spin as the clutch engages when starting up again. Always carry shovels and, if the vehicle is fitted with a capstan winch, carry a sturdy rope and a 1.5m (5') fence post for use as a 'dead man' when winching. You may have to lower tyre pressure to 'emergency soft' to drive over such areas.

i   Take extra care when working alongside large machinery. The operator is unlikely to hear or see you, so watch out for him. Wear a protective helmet. Work out signals in advance when directing the operator from a distance. Never hang onto the cab or the cab door of the machine when in use.

j   It is best to avoid working at a cliff foot, for fear of rock falls or earth slips. Wear a safety helmet if such work is essential. Never work under an overhang. Do not work within 6m (20') of a cliff edge unless absolutely necessary, eg to complete the end of a strip of fencing or to remove dangerous or unsightly debris. If you do have to work near the edge, follow these precautions:

(i)   Check the amount of undercutting before starting work.

(ii) Rope off a 'no go' area towards the edge, using rope or bunting, to warn other workers and passers-by.

(iii) Tie a rope, shorter than the distance to the edge, to a secure support (eg a stake or tree) with the other end around your waist. Use bowline knots at both ends.

Clothing

The aim is always safety and comfort first. Requirements vary depending on the weather and the type of work.

a   Loose cotton clothing is most comfortable in hot weather, but overalls or fitted work clothes are safer when using edged tools and are best for most work. Carry a pullover and parka or anorak since it can quickly become chilly when the sun drops and the wind rises. For dealing with sea buckthorn, really tough outer gear such as a 'Barbour' jacket is important to protect you from thorns.

b   Boots. Heavy leather work boots with metal toe caps and spiked or deep moulded soles are best for construction, fencing, tree clearance and other jobs involving sharp or heavy implements and materials. Wellingtons are best in shallow mud and water if edged tools are not being used. Plimsolls or other light shoes are safe only for tasks such as marram planting which do not require sharp tools.

c   Gloves. Bare hands provide the best grip when using tools, but for general protection wear heavy-duty leather-palmed work gloves. Other types may be required in certain situations, eg when fencing with barbed wire or using a power chain saw. Gauntlet-type hedging gloves are best when tackling sea buckthorn, since ordinary work gloves will not turn thorns and do not protect the wrists. Suppliers include W G Todd and Son, Rannock House, Crescent Green, Kendal, and The Smithy, New Invention, Bucknell, Shropshire. A pair costs about £24.00 (1986 price).

Rubber gloves are warmer and less slippery than other types when working in water, although they do not protect against sharp objects. When handling herbicides in concentrate or solution, it is best to wear disposable polythene gloves, since leather gloves are not waterproof and there is a danger with rubber gloves that you may not notice if small leaks develop.

d   Hat or helmet. An old cloth or leather cap is fine for general work. One with a brim will shield your eyes against sun. When felling trees or working near machinery wear a plastic or metal helmet. This must be internally adjustable to fit the head, and preferably should be fitted with a wire mesh visor, and with ear protectors when working near machinery.

e   Sunglasses with polarised lenses are useful to protect your eyes from glare.

f   Goggles or eye shields, for use when cutting sea buckthorn or other thorny scrub (alternatively you can wear a safety helmet with a visor). Eye protectors should be marked with the British Standard Kitemark and the number BS2092. If impact resistance is required, they should be marked as Grade 1 or 2. When mixing herbicides in the field, or spraying with herbicide, wear chemical-splash-proof goggles (see Brown, 1975, for details). Goggles are also useful to shield your eyes from blown sand on windy days.

g   'Chaps', for use when cutting sea buckthorn or spraying regrowth. These are the only sort of overtrousers which let you bash into buckthorn stands without fear of a disabling thorn below the middle. Chaps of the design shown below have had many years of use at Braunton Burrows NNR, Devon. They are made up from tanned cow hide ('back' leather, not the softer 'belly' leather) by a local saddler. Although expensive (£22 in 1975), they should last for many years of heavy work. Note that the legs are separate, and each has a flap that goes over the fly with a popper stud. The slit on the outside of the leg is to provide ventilation and to allow you to take them on and off over boots. The straps fit over the wearer's belt and should be adjusted so that the chaps sit well down over the tops of the boots.

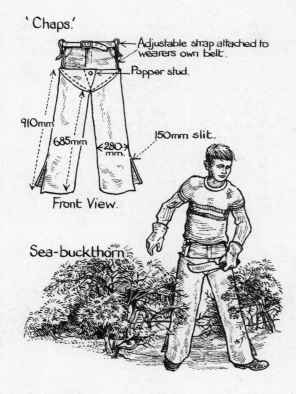

'Chaps.'

Adjustable strap attached to wearers own belt.

Popper stud.

910mm

685mm

280 mm.

150mm slit.

Front View.

Sea-buckthorn

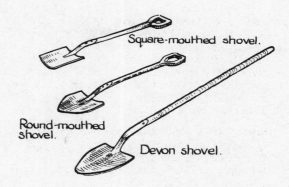

Square-mouthed shovel.

Round-mouthed shovel.

Devon shovel.

Tools and Equipment

FIRST AID

Keep a first aid kit available at all times. The BTCV can supply standard first aid kits which comply with the 1981 Health and Safety Regulations (First Aid). For six to ten people, the contents are:

1 guidance card
20 individual sterile dressings
2 sterile eye pads with attachments
2 triangular bandages
2 sterile coverings for serious wounds
6 safety pins
6 medium size sterile unmedicated dressings
2 large size sterile unmedicated dressings
2 extra large sterile unmedicated dressings

From experience on tasks, the following are also found to be useful:

100mm (4″) crepe bandage
tweezers
scissors
insect repellant
antihistamine cream for insect bites
sunscreen cream
mild antiseptic cream
eye lotion and eye bath

EARTH MOVING AND PLANTING

a   Round- or taper-mouth shovel for loose soil, sand and shingle, or square-mouth shovel for working off a smooth 'floor' or shovelling board. A Devon shovel is ideal for use in stony ground and deep soft sand.

b   Heavy-duty treaded digging spade, for general use

c   Trenching spade with triangular, slightly bevelled blade, for use in compacted wet sand or for planting marram in hard, stony ground. Small, light ex-WD spades are ideal. A Schlich planting spade can also be used in these conditions.

d   Heavy-duty digging fork

e   Mattock, grubbing or pick-ended for general use

f   Dibber, as an alternative to a spade, for making holes to plant marram and other grasses in soft ground. Purchased dibbers are steel shod and usually have a 'T' grip. The top half of a broken spade handle, tapered at the end and sharpened to a point, does just as well in sand and soft ground. A short crowbar may also be used.

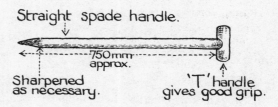

Straight spade handle.

750mm approx.

Sharpened as necessary.

'T' handle gives good grip.

g   Wheelbarrow. The best type is heavy-duty steel, with a single wheel and long handles for leverage and balance. Pneumatic tyres are essential for work in soft ground. Capacity should be about 0.08 cubic metre (3 cubic feet) since bigger barrows are hard to handle when full. Rubber handles are unnecessary and tend to come off when least expected. A hand barrow, for use by two or four workers is useful for moving small loads short distances over rough terrain.

CLEARANCE

a   Bow (bushman) saws, 530mm (21″) and 760mm (30″) sizes for most purposes including rough cutting of fence posts, 910mm (36″) size where a chain saw cannot be used

b   Two-man cross-cut saw, for large trees and cutting sleepers

c   Axe

d   Billhook

e   Power tools such as the power chain saw and scrub cutter may be useful but are hazardous, should only be handled by trained operators and should not be used in water.

CONSTRUCTION AND FENCING

General purpose

a   Carpenter's hand saw

b   Hack saw

c   Claw hammer

d   Lump (club) hammer, 1.8kg (4lb) size

e   Sledge hammer, 6.3kg (14lb) for heavy work

f   Crowbar

g   Wrecking bar ('swan neck')

h   Combination or slip-joint pliers

i   Screwdrivers, assorted sizes

j   Wood chisels, assorted sizes

k   Cold chisel

l   Brace and assorted bits, for wood

m   Hand (ratchet) drill and assorted bits, for various materials

n   Spirit level

o   Try or combination square

p   'Surform' plane

q   'Stanley' trimming or retractable knife

r   Flexible tape rule

s   Plumb bob and line

t   Paint brushes, assorted sizes

Additional fencing tools

a   Fencing pliers

b   Heavy-duty wire cutter ('bolt cropper')

c   Tinsnips, for cutting netting

d   Mell, maul or 'Drivall', for knocking in stakes and posts

e   'Shuv-holer' (post hole digger) for removal of earth and sand from strainer post holes

f   Wire strainer (eg 'Monkey Strainer') for tensioning wires to strainer posts

FIRES

a   Matches

b   Solid fuel fire lighter or container of paraffin

c   Pitchfork

MISCELLANEOUS

a   Hand winch, for scrub and tree clearance, lifting and hauling. The BTCV use the 'Tirfor TU16' winch which has a 760kg (15 cwt) safe working load, with 18m of 11.3mm diameter galvanised maxiflex cable, which has a 1620kg (32cwt) safe working load, fixed with a large eye hook. 'Tirfor' winches are made by Tirfor Ltd, Halfway, Sheffield S19 5GZ. An additional length of cable is useful.

b   Rope, for dragging brushwood, rubbish etc. Terylene rope is best, 50–75mm (2–3") in circumference. Nylon rope stretches too much and natural fibres rot quickly unless they can be thoroughly dried after use in wet conditions.

c   Sharpening stones. Curved billhooks are best sharpened with a canoe-shaped (flat oval) or cigar-shaped stone. Axes can be sharpened with a canoe-shaped or flat rectangular stone. Flat round axe-stones, although commonly used, are dangerous and difficult to hold.

d   Flat files, for taking out nicks and major sharpening of edge tools. Two types are useful, 250mm (10") bastard for spades and for preliminary filing of axes and billhooks and 250mm (10") fine mill for final filing of axes and billhooks. Files must be fitted with handles for safety.

e   Buckets. Use heavy-duty rubber buckets, not metal or plastic ones which break too easily.

f   Binder twine (eg old bale strings)

g   Old hessian or polythene sacks (eg fertiliser sacks) for transporting marram plants, stones etc and for keeping small tools collected and out of the sand (plastic sheeting can also be used for the latter purpose).

h   Old fish netting, for carrying brushwood, transporting bundles of grass offsets and for various stabilisation uses. Netting can be suspended from stakes about 300mm (1') high over newly planted areas to cut wind disturbance and help keep people away (perimeter fencing may also be necessary for the latter purpose) or it can be pinned directly on newly planted or seeded surfaces to help retain the soil. Wide-mesh netting should be used to protect transplanted offsets but fairly narrow mesh (eg 25mm, 1") is better for seeded areas. Nylon netting can be removed for reuse but natural fibre netting may be left in place to rot.

i   Knapsack sprayer, horticultural type. For spraying herbicide, a mist nozzle is required (see Brown, 1975, for details), while for spraying non-bituminous sand binders an 'uncloggable' nozzle with a wide coverage and reservoir pressures of at least 30psi (8.3g/m^2) is preferable. A watering can with the holes of the rose enlarged can be substituted if necessary for distributing binders.

j   Water carrier, 22 litre (5 gall.) for use when diluting herbicide or sand binders

k   Rags for wrapping edged tools and for cleaning

l   Puncture repair kit for waders and wellies: old inner tube, a tin of rubber solution, sand paper and scissors

m   Book of tide tables

Tool and Equipment Maintenance

a   Clean tools immediately after use. Wash and scrape muck off blades and handles, to keep them easy to use and to avoid blisters next time.

b   Hang waders upside down to dry. If just left in a heap they get smelly and rot at the folds.

c   Edged tools are safest when sharp. Stop work as often as necessary to touch them up with a sharpening stone, but if you nick a tool badly and have a replacement available save filing for the work bench. Tools dull very quickly when used in sand.

d   Spades are sharpened by filing into rather than away from the metal. Filing softens the metal so have a blacksmith temper their edges occasionally, if possible.

e   Oil or grease metal parts of tools after use. This is especially important in coastal areas since salt accelerates rusting. Soak new hafts in linseed oil before use.

f   It is easy to lose tools in soft sand and mud. Paint the handles red, orange or pink to make identification easier. Keep them in boxes, sacks or on a polythene sheet when not actually in use so that they can be located when needed.

g   Clean and lubricate hand winches after every task, if used in wet, mucky conditions. 'Tirfor' and similar winches have two side casings bolted together. Take these off, clean all parts including the cable, grease the working mechanism and replace the casings. Keep the lever in the release position when feeding in the cable to prevent it fraying or jamming. If used in dry conditions, you only need to clean and grease it occasionally but you should oil it periodically with gear oil.

h   Hose down the undersides of vehicles daily, using fresh water, when working in a salt-laden environment.

Organising Group Work

Volunteers should see that they are part of a team which is determined to do things as efficiently and enjoyably as possible.

a   The leader should first explain the task and set the day's objective. Where a task is dishearteningly big and apparently endless, it helps greatly to see at the end of the day that a measurable amount has been accomplished.

b   Small groups should work methodically on one goal at a time, rather than on several things none of which may get done by day's end. Larger groups may, of course, do several things if they are sure of finishing them.

c   If some jobs are unavoidably colder or more tiring than others, switch people around from time to time to spread the burden.

d   Logistics pose a major problem on many coastal tasks. Supplying and transporting materials is the essential factor in a task's success, whether the work be transplanting marram, laying mulch or brushwood, constructing fences, spraying fertiliser and binder or building boardwalks.

e   Even in simple, slow tasks it is often most efficient to break down the work force into small groups of three to six people since this allows them to develop teamwork and help each other as necessary.

f   The leader's main problem in 'linear' tasks such as fencing and boardwalk construction or fertilising and binding is to reduce bottlenecks to a minimum so that all volunteers are employed as steadily as possible whatever their job. Too often a large group does a job which is best done by just a few people. On such tasks it is also a good idea to stockpile materials along the route in advance, to avoid delays while waiting for materials and to reduce the danger of people tripping over tools or colliding with fellow workers when fetching heavy materials. If at all possible, tasks should be planned with varied work so that 'excess' volunteers can be put to use elsewhere if they are not needed on the main job.

g   Foreshore work times may be restricted because of tides or weather. Consult tide tables well in advance when planning the daily work routine, and keep up with weather forecasts. Have backup work available if there is a chance that tides or weather may make it impossible to carry out the main task on certain days.

5 Dune Profiling and Stabilisation

This chapter covers techniques of re-contouring dunes using machines, the construction of wave barriers and sand-trap fencing, and the use of thatching, mulching and binding to stabilise unvegetated surfaces. For the principles of dune stabilisation see the chapter on Management Planning.

Wave Barriers

Sea defences are beyond the scope of this Handbook, but it is appropriate to mention a few types of wave barriers which may be useful in large-scale dune protection programmes and which are suitable for construction by groups of volunteers.

GENERAL POINTS

Uses

The main uses of coastal wave barriers of the sort described below include:

a   Deflecting currents and tidal scour from eroding sections of beaches and dunes

b   Shielding vulnerable foredunes from high tides and storm waves

c   Blocking the mouths of blowouts or other low-level gaps in foredunes near the sea

d   Providing a basis for preliminary sand buildup to encourage the formation of embryo dunes

Other considerations

a   Wave barriers should be of porous rather than solid construction, so that they slow the waves and cause them to lose energy and drop their load of suspended sediments. Solid barriers usually cause scour in the same way as solid wind barriers (see the diagram under point a, page 24) or the unequal buildup of beach material on either side of the barrier.

b   Ideally wave barriers or their component parts should be able to shift with the force of the sea yet retain their overall structure. It has been found that for large-scale coastal defences, interlocking polyhedrons are stronger and more effective than solid walls. Small-scale designs cannot always accommodate this factor, but gabions (see below) have considerable flexibility and are often a good choice where exposure is not too great.

c   It is important to prevent scour or weakness at the ends of wave barriers. If barriers project out from the dunes, their seaward ends must be far enough out that scour does not endanger the dunes and their landward ends should run well above the line of storm tides. If they run along the beach, their ends should be brought gradually in toward the dunes at either end.

DESIGNS

Fencing

Most fencing, although useful to trap wind-blown sand or control access, is too weak to withstand wave action. Even large posts (eg railway sleepers) may be undermined by the sea so that fences rapidly deteriorate and must be repositioned frequently.

The box system of brushwood fencing used on the East Lothian coast, and similar systems of brushwood or chestnut paling fencing used on the Sefton coast can be effective against wave action, as well as in trapping blown sand. These are described below.

Note the following:

a   The very nature of the problem means that fencing material cannot last many years, and normal wave action and the occasional storm will damage or completely remove the fencing. When erecting fencing primarily as wave barriers, which are unlikely to be permanently buried by sand, it is important to consider what maintenance is likely to be needed to keep it effective, and who will undertake this. This type of work is a constant battle, and constant maintenance with some replacement of materials is likely to be needed.

b   Chestnut paling is reckoned to have a life of about two years at the best when used as a wave barrier. It is not considered worth trying to lift and re-use any chestnut paling which does get buried by sand, as the lifting loosens the sand that has accumulated. It is important to repair chestnut paling immediately after any storm damage loosens it, or it will be removed by the next storm or high tide. Re-attach paling to posts, and join in new sections as required (see p48).

c   Brushwood does not have to be held in position by wire fences, and is better simply set in holes in the sand, provided loss to firewood-gathering and vandalism is not too great a problem. The post and wire fence serves little purpose, and is a nuisance to clear up if it becomes damaged. The brushwood should last two to three years before it breaks up.

d   Post and wire with brushwood or chestnut paling will usually be needed where the wave barrier also acts as an access control fence, to stop people moving back from the beach onto the foredunes.

e   The size of the 'box' depends on the severity of erosion and the requirement for trapping sand blown longitudinally along the beach.

The box system of 'Dutch' fencing shown below has been used to reduce tidal erosion of dunes at Hedderwick on the East Lothian coast. The box construction absorbs the impact of incoming waves, while the entrenched brushwood resists tidal scour and remains in place to trap wind-blown sand. It is important to thatch the eroded sand face (see p81) to increase its stability so that plants can grow. You need to set the distance between fences and their height by trial and error, but if this is done correctly the build-up can be rapid.

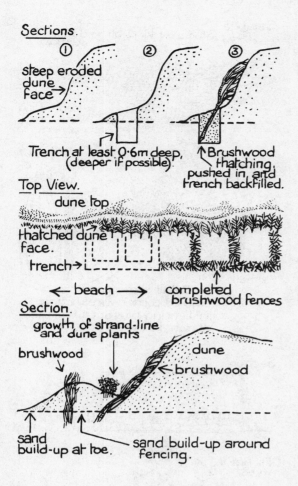

Sections.

① steep eroded dune face

② Trench at least 0·6m deep (deeper if possible).

③ Brushwood thatching pushed in, and trench backfilled.

Top View.

dune top

Thatched dune face.

trench →

← beach →

completed brushwood fences

Section.

growth of strand-line and dune plants

brushwood

dune

brushwood

sand build-up at toe.

sand build-up around fencing.

At Gullane, another site on the East Lothian coast, a box system with spurs has been found effective in protecting the foredune face.

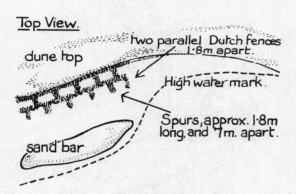

Top View.

dune top

two parallel Dutch fences 1·8m apart.

High water mark.

Spurs, approx. 1·8m long, and 7m. apart.

sand bar

As shown above, the protected stretch of dune has two 'Dutch' fences parallel to its face, about 1.8m (6′) apart. The spurs are about 2m (6½′) long and 7m (24′) apart, at right angles to the main fences. These fences, besides trapping windblown sand, force the waves to break farther offshore. This has caused a sand bar to form just to seaward of the breaking waves, where the waves drop their load of sand. The bar pushes the tide line still farther seaward, giving added protection to the dunes.

Experience with fences in the severe winter storms of 1977–78 suggests that, even when the sand in the boxes is repeatedly washed away, the fences should remain intact for renewed sand collection provided

the brushwood is entrenched as deeply as possible with some side branches buried to act as anchors. Where even this is inadequate and the boxes are demolished by waves, it is likely that the battle is a losing one and that damage will occur no matter what measures are attempted to safeguard the dunes.

The following pattern of post and chestnut paling fencing is used at Ainsdale, Merseyside. The fence serves several purposes. The 'boxes' trap sand, whichever way the wind blows, and build up a low dune, as shown. The dune helps provide a buffer against wave action. If the dune is eroded by storms or high tides, the fencing should remain as a barrier, although damage is inevitable in exceptional conditions. The fence also discourages access from the beach into the foredunes, except when it is fully buried by sand. The posts are of tanalised timber, 2m (6′6″) × 100mm (4″), knocked in 1m (3′) by a 'Unimog' mechanical post driver. The chestnut paling is three strand, 1.07m (3½′) high with pale spacing of 75mm (3″), supplied in 9.2m (10yd) lengths.

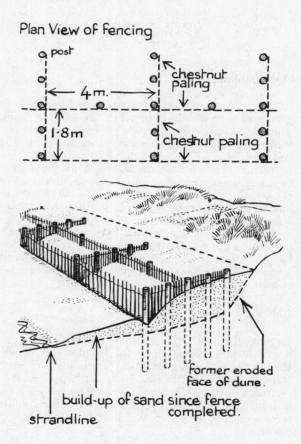

Plan View of fencing

post

chestnut paling

← 4m. →

1·8m

chestnut paling

build-up of sand since fence completed.

former eroded face of dune.

strandline

The other designs shown, used at Formby, Merseyside, serve similar functions, but are built of cheaper materials and have more widely-spaced spurs. Only a single longitudinal fence is built, and the spurs are unenclosed on the seaward side. This does not build up as much sand as the box design above, and is also less robust. It is however very much cheaper to erect. The length and spacing of the spurs varies according to the dune profile required, the spurs being longer to make a wider dune, and closer spaced to trap more sand. The spurs can be made of chestnut paling, brushwood and wire or brushwood only. A post spacing of 1.8m (6′) or 3.05m (10′) on the longitudinal fence is useful, being exact divisions of 30 foot, which is the standard length for rolls of chestnut paling. This avoids having to join lengths of paling between posts. The closer spaced posts make a more robust fence.

Some examples of spur length and spacing.

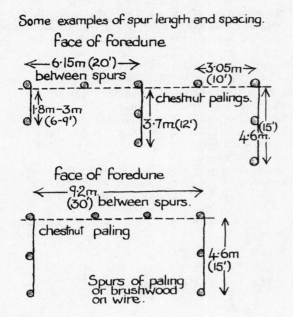

Stone banking

At White Sands, East Lothian, an eroded beach-grassland edge which drops 1.2–1.5m (4–5') to a stony beach has been repaired by the simple expedient of throwing stones from the beach against the bank. The beach is sheltered so only a minimal amount of protection is needed against waves. While isolated boulders might promote scour, many smaller stones can be built up into a protective facing which evens out the gullies caused by people jumping down. No effort need be made to achieve the correct slope because as people descend the stony bank it gradually develops a more stable angle of rest. After this happens, the surface, which by this time has trapped some sand, may be planted up with sea lyme or other grasses.

Gabions

Gabions are most useful in somewhat sheltered conditions. If exposed to the full brunt of the waves, the motion of the rocks within the gabions may wear through the wire of the baskets as has happened at Northam Burrows, Devon. This problem can be minimised by packing the baskets by hand and adding more stones as necessary after initial settling has occurred.

Large prefabricated gabions are made by River and Sea Gabions (London) Ltd, 2 Swallow Place, London W1R 8SQ and by The BRC Engineering Company Ltd, Stafford ST17 4NN. River and Sea Gabions Ltd recommend that their 'Maccaferri' gabions should be assembled and filled as shown below.

Smaller home-made gabions, using chain-link fencing rolled into stone-filled 'sausages' which are 'stitched' with straining wire, have been used at Braunton Burrows, Devon, to help block a tidally eroded gap in the dunes, and at Lindisfarne, Northumberland, to protect a tern nesting island from tidal scour. The design is shown in cross-section below. Further

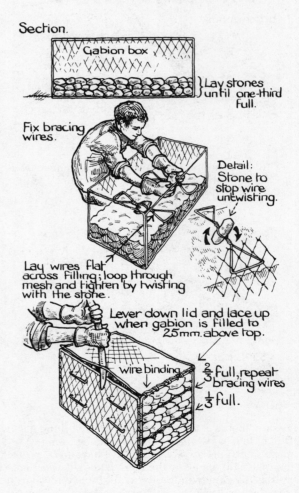

details and construction methods are given in 'Waterways and Wetlands' (BTCV, 1976).

Although this design is only suitable for blocking small waves, it can easily be added to in succeeding years if it becomes covered with trapped sand and the materials are cheap, readily available and easily handled by volunteers.

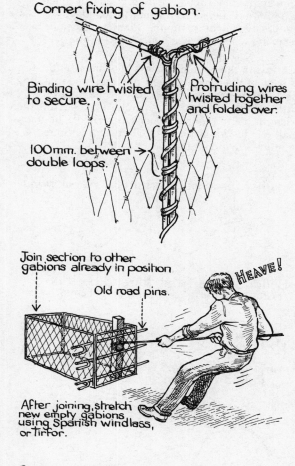

Corner fixing of gabion.

Binding wire twisted to secure.

Protruding wires twisted together and folded over.

100mm. between double loops.

Join section to other gabions already in position

Old road pins.

HEAVE!

After joining, stretch new empty gabions using Spanish windlass, or Tirfor.

Section:

375mm. approx.

Wire stitching.

Chain-link fencing - folded up around stone-fill.

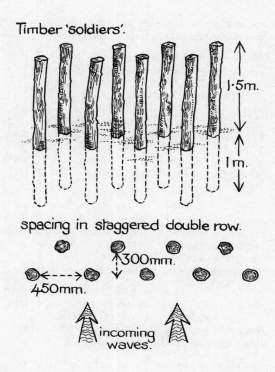

Timber 'soldiers'.

1·5m.

1m.

spacing in staggered double row.

300mm.

450mm.

incoming waves.

Timber 'soldiers'

This technique has been used by the National Trust at Formby on the Sefton coast, Merseyside, to break the force of the waves where they were undermining a small pine wood on the seaward edge of the dunes. The 'soldiers' are set 1–1.2m (3–4') into the sand, in a double row, staggered as shown. In this case unpeeled local pine was used, 2.4–2.7m (8–9') long by 75–125mm (3–5") diameter, but any available large timbers would be suitable.

Timber groynes

Timber groynes are beyond the capabilities of most volunteer work groups, and require careful design and digging-in to be effective. Aaron (1954) discusses methods and materials. Gaskin (1970) gives a detailed plan for a system of straight and zig-zag permeable groynes used in conjunction with wave screens at Culbin Forest, Moray. It is important that any such system ends gradually with successively shorter groynes, otherwise scour may occur around the ends.

Contouring

GENERAL POINTS

Uses

The uses of contouring include:

a   Lessening the windward slopes of dunes or blowouts which are too steep to permit an effective use of fences or a good growth of dune grasses

b   Filling in blowouts and decapitating remnant dune peaks to achieve a regular dune crest and profile which reduces problems of wind funnelling and scour (see second diagram on page 24).

c   Remove excess drifting sand from rapidly accreting dunes

Other considerations

It is almost always easiest and cheapest to contour by mechanical means, except on the smallest scale, where the work may be suitable for volunteers. Volunteers can carry out site protection once the earth moving is finished. In the last few years, bulldozers have increasingly been used as a means of contouring badly eroded dunes in Britain. As the expertise of dune management has developed, the confidence to take these rather drastic measures has been gained. Points to note are:

a   Contouring by bulldozer is immediate. In a few days many tons of sand can be shifted, which might take years, if ever, for fencing to accumulate. It is difficult to effectively position sand-trap fencing in eroded dunes, as the complex pattern of humps and hollows creates wind tunnels and eddies that make the effect of the wind hard to predict. The wind may also re-erode fences that have been buried, so that in spite of taking measures, the system is locked in an eroding pattern that cannot be broken without first shifting sand mechanically.

b   Eroded dunes can be contoured to a fairly safe profile, so that even before marram planting or other stabilisation work commences, there should be little danger of major wind-blow. The smooth profile means that there is nothing to create turbulence. If the contoured dune is not high enough after bulldozing, and more sand is required, it is relatively easy to then build effective sand-trap fences as the smooth profile ensures a fairly predictable movement of sand by the wind.

c   Use of a bulldozer can look rather drastic, and an unusual way of 'conserving' the dunes. Work is normally done in early spring, before many visitors are around, but care should be taken to inform local residents so that there is no misunderstanding about the aims of the work.

d   Plan machine use carefully, to avoid secondary erosion. Bulldozers should not be used where they will damage existing vegetation. If possible, provide access from the beach rather than through the dunes.

e   Save any existing remnants of vegetation, so that it can be re-planted. Dig up all the marram before the bulldozer starts, and keep the plants moist in fertiliser sacks (see p72). In some cases it may be possible for the bulldozer driver to carefully sweep whole tumps of vegetation from one place to another.

f   Theoretically, windward dune faces should be regraded to a slope of as little as 3°–6° (1:20–1:10), provided the site is wide enough and there is adequate sand. In practice, space and sand are normally limited, and it is necessary to grade to a maximum of 1:2 for hard planting or 1:5 for mechanical sowing of marram (Adriani and Terwindt, 1974). Do not build dunes in low areas where the spoil must be taken from the beach storm platform, since this lowers the buffer zone between the dunes and storm tides.

EXAMPLES

Two of the areas in Britain where bulldozing has been used on quite a major scale are on the north coast of Cornwall, at Hayle, Perranporth and Constantine Bay, and at Formby on the Sefton coast, Merseyside. Many of the details which follow, both of contouring and fencing, are based on the work done in these areas.

To shift sand, a caterpillar tracked vehicle is needed. Suitable machines are the Caterpillar D6 which has a 1.8m (6′) blade, or the D8, with a 2.4m (8′) × 4.2m (14′) blade. Hire prices in Cornwall in 1986 were £22 and £30 an hour respectively. The larger machine is normally preferred, as it can get the job done more quickly. The D8 can move 5–8 tons of sand per sweep, and at Hayle was used to shift 80,000 tons of sand over an area of about 7 acres. On the Sefton coast a D6 is normally used, and is reckoned to deal with about an acre a day. Each area has been fortunate in having the services of the same local driver for several years, thus building up expertise in sand dune contouring. On the Cornish sites the general aim is to re-grade to a 1 in 3 gradient. This has proved to be stable, and so far there has been no problem with wind blow in the

period before planting is finished. A netting fence (see p49) is erected along the landward side as soon as possible, by way of insurance. Planting is begun in late spring when the weather begins to improve.

In Cornwall, the operator works by starting at the top and back of the eroded dunes, pushing the remaining peaks into the troughs. This creates a fairly level broad-topped ridge called a 'bench'. The bench is then pushed down in oblique sweeps as shown. The tracks remain visible for a short time, but soon become obscured by wind action.

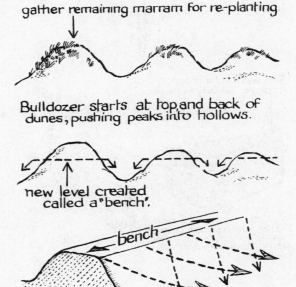

gather remaining marram for re-planting.

Bulldozer starts at top and back of dunes, pushing peaks into hollows.

new level created called a "bench".

'bench' is pushed down, in oblique sweeps.

Contouring is only the first stage, creating the basic dune shape, on which the new 'landscape' is formed. This involves delineating pathways by barriers or access-control fencing, and planting marram to stabilise the surface, and continue the process of dune building by trapping more sand. Sand-trap fences are usually also constructed, and may double as access-control fences to discourage people going into the newly-planted areas.

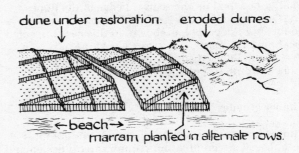

dune under restoration.   eroded dunes.

←beach→

marram planted in alternate rows.

The resulting dune profile is very even, and will look 'un-natural' compared to any eroded dunes nearby. This even profile will become more complex over the years, with the effects of the wind, vegetation, public pressure and further management.

An interesting example of bulldozing curing a problem that sand-trap fences had failed to solve is at Trearddur Bay, Anglesey. Here the sea wall had caused the wind to scour away the sand to leeward, leaving a drop of several feet behind the wall. The sand was blown across the car-park, and was in fact causing problems as it partly buried the public toilets. Sand trap fences had failed because they were in the sheltered lee of the wall. A bulldozer was used to move the sand from the leeward side of the car-park up against the sea wall.

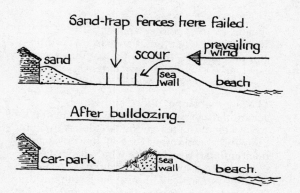

The work was done over a period from January to April, and there was enough seed and plant material within the sand to create a good cover of vegetation by the summer. The area was fenced off with chestnut paling, leaving paths from the car-park up to the sea wall and beach.

Fencing

GENERAL POINTS

Uses

Fencing may be used for a number of purposes directly or indirectly concerned with dune stabilisation, including:

a   Trapping sand at the eroding windward faces of dunes to help maintain their positions and stop blowing sand smothering planted vegetation

b   Creating new embryo dunes in front of existing foredune ridges. In eroding systems the new dunes protect the existing foredunes, and in accreting systems the new dunes reduce sand supplies to the foredunes. In eroding systems the gain may only be seasonal, with sand accumulating in the summer, and eroding in the winter and early spring. In this case fencing is required as a permanent fixture (see p42).

c   Reducing the scouring effect of wind in blowouts and at the same time trapping sand to help fill them in

d   Indicating dune restoration areas, alone or with other fencing and signposting, in order to reduce access

e   Closing off and helping fill in access routes and channelling people onto boardwalks or other non-erodable surfaces

f   Providing sheltered bases or 'nests' for people in areas less easily eroded than the dunes themselves, eg in front of or between dune ridges

Fences which are designed or sited primarily for the last three reasons are discussed further in the next chapter. Even fences which are designed primarily to trap sand affect public access and can be sited in part to restrict use of the dunes.

Other considerations

a   Fencing is the best way to trap sand where so much sand accumulates that marram grass and other plants cannot survive on their own. Such areas are unusual, however, and it may be possible even here to alter the pattern of deposition so that more of the site becomes suitable for planting.

b   Wherever possible, coordinate fencing with planting so that when the fence becomes buried or is removed for reuse the vegetation remains to continue trapping sand. Fences should remain in place until the plants have a chance to become established and can cope with the amount of sand blow.

c   Often, fencing and planting can be carried out at the same time. Where fencing is likely to cause an immediate rapid buildup of sand, wait until this has occurred before planting in the accretion zone. In the meantime, use a mulch to help stabilise the sand surface.

d   Planting is most successful downwind of fences, but you can also plant a strip just to windward after the fences are at least half buried. This helps broaden out the resulting dune profile.

e   Fencing is relatively expensive and laborious. You can reduce costs by using local materials, such as brushwood, or by retrieving fences for re-use before they become buried. Retrieval requires close monitoring of the sand buildup, is usually very time consuming and difficult and almost always disrupts the sand surface. For these reasons it is best, if possible, to use cheap, disposable and biodegradable designs and let them become buried so that some material remains in the sand to help bind it.

f   Fences seldom keep their alignment and may be badly damaged by storms, but they will continue to function as long as they remain exposed and at a steep angle to the wind.

g   The object of sand-trap fencing (with the exception of 'piggy-bank' fencing, p42) is to become quickly and permanently buried so that no trace remains. The job should not be considered completed until the resulting sand mound is planted and stabilised. Fencing that is not working should be removed.

h   The success of sand-trapping fences depends on such factors as the supply of blown sand, wind speeds and fence placement and design (see below). In suitable locations, fences on coastal sites in Britain may accumulate 0.9–1.8m (3–6') of sand in a year.

DESIGN AND PLACEMENT

Porosity

Optimum porosity (the proportion of holes to solid material) for a sand-trapping fence, at right angles to the wind, is between 30% and 50%. At lower porosities there may be a reverse flow of sand at low wind speeds and scouring at high wind speeds. At higher porosities the wind is not slowed enough to drop the maximum load of sand. The optimum porosity for shelter fences is about 35%–40% so this is the range to aim at when erecting fences which serve both purposes (Phillips, 1975). The porosity of the material used for fencing affects both the amount of sand trapped and the shape of the 'dune'.

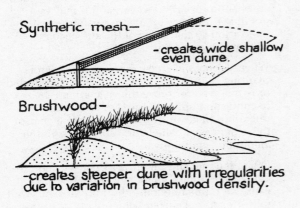

Synthetic mesh— —creates wide shallow even dune.

Brushwood— —creates steeper dune with irregularities due to variation in brushwood density.

Chestnut paling— —creates steepest dune, with notch, caused by scour around pales.

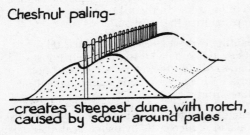

Brushwood tapering to sand surface.

Sand build-up and scour

a   The effect of a porous fence on wind speeds determines the way in which sand is trapped. If the fence is at right angles to the wind, the greatest reduction in wind speed occurs in the area from five to ten times the height of the fence (5h–10h) downwind. Here the wind is reduced to about 25% of its free speed. There is also a smaller, but still effective, slowing of wind on the windward side of the barrier. Along a narrow strip just to both sides of the fence the wind is at full speed, causing a notch effect at the fence (Searle, 1972). Because winds are frequently at angles other than 90° to the fence, this effect is minimised and most sand tends to accumulate about 1.2m (4') behind the fence in the general pattern shown on page 24.

b   Around the ends of the fence, turbulence produces wind speeds of about 110% of free speed. This can cause scour unless the fence ends are positioned in areas which are already as stable as possible or brushwood is used as shown below, to finish the fence.

c   The velocity of wind required to transport sand is given on page 9. It is the bottom 600–900mm (2–3') of fence which traps most sand since even at high wind speeds the sand remains quite near the surface. While a strong wind moves much more sand than a weak one, the ratio of sand trapped by the fence to sand in motion is greater at low than at high wind

speeds. Even so, more sand actually accumulates when wind speeds are 25 mph–30mph (40km/h–48km/h) than at lower speeds, especially where two rows of fences are used in parallel series (Phillips, 1975, p12).

d   The angle of slope of the sand which accumulates around the fence, and the depth of any notch at the fence line, are determined by the wind speed rather than by fence design or positioning. Provided the wind speed stays constant for a long time, the profile reaches equilibrium with sand on the lee side building up about as high as the fence and with the lee slope being very shallow.

Positioning

a   In general you should orientate fences at right angles to the dominant winds (winds of greatest force) for maximum sand buildup, provided these winds occur fairly often.

The best sand-carrying winds are strong and dry. In Britain this means winds from the north or northeast provided the site is suitably exposed. Strong winds from some other quarters may transport surprisingly little sand if they occur with heavy rains and high wave levels.

The easiest way to determine fence alignment is to observe how the sand moves on a really windy day and to position the fences about 1.2m (4') in front of where you want the most sand to build up. Since fences are often moved or replaced every year or so, it is usually easy enough to adjust the layout in accordance with the observed pattern of sand buildup.

b   Damp depressions on the beach cut the amount of loose sand which can be blown by the wind. Position fences some way back from creeks, layers of shells and other moisture-retaining areas.

c   Ideally, you should site fences along or in the lee of areas of fine sand, not coarse sand or 'beach gravel' which is seldom set in motion by the wind. Unfortunately, such areas are often within reach of high storm tides so some compromise may be necessary.

d   Position fences no lower than 1m (3') vertical distance above the mean high water level. Even at this level wave damage is possible and it is usually best to keep fences 2m (6') above MHW.

When in doubt about water levels, or where there is rather little room between existing dunes and the sea, place the seaward fences at the strandline or where dune-building grasses are starting to colonise the beach. Where other indicators are absent, set the fences no more than 7–9m (24–30') in front of existing dunes. You can extend the fences seaward later if necessary, but it is generally best to leave room for embryo dunes to develop to help protect the main dune ridge.

Where it is essential to protect a foredune ridge which is being eroded by storm tides, try one of the systems of fencing described on page 00.

e   Where you want to develop a dune ridge, it is best to erect fences in straight parallel rows about four times the fence height (4h) apart. With fences of normal height (1m) this results in a 4m spacing. On open flat areas, use a spacing of six times the height, and on leeward slopes use a wider spacing of eight to ten times the height (CCS, 1982). Transverse fences may be needed, as detailed below. The greater the number of rows up to a limit of four, the greater their sand trapping efficiency and the less the amount of scour and size of the notches at the fencelines.

f   In normal conditions, straight fences work better than either spur or zig-zag patterns except at very low wind speeds (Phillips, 1975, p10). However, spurs at right angles to the main fences improve performance where the backshore is narrow and sand supplies are low or where occasional strong winds blow parallel to the main fences and scour between them.

The Countryside Commission for Scotland (CCS, 1982) recommend that spurs or transverse fences should be spaced half as much again as the main fences, as shown below.

Normal fence spacing on backshore zone.

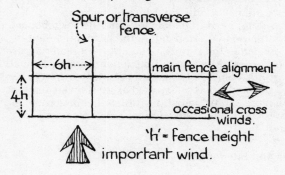

Fence spacing on flat, open areas.

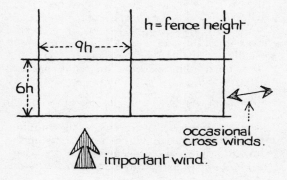

Hewett (1973, p57) recommends using a spur or zig-zag design wherever dunes have formed along the line of the prevailing wind, rather than at right angles to it. When in doubt, start with simple straight fences and observe their performance before modifying the design.

g   Dune ridges can be built up most easily by a programme of sequential fencing carried out over a period of three to five years or so. Of the various ways to do this (eg Phillips, 1975, figure 10), the method recommended by Adriani and Terwindt (1974, p52) is simple and effective. They suggest using low fences (about 1m, 3' high) at first to achieve width, followed by higher fences (about 2m, 6') to develop height. The diagram shows how to do this.

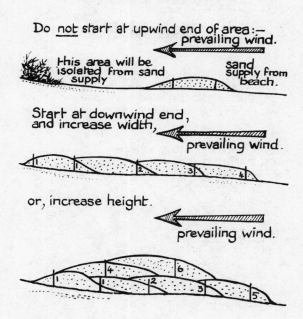

h   Fences on gradual slopes trap more sand than fences on the flat. But on steep slopes, fences shelter only a small area in relation to their height so that sand buildup is highly localised and erosion is likely to continue between rows. To prevent this, contour very steep dunes before fencing them. Where this is not possible, you can place fences close together in series to reduce scour, but where sand supplies are relatively meagre only the first fenceline is likely to trap much sand (Wilcock and Carter, undated, p3). In this situation, fences – especially those near the dune crest – are likely to be undermined by scouring on the windward side.

Blowouts, corridors and bowls

a   When fencing blowouts and other gaps in dune ridges, first concentrate on trapping sand at the downwind end. If you first fence the mouth, or upwind end, you will cut off the sand supply to the rest of the area. Extend the fences as far up the slopes as possible, since a great deal of sand moves along the steep sides of blowouts.

b   When filling a corridor, space the fences as shown (CCS, 1982). There is no need to build transverse fences as winds are funnelled through the gap. Make sure that the fence ends

41

are extended into the sides of the dunes, so that scour does not occur.

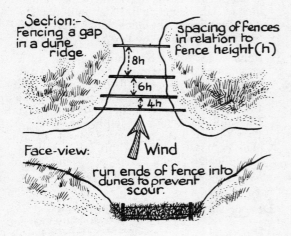

Section:- Fencing a gap in a dune ridge.

spacing of fences in relation to fence height (h)

8h

6h

4h

Face-view:

Wind

run ends of fence into dunes to prevent scour.

c   In eroding bowls, wind patterns are complex, and a box system of fencing is the most satisfactory, so that sand is trapped whichever way the winds blow.

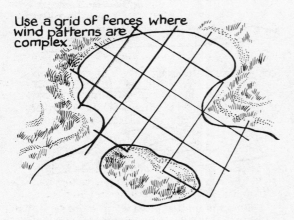

Use a grid of fences where wind patterns are complex

Contoured areas

Where large areas of dune have been bulldozed, sand trap fencing may be needed in addition to marram planting, to continue the process of dune building. In North Cornwall, the basic plan is a grid of fences, creating boxes about 25m square. It has been found that wind direction and the amount of sand blow is difficult to predict, especially on sites where the local topography of cliffs, headlands and valleys complicates the wind pattern. These fences are economical to build in terms of straining posts, as each one can be used in more than one direction. The grid makes an obvious and formidable obstacle which discourages people going into the area, and divides the area up to ease the rather monotonous job of marram planting. Sand is first trapped in the corners of each box, gradually building up until the whole level has been raised. More boxes are then built as necessary. In this case the fences are of strained wire and 'strawberry netting', but other types of material are also suitable (see p49). No attempt is made to retrieve fence material, as this is too time consuming and disturbs the accumulated sand. However, once sand has stopped building up, any fence wire or netting showing at the surface is removed and disposed of to keep the site tidy.

Access routes are usually needed through restored areas. The plan below shows the layout of fencing used at Hayle, near St Ives in Cornwall. This is a heavily used access point from a large caravan site to the beach, which started as a footpath, and eroded to a 100ft deep gully. A seven acre area was contoured by bulldozer, and then fencing was carried out.

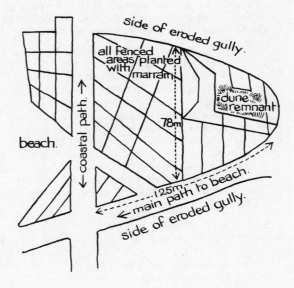

side of eroded gully.

all fenced areas planted with marram.

dune remnant

78m

beach.

coastal path.

125m

main path to beach.

side of eroded gully.

Where an area is at an acceptable height and profile after bulldozing, and wind blow is unlikely to be a problem, sand trap fencing is not necessary. However, access control fencing will be needed to keep the public out of the newly planted areas. See page 63.

Fencing Materials and Techniques

MATERIALS

There are many different types of materials which can be used for sand dune fencing, and the best choice for any situation will depend on the factors detailed below. Often the simplest and cheapest materials are also the best. Most sand dune fencing has a relatively short life, compared to fencing elsewhere, and is liable to be either buried or exposed as sand levels change. The more sophisticated the design and materials, the more work is likely to be involved in repairing or removing it.

Use and intended life

a   If the fence is required only for sand trapping, and will hopefully be buried within a few months, the cheapest, degradable material such as brushwood is the most suitable. Where brushwood is not available, the next best material to use is the cheapest obtainable synthetic material, supported on non-preserved posts and mild steel wire. A life of a year is usually acceptable, as if the fence has not become buried in that time, it possibly never will.

b   Some sand trap fences are designed to trap sand seasonally, the sand then being eroded back seawards during winter storms, or blown into eroded dune areas by winds from a different direction. The aim of this 'piggy bank' fencing is that it remains in position for as many years as possible, the sand accumulating and eroding on an annual cycle. In this case the fencing should be as permanent as possible, usually built of tanalised posts and 4.00mm mild steel wire, supporting chestnut paling or strong synthetic fabric. Brushwood can be used, either alone or attached to post and wire fencing, but will only have a life of about two years before it breaks up and needs replacing. Timber slat fencing (p49) is also suitable. Two examples of this type of use are shown below. See also page 34.

vulnerable foredune face, protected by seasonal dune

seasonal dune, formed in spring and summer, and washed away by winter gales.

winds

fore-dune

co-dominant wind

occasional cross-wind

blows sand into blow-out

blow out

sand trapped by fences

co-dominant wind

c   For access control purposes, fences need to be suitable for the anticipated public pressure. Normally, such fences will be needed to last for several years, before changing sand levels affect them. However, in areas recently restored with planting, sand build-up may be rapid, so that access control fences need lifting or replacing after only one season.

A whole range of materials can be used for access control fences. Brushwood or chestnut paling are suitable where their ability to trap sand is not going to cause problems. Chestnut paling is useful because it can be lifted and re-used. It can also be erected with a gap at the bottom so that it does not trap sand (see p65).

d   Wave barrier fencing (see p34) is probably the most difficult to build, as it is so vulnerable to destruction by the sea. Brushwood only, set in

holes about 600mm (2') deep, can be effective, and if this is lost, at least there is no high material cost wasted (although labour costs for handling this material may be high). Otherwise, a post and chestnut paling fence is probably the best type to use.

Vandalism

A problem closely related to access is that of vandalism. Particularly vulnerable is any material which can be removed for beach bonfires. Losses of brushwood can be reduced by attaching it to post and wire fences (see p46). The deeper posts are buried in the sand, the more difficult it is to remove them. Chestnut paling needs to be kept in good repair to discourage people helping themselves to any loose pieces.

Where vandalism is a more serious problem, chestnut paling and other types of wooden fencing are unlikely to last long, and post and wire fencing will be necessary, with strong synthetic material such as 'Wyretex' (see p49) for sand trapping. Thicker wire, of 3.15 or 4.00mm diameter, is more difficult to cut than thinner wire. It is dangerous to cut any wires while they are under tension, and particularly high tensile wire. High tensile 3.15mm wire retains its springiness, even when persistently climbed on.

Good layout of fences and paths, with clear signing, greatly reduces damage caused by people inadvertently finding themselves on the wrong side of a fence, and causing damage when they climb over or break through. For more details on access control fencing, see the chapter on Access Management.

Labour, access and availability of materials

a   Brushwood fencing is much more labour intensive than other types of fencing, because of the time required to cut, gather and transport the material, as well as the time taken to erect the fence. However, where brushwood is being cut anyway as part of management within the dune system, or is available by the lorry load from elsewhere, the time factor is less significant. It is a job suitable for volunteers, as many hands can be employed, and the work is not as skilled as some other types of fencing.

b   On remote sites, and those where brushwood is not available locally, other material must be used. Synthetic netting or pre-fabricated timber slat fencing can be brought in, and is quick to erect, so making the best use of labour which is only available for a short time, such as on a volunteer project. On remote sites, it may be important to use the most lightweight material available.

c   Labour to maintain fences is also an important factor. Where no maintenance is likely, either 'cheap' materials such as brushwood, or low-maintenance materials such as timber slat fencing are most suitable. Chestnut paling usually requires regular maintenance.

d   Strained wire and chestnut paling fences can be erected quite quickly by a few skilled people. In places where machinery can get access, a mechanical post driver can be used which speeds up the job considerably.

Appearance

Sand dunes are amongst the most natural habitats in Britain, and even those which are damaged and degraded by erosion remain essentially wild and un-managed places.

a   Fencing should not mar this natural appearance. Most sand fencing which is well-built and maintained is acceptable, given that repair of the dunes is necessary. Effective sand-trap fencing rapidly becomes filled with sand, and access control fences need not be an eyesore. Fencing that is poorly maintained or vandalised, or sand-trap fencing that is not functioning will always be an intrusive element.

b   Fencing that is neat and tidy in appearance is more likely to be respected by the public than fencing which is poorly constructed or badly maintained.

c   Sand trap fencing which follows a smooth line, for example along the front of the foredunes, and is of even quality and porosity throughout will trap sand evenly, making a long even dune which matches the natural sweep of the beachline. Such dunes are less likely to erode, because there is nothing to create turbulence. Fencing of a patchy uneven quality will create patchy results.

Length of fence

Strained wire fences are not usually worth erecting over lengths of less than about 10m, because the main effort, time and expense goes into erecting the straining posts, which can be used over a much greater distance. Therefore, synthetic fabrics which need supporting on tensioned wires are better suited to longer fence lines. Chestnut paling should not be highly tensioned, and for most fences on sand dunes, straining posts are not required (see p48). Wire for supporting brushwood does not have to be highly strained, and therefore can be erected over short distances without straining posts.

TECHNIQUES

There are two basic types of post and wire fence used on sand dunes:

a   Strained wire fences. These fences are usually over 10m in length, and are used either for access control, or to support synthetic netting for trapping sand. The fence has a straining post at either end, which takes the strain of the wire. The intermediate posts strengthen and stiffen the fence, and hold the wires at the correct height. When constructing the fence, wire strainers such as 'Monkey' strainers are used at the straining post to pull the wire tight. Either mild steel wire or high tensile steel wire can be used, the latter requiring stronger straining posts. The wire is fastened off at the straining posts, but at the intermediates is held by a staple driven far enough to just touch, but not grip the wire.

b   Non-strained wire fences. These are short lengths of wire and brushwood or chestnut paling fence. No straining posts are built, so the wire cannot be tightly strained but is merely tensioned by hand, and fastened to each post with a staple which grips the wire (though does not distort it). The strain is thus held equally at each post. Monkey strainers are not used. The posts are normally spaced closer together than are the intermediate posts of strained fences.

Straining posts

The following method should be sufficient for most sand trap fences. If necessary the post can be strengthened by fitting a 'Spanish windlass' (see p50). Where long lengths of strained fencing are being constructed, one of the designs of strainer shown for access control should be used (see p63).

Use a post about 125–150mm diameter (5–6″) and long enough for at least 1m (3′) to be below the surface. Dig out a large stepped hole before placing the post. Then nail anchor plates, about 1m (3′) long, in opposite pairs as shown. Backfill the hole, treading it to pack the sand firmly. If there is water nearby, it can be sprinkled on every 50mm (2″) layer, to settle the sand.

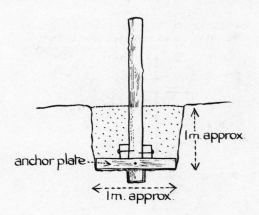

Other posts

The usual method of erecting posts is to dig a hole 760–900mm (2½–3′) deep, using a shuv-holer. Place the post in position, and then backfill, tamping the sand with an upturned post. The tamper can be used to 'collapse' the side of the hole against the post, then the upper part is filled by shovelling.

Hole digging is easy enough in deep sand, but can be a slow job on sites where there is a buried beach line of shingle which is hard to dig through. Do not put posts in less than 760mm (2′) deep, or they may be easily loosened and removed by vandals.

Alternatively, posts can be melled into sand with a 'Drivall' or mell. This is quicker than digging, but does not usually get the post as deep or as firm in the sand as when the post is set in a dug hole. Where access by machine is possible, posts can be driven in quickly and firmly by a tractor mounted post driver.

Wire and fastening

Wire is sold by weight, and therefore the thicker the wire the higher the cost. Weight for weight, mild steel and high tensile steel wire are a similar price. Never use barbed wire in sand dune fencing, as it can be dangerous if it becomes partly buried.

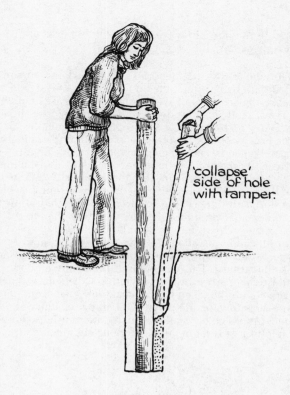

'collapse' side of hole with tamper.

Do not use more staples than necessary; usually two per wire should be enough. All stapling damages the wire galvanising, so reducing wire life, and adds to the non-degradable content of the fence. Staples can be dangerous if they work free and lie loose in the sand.

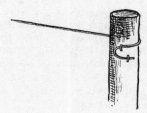

Always hammer staples at an angle, so the two points enter different grains in the timber. This lessens the chance of the wood splitting. At straining posts, hammer the staple so that it grips the wire, but not so far that the wire is severely distorted and the staple head flattened. At intermediate posts, the staple serves only to locate the wire at the correct height. It is therefore sufficient to hammer the staple so that it just touches, but does not grip the wire. This holds the wire so that it does not wear against the staple when moved by the wind, but allows it to move if for example a weight is leant against the fence.

BRUSHWOOD FENCING

Brushwood fencing is most suited to areas having a plentiful supply of cuttings from nearby scrub thickets or forestry plantations. You can use any sort of brush as long as it retains its density. Sea buckthorn is ideal, provided you cut it in autumn and leave it to die over the winter. Otherwise it may resprout when 'planted' in fences. All brushwood fences are tempting sources of firewood, but sea buckthorn is too thorny and hard to burn to attract much interest. Conifer thinnings burn easily and are more likely to be taken. Spruces and firs are better than pines and larches because they have a flatter spread of branches and so remain bushy even when the needles have dropped off. Pines and larches, with their curved or twisted branches, become thin and ragged once they have dried.

Bacon (1975, p8) recommends Norway spruce (*Picea abies*) as ideal, followed by Sitka spruce (*P sitchensis*), Douglas fir (*Pseudotsuga menziesii*) and western hemlock (*Tsuga heterophylla*) in that order.

Another good source of brushwood material are unsold Christmas trees (usually *Picea abies*). Their value drops to nothing on Christmas Eve each year, and if you find a garden centre or shop which has over-purchased, the manager may be glad to get rid of an embarrassing surplus. A further advantage is that cut trees are packed 'flat' for delivery from the plantations, thus onward transport is fairly economical. The flattened shape is also useful when fence-building. In some places sand dune managers have also asked members of the public to bring along their discarded trees after Christmas. Although this may not amount to very much in terms of brushwood, it can be a good publicity exercise to encourage interest from local people.

For long lengths of fence supporting synthetic netting, and for access control fencing, high tensile wire can be used. This has the advantage over mild steel wire of greater springiness, and retains its tension under changing temperatures and if people climb on it. It needs properly constructed straining posts, and must be unrolled and handled with care, as weak points can develop if the wire is kinked. The 3.15mm diameter size has been found satisfactory in use. On sand dunes, it can be strained at least 100m between straining posts, taking it around turning posts as necessary. Much longer strains are possible in firm soils. The best method of fastening high tensile wire to straining posts is to use spiral fence connectors, which grip the wire as shown. These are available from major fencing suppliers. Note that only one staple is needed, to locate the wire at the correct height.

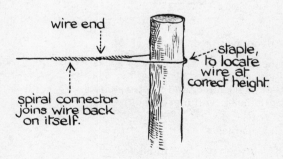

wire end

spiral connector joins wire back on itself.

staple, to locate wire at correct height.

Mild steel wire can also be used, and is suitable for straining over lengths of up to 50m between straining posts. The size normally used is 3.15mm, which is reasonably easy to handle, but needs wire cutters or a hacksaw to cut, so discouraging petty vandalism. The 4.00mm size can be used as a greater deterrent, but is more expensive and slightly more awkward to erect because of its relative non-pliability.

If spiral fence connectors are not used, the wire should be fastened off at the straining post as shown.

Virtually any brushwood can be used. The important factor is the time taken to gather and transport it (see below). Loppings from roadside trees or parks that have anyway to be put on a lorry for disposal may be worth obtaining, especially where this helps the authority concerned by saving on disposal costs.

Most brushwood has a life of about two years before it starts to break up, which is ample time to allow for sand build-up. Buckthorn lasts about five years, and is therefore better used for access control fencing, or for erosion control on inland blowout, where there is no sand supply and the aim is to prevent further sand loss and allow natural regeneration to take place.

Collecting and bundling brushwood

Collecting and bundling brushwood is a good job for winter, when felling is likely to be underway and when sheltered work is at a premium. Ideally, the plantation should contain the desirable species, be accessible for transport in all weathers, have been brashed within the past year and certainly no more than three years previously (the branches become brittle with age), have an abundance of brashings and a minimum of honeysuckle, bramble and thorn for efficient collection, and be as close to the work site as possible to reduce transport costs. The last consideration is the least important, up to a distance of 20 miles (32km), since loading is more time-consuming than transport within this distance (Bacon, 1975, p8).

Once you find the plantation, you may be able to persuade the landowner, forester and gamekeeper to let you collect brushwood free of charge since clearance reduces fire risks, improves access for future forestry work and may be used to open up the forest floor for pheasants (you may have to leave brushwood around the plantation edge, for cover).

Bundling the brushwood reduces the work time and effort by two thirds compared with transporting it loose. Lay out lengths of twine (old baler twine is ideal and may be available free from farms) and place branches across them, with the butt ends one way, so that the tied strings will be at the balance points of the bundles. Grade the branches roughly into two sizes, or as required. Use one string per bundle for branches up to 1.5m (5′) long, two strings for 1.5–3m (5′–10′) long branches. Brash over 3m (10′) long is not worth the effort in handling. Tie the string with a slip knot, pull it really tight and secure it with a half-hitch.

You can leave bundles in the woods for up to twelve months (three months for brash with needles on) provided you prop them against a tree trunk so that they keep dry. Bundles propped at the edge of the wood or under a light canopy may deteriorate due to vegetation growing up through them.

Dutch fencing

The original Dutch fencing was of cut reeds or willows, being the only material available in the fenlands of Holland, which was set into a trench dug in the sand. This technique is still used. In Britain, any available brushwood can be used, such as Christmas trees, conifer brashings, loppings of birch, alder etc. Sturdy, well-branched material can be set singly into holes dug in a row in the sand. The holes should be 450–900mm (1½–3′) deep, depending on the height of the brushwood, and the rapidity with which sand is expected to accumulate. Brushwood used

within the range of wave action should be set as deeply as possible.

Thinner, less sturdy material should be bundled and tied with baler twine, the bundles being of a size to make the brushwood stay upright, and dense enough to trap sand. The bundles can be set in holes, or in a trench 750–900mm (2½–3′) deep. Space the holes, or the brushwood within the trench, so that the porosity of the fence is as even as possible along its length. Normally the holes or bundles should be 300–450mm (1–1½′) apart. Make sure that there is plenty of brush at the base of the fence, or the wind will simply scour underneath. If necessary shorten the bare part of the main stem. Christmas trees are well branched to the base, and where sand accumulation is likely to be rapid, can be set about 450mm (1½′) deep. Some species may resprout, particularly willow, poplar and sea buckthorn. This can be useful on badly eroded sites where any growing vegetation is beneficial, but care should be taken that undesirable species do not spread into valuable parts of the dune habitat. Sea buckthorn is a particular menace, and cuttings should be left for several months before use in fencing.

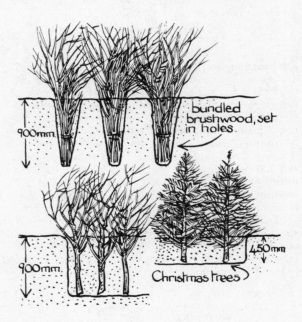

Advantages:

Cheap
Biodegradable
Can be used for sand trapping and access control
Suitable for voluntary labour

Disadvantages:

Brushwood can be vandalised
Bulky to transport
Some material may sprout (though this can be useful)

Post and wire fencing with brushwood added

This is more durable than Dutch fencing, as the wire holds the brushwood in place against wind and wave action, and discourages vandalism. All sorts of brushwood can be used, including material which may be too short to use in Dutch fencing. Post and wire with brushwood is recommended where fencing is needed for both access control and sand trapping, and where the fence may need to stay in position for several seasons. It should not be necessary to use post and wire where sand is expected to accumulate within a few months.

Post and wire with brushwood is more time consuming to erect than Dutch fencing, and is more expensive in materials. It is also a nuisance to clear up if it becomes damaged or undermined. Whether or not wire is necessary depends very much on the location of the site, and the amount of supervision and management it receives. Remote sites, or those which are heavily used for recreation but are not constantly managed are likely to need the insurance of post and wire. By contrast, on some parts of the Sefton coast, Merseyside, the move is away from using post and wire, as it has been found that with sufficient labour and supplies of brushwood it is possible to quickly place effective Dutch fencing. If done over the winter, this should be mainly buried by the start of the busy summer season. The area is closely wardened throughout the year.

Advantages:

Reasonably durable
Discourages vandalism
Access control use

Disadvantages:

Slow to build
Cost of post and wire
Not biodegradable

Several designs have been used:

a   Brushwood between parallel wires. This design can be varied to suit local conditions and materials. Bacon (1975, p7) recommends the type shown below, which has been used on National Trust sites on the Northumberland coast. You can use old net stakes and baling wire for economy, since even if the fences start to deteriorate in four to six months they should be well buried by that time.

Knock the posts in securely. Using a stake or crowbar, pitch holes in two rows, 150mm (6″) apart, to take the brushwood. Make the holes 300–600mm (1–2′) apart within the rows, and at least 300mm (1′) deep. Push sturdy 1.8–2.4m (6–8′) branches into the holes, with their curvature towards the centre. Secure them with 2.50mm wire, running each side of the double row from post to post, about 900mm (3′) above ground level. Place intermediate ties at 900mm (3′) intervals between the posts. Trim off the tops of the branches as necessary. This not only looks neat, but means that the fence should fill to the top, with no line of odd protruding branches remaining to mark its position.

Variations on this design, which have worked well on a number of work sites, include using 2.1m (7′) unpointed posts for greater security in soft sand, using shorter branches to make a somewhat lower fence where brushwood is scarce, placing the wires near the top of the fence, and twisting the wires together with a wrecking bar to tighten them around the brushwood.

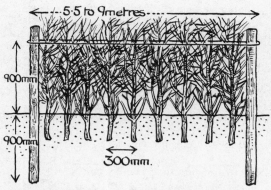

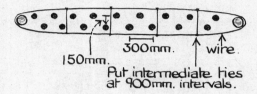

Plan View showing holes for brushwood.

This latter technique is done to tension the wires after the fence is complete. However, it can also be done at more frequent intervals while the fence is being built, to hold the brushwood securely in position and deter firewood gatherers. Some slack must be left at each end of the wire, which is taken up as the wire is twisted. This does tend to make a rather gappy fence, so additional material may need to be added, tied to the horizontal wires.

b   'Woven' brushwood fences. This design uses more stakes and wire but less brushwood than the fence described above, and is best employed where brushwood is scarce and where stakes can be firmed securely so that the wire can be tensioned.

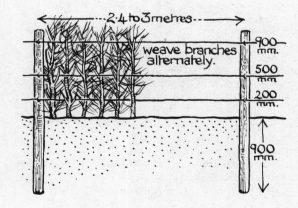

Such fences should last at least a year. Care must be taken to weave the brushwood closely so that an even cover is made. This can be quite difficult, especially with sparse material such as pine or larch. Very twiggy material such as birch is probably the best.

c   Tied brushwood fences. For Christmas trees and other bushy material it is easier to omit the middle wire and attach each piece by tying its 'trunk' or main stem to the top and bottom wires. A spacing of 200–300mm (8–12″)

between stems is usually sufficient. The quickest method of attachment is to use sack ties, twisted into place with a wire tying tool or ratchet screwdriver. Otherwise, just attach with short lengths of baling wire, twisted to tighten.

Post-and-rail fences with brushwood added

These are suitable for use on machair-edge restoration work.

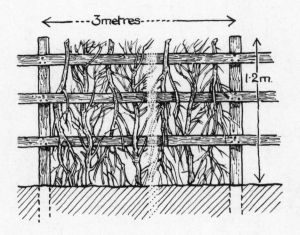

These fences are most easily made and last longest if sawn tanalised fence posts and rails are used.

Brushwood-and-stake fencing

These low barriers have been used successfully at Holkham National Nature Reserve, Norfolk, both to trap sand and to divert people onto an adjacent boardwalk.

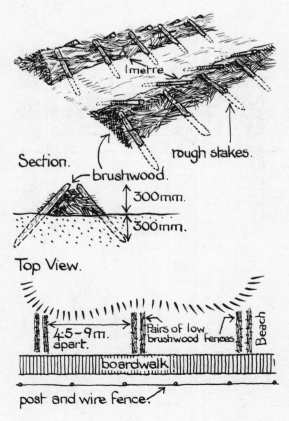

Fences are positioned at right angles to the walkway across a wide gap in the fixed dunes. They are placed in pairs, each fence about 1m (3′) from its partner. This discourages people from walking over the low fences and creates strips of protected sand in which plants can grow.

With pairs of fences installed at 4.5–9m (15–30′) intervals along the gap, most people are dissuaded from walking in the fenced area and keep to the boardwalk.

The fences are quick and easy to make using cuttings and fallen brush from nearby plantations. Brushwood is laid flat on the sand and held with rough stakes driven in at an angle. No digging is required and the turf remains relatively undisturbed. Where the brushwood has convenient branches these can be woven over the stakes to help hold the fences more tightly together.

Chestnut paling

With the increasing cost of transporting brushwood, chestnut paling is becoming more competitive as a material for sand trapping. It is quicker to erect than wire and brushwood fencing, so is useful where labour is limited. It is more effective than brushwood for sites which are subject to wave action.

The type commonly used is 1.07m (3½′) high, with 75mm (3″) pales and 75mm (3″) gaps, joined with three double strands of wire. It is supplied in 9.2m (10yd) lengths. This should be supported on 2m (6′6″) posts of approximately 100mm (4″) diameter, set 1m (3′) in the sand. Space the posts at 1.8m (6′) or 3m (10′) intervals, depending on the site and pressure of use. The paling should not be tightly strained, as the wire used to bind the pales is not suitable for tensioning.

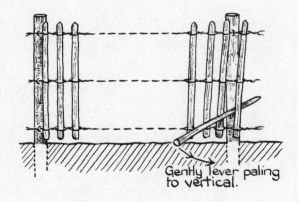

There is also no satisfactory way of securing the wires if the paling is pulled tightly, as in order to stop the wires slipping at the staple, the staple has to be driven in so far that the wire is damaged. Use one staple per strand at each post, hammered to grip but not distort the wires. First attach the paling to the end post, then pull by hand at the next post and staple, or gently use a crowbar or spade as a lever, as shown. Do not over-do this, or the pale will break. The pales should remain vertical and parallel to the posts. If possible arrange it so that joins in the paling coincide with a post. If not, simply join the lengths by twisting the free ends around the first pale of the next length, to imitate the method of manufacture. Do not twist the wire more than necessary or it will snap.

Slabwood fencing

Fencing using slabwood is not recommended, as the usual width of 75–125mm (5–7″) is too wide, in effect making the fence too solid, and causing scour at the base and between the slabs. It is also vulnerable to firewood-gathering.

Timber slat fencing

The Countryside Commission for Scotland have devised a system of timber slat panels, using slats 75mm (3″) by 8mm, with 75mm (3″) spacing. This method is useful on sites where brushwood is not available, as the panels can be assembled in a workshop and quickly erected on site. Full details are given in their information sheet 5.2.5 (CCS, 1982).

SYNTHETIC MATERIALS

A wide range of synthetic fabrics have been tried for sand trapping. Note the following:

a   Most of the materials require attachment to a strained wire fence. This can be of either mild steel or high tensile steel wire, depending on the length of run, and the ability to erect secure straining posts.

b   Materials vary in their porosity, and thus in the shape of the dune they create. However, all create a uniform profile along their length, because of the uniformity of product.

c   Materials vary in their durability against waves, wind, ultra-violet light and vandalism. The estimated time required for sand filling must be weighed against the estimated life of the product. Degradability is a useful quality once sand-trapping is complete.

d   All materials are light and easy to handle, compared to brushwood or timber slat fencing.

Advantages:

Lightweight
Useful for remote sites
Quick to erect
Creates uniform dune

Disadvantages:

Expensive
Difficult to achieve durability against wind and vandalism, with degradability

A summary of the available materials follows:

Enkamat

This is a flexible three-dimensional matting, originally designed for laying on banks of ditches, roadsides and reservoirs, to stabilise the surface and allow vegetation to become established. It has also been found to be useful as a vertical fence, for sand trapping. Enkamat is made of filaments of black nylon welded together to form a tough mat with 95% free space. It is available in various thicknesses and widths, with or without a backing material on the 'flat' side. The type which appears to be the most effective is 7020, which is 20mm thick, and has no backing material. This is available in either 1 or 5m widths, of which the

former is suitable for sand fences. It should be attached to posts spaced at 2m intervals, using three strands of 3.15mm wire threaded through the material and stapled to the stakes. Although black in colour, Enkamat is not too obtrusive as the 'pockets' rapidly get filled with sand. As it tends to trap sand within it, this material makes a fairly steep-profiled dune. It is difficult to vandalise.

Wyretex

This is a reinforced fabric of ultra-violet and acid resistant polypropylene and galvanised steel wire, twisted together and then woven. It is manufactured in Scotland, and used for erosion control on banks, as a foundation for roads and tracks and many other uses. Various grades are available, according to the density of the weave. Grade 4 or 5 is suitable for sand fencing. Wyretex is very strong, resists wind and wave action, and is difficult to vandalise. It is a fairly unobtrusive grey colour.

Posts should be spaced 3m apart for mild steel wires, and up to 6m apart for high tensile steel wires. Wyretex is manufactured in 1½m widths, and is best used to full height on 2½m posts. Where this height is not required, the bottom ½m can be buried in the sand, although this is only serving a useful purpose if undercutting occurs. Thread a top and bottom wire through the fabric, in approximately 300mm-long 'stitches'. At the posts, fasten the fabric with a vertical batten nailed every 300mm, or alternatively a piece of wire stapled vertically. Do not staple direct through the fabric, or it may tear.

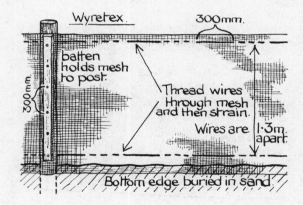

Strawberry netting

Cornwall County Council originally started using this material when they were offered a cheap job lot which had been inadvertently manufactured to the wrong width for strawberry protection. It has proved successful for sand trapping, and is now manufactured in a one metre width, for this purpose. It is a lightweight material, and is not ultra-violet resistant, and thus deteriorates after only a year. However, this has been found sufficient as expertise is gained in positioning of fences, and is a positive advantage as little clearing up is needed of odd lengths or ends which remain exposed. The netting is used double, which makes the fence only slightly cheaper than using Enkamat. An advantage is its pinky-buff colour, which fades to become almost invisible amongst the dunes.

The netting is supported 75mm (3") from the top and bottom edge by 2.50mm mild steel wires, stapled to 75mm (3") by 1.1m (43") posts at 5m (16') intervals.

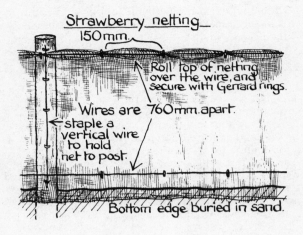

The staples are 30 × 2.50mm, galvanised. The netting is attached to the wires with Gerrard (Gordian) ring gun staples every 150mm (6"), and to the posts with a vertical wire stapled to grip the netting against the post. A shallow trench is dug to fit the bottom wire and lower edge of netting, and is backfilled to complete. Formerly, 'A' frame strainers were used to support the fence, but these are no longer found necessary, as from better knowledge of fence placement, the fences are quickly buried. Instead, the end posts are held firm by 'Spanish windlasses'.

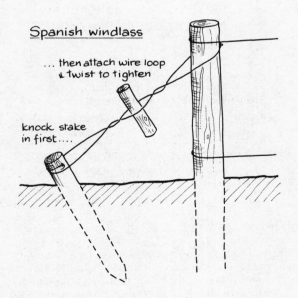

Tensar

Netlon Ltd manufacture a range of 'Tensar' fencing and windbreak products, and recommend 'Shelter Shading' for sand fencing. This is made of high density polyethylene, 1.5mm thick, and with 42% porosity. It is available in 10 × 1m and 30 × 1m lengths, and should be supported on 100mm diameter posts at 3m intervals, attached by battens nailed to the posts. The material can be tensioned using Monkey strainers, attached to a 50mm batten or steel pin threaded through the mesh. Do not over-tension. Lengths are joined by overlapping the ends and threading a batten through the two thicknesses. 'Tensar' is satisfactory if it remains taut, but if it slackens as sand gathers against it, the weight can cause failure of the fence. Extreme conditions of sunlight and wind at the coast may mean a life of only one year before it deteriorates. Being black, the material is rather obtrusive.

Paraweb

Paraweb is made of terylene filaments, encased in black polyethylene, and is claimed to be durable in extreme conditions of sun and wind for over 15 years. The material is made of 50mm wide horizontal webs, joined with vertical webs, to give 46% porosity. Suitable widths for sand fencing are 1m and 1.4m, supplied in 30m lengths. Like Tensar, it is effective while it remains taut, but can fail from the weight of sand accumulation or undermining by wave action, leaving a tangled mess which is an eyesore and a nuisance to clear up. Both Tensar and Paraweb have the advantage that no wires are necessary, thus lessening the non-degradable content of the fence.

Paraweb can be tensioned with Monkey strainers, and should be attached to posts with battens or special staples available from the manufacturers. The webbing should not be punctured by staples or nails, unless finishing off loose ends not under tension.

Synthetic materials: suppliers

Enkamat	MMG Erosion Control Systems, Waterloo House, Kings Lynn, Norfolk PE30 1PA Tel 0553 774423
Wyretex	Malcolm, Ogilvie and Co Ltd, Constable Works, Dundee DD3 6NL Tel 0382 22974
Strawberry Netting	Mr. M Cain, Manor Cottage, Dark Lane, Chew Magna, Avon.
Tensar	Netlon Ltd, Kelly Street, Blackburn BB2 4PJ Tel 0254 62431
Paraweb	ICI Linear Composites Ltd, Hookstone Road, Harrogate, N. Yorkshire HG2 8QN Tel 0423 68021

6 Access Management

This chapter describes basic principles and methods of directing and limiting public access on sand dunes. Further details and techniques are given in other handbooks in this series: 'Footpaths' (Agate, 1983) and 'Fencing' (Agate, 1986). The information sheets produced by the Countryside Commission for Scotland include one on beach recreation management (CCS, 1984), with others covering designs for boardwalks, car barriers and other items.

Access management is needed initially to prevent or reduce erosion of dunes, and to protect dune stabilisation works. Secondary work may include the creation of educational and recreational features such as nature trails, view points and pony tracks, as alternatives to free range use of the area.

Factors to Consider

GENERAL PRINCIPLES

a   Successful access control requires a unified strategy determined by site conditions and local patterns of public pressure. Coastal access control usually involves restricting access to sensitive areas, such as unstable foredunes, while channelling people along attractive erosion-resistant routes through or around the restricted areas.

b   It is vital for the success of dune restoration schemes to get access working for you, not against you. This means sorting out parking and access first, before doing major planting or fencing work. Otherwise you will be constantly struggling against the force of public pressure and trampling.

c   Some parts of the coast withstand public pressure much better than others. Foreshores and beaches can tolerate high densities of people and, where the foreshore is strongly accreting, can even take vehicles without serious damage. Slacks, stable backdunes and dune grasslands withstand more intensive use than exposed dunes near the sea. By allowing relatively free access to seashore and inland 'buffer zones', pressure may be relieved on the more sensitive areas between. Selected areas within the buffer zones can be developed as 'honey pots' to divert attention from elsewhere. 'Furniture' such as picnic tables and children's play equipment and features such as bare slopes for sliding provide positive inducements for people to stay in a particular area.

d   Access control begins at the car park. Its location and capacity, along with any auxiliary (eg roadside) parking, set the approximate maximum number of visitors during peak periods. The first way to reduce pressure is to prevent parking along trackways, and confine it to car parks of a size and design consistent with site requirements. Sometimes existing de facto car parks must be tolerated, but they should be made official by having their boundaries set and signposted.

e   Once parking is under control, the main task is to channel people from car parks to the beach. Most visitors are interested in little else, and they will beat their own paths to the sea unless suitably attractive routes are provided.

f   Dunes are of secondary interest to most people except on windy days and at high tides when they provide shelter and play areas for children. High dunes may also be used as viewpoints. These needs can be catered for by providing 'nests' for family-sized groups, for example by mowing the grass on the lee edges of foredunes and in dry slacks, or by clearing picnic sites within thickets of backdune scrub. Such areas must be sited with care and the paths to and from them should be aligned to limit erosion in the immediate vicinity.

g   Existing public rights of way must not be obstructed no matter how convenient this might be from the site manager's viewpoint. Sometimes routes can be redirected but to do this legally is a slow process and may do more harm than good if it arouses local opposition. It can often be more effective to provide attractively surfaced, landscaped and signposted alternatives to existing rights of way. However, this may cause problems in later years if the new route is also claimed as a right of way.

h   Nature trails attract visitors who want general site access, but they create additional pressure where it may previously have been low. Such trails often become eroded around view points. At some coastal sites, such as Braunton Burrows NNR, Devon, nature trails have been tried and abandoned for this reason. Elsewhere, as at Ainsdale Sand Dunes NNR, Merseyside, trails are open only on an advance-booking quota system so that use can be monitored and restricted as necessary. Another approach, as at Oxwich NNR on the Gower Peninsula, is to shift nature trail routes occasionally to 'rest' over-used parts of the dunes.

i   Access control measures must be in keeping with the character of the environment. Car parks, fences and signposts are often obtrusive on the coast and, particularly in wild and remote areas, erosion may be no more unsightly than controls.

j   Access control usually requires back-up in the form of wardening and strong byelaws. Wardens can deal with careless or thoughtless visitors and with egg collectors and poachers who are undeterred by signs and fences. But without byelaws a warden can do little aside from friendly persuasion. On some sites, vandalism and trespass are major problems and wardens are equipped with portable radios. On these sites, too, good relations with the local police are vital so that serious offenders can be prosecuted.

Car Parks

The location, size and layout of car parks are important factors determining access to dunes and beaches. The location of the car park in relation to the beach is considered first.

Distant from beach

Access from car parks that are distant from the beach is often relatively easy to manage, as people have fewer options. The access is likely to be initially through scrub or fixed dune, which is the most stable part of the system, with few problems of path construction. Car parks and paths cut through scrub are usually simple to manage as there is no temptation for people to leave the designated route. The free-draining soils mean that the surface can stay usable even in wet weather, unlike such enclosed paths on heavy soils. However, where artificial surfacing or boardwalks are needed, the path may be expensive to install or maintain, because of the length involved. Fencing may not be needed though, as people are less likely to stray once they are on a path which is comfortable to walk on and is perceived to be taking the quickest route to the beach.

Near the beach

Access from car parks near the beach can cause problems, as people tend to take short cuts when they are within sight and sound of the sea. The usual pattern is as shown, with people spreading seawards from along the edge of the car park, either walking through the gullies, or scrambling to the top of the dunes for the view. Thus the whole zone between the car park and beach can become eroded.

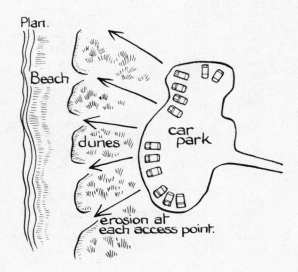

The most severe restriction to access would be made by fencing the whole car park, leaving only one access point taking visitors along a surfaced path or boardwalk to the beach. Although this is the cheapest solution in terms of path building costs, it will be expensive in initial fencing costs, as on most sites a fairly formidable barrier will be needed to stop people short cutting. Frequent repair may also be needed. A better solution is likely to be found in making two or three paths, with any fencing as more of a guide than a restrictive barrier. These paths can be treated in different ways, as has been done at Formby, Merseyside. Here one route has a boardwalk along much of its length, making it suitable for pushchairs and wheelchairs. The central path has gravel surfacing plus some boardwalk, making it suitable for average use. The southern path is the most heavily used, and is a wide path up and over a dune which is treated at

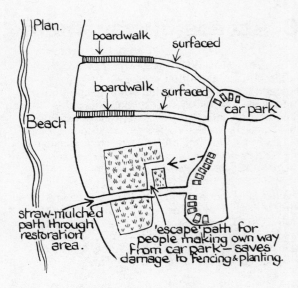

least twice a year with a straw mulch (see p56). There are likely to still be some people who will wander between the paths, but this can be contained by using brushwood, thatching and fencing at strategic points where people may be tempted off.

On the beach

Parking on the beach is traditional in some areas, where there is space and the sand is firm enough. Examples include Ainsdale, Merseyside, and Ynyslas, Dyfed. This does away with the problems of access through the dunes, although other problems are created.

Firstly, some restriction of parking is preferable, or the beach becomes no safer than a highway. On the Southport to Ainsdale beach there is a four mile stretch where cars can park, from backshore to waters' edge. This is perfect for the few on quiet days, but can be extremely hazardous when several thousand cars turn up on summer weekends. Effective barriers are difficult to build and maintain on the beach, because of the action of the waves. There is also understandable opposition from users when existing patterns of use are changed. Car barriers are described on page 66.

The second problem is that people will still wish to walk and sunbathe amongst the foredunes, and can gain access all along the backshore. Although this use also occurs on beaches with no car access, the problem is not so severe as people tend to congregate on the part of the beach nearest the car park, toilets and other facilities. Fencing may be needed to discourage this use, as at Ainsdale. This is inevitably expensive and difficult to maintain, as any fencing along the backshore is vulnerable to wave action.

Size and layout of car parks

The size of the car park and the restriction of off-road parking outside the car park determines the number of people able to use the beach and dunes on a busy day. Many car parks become full on summer weekends. In addition on some sites there will be people who walk from nearby caravan sites, railway stations and residential areas. The layout of the car park is important, as an orderly layout allows capacity use whilst minimising harrassment to all concerned. There are two basic types of layout for car parks, being either parking in small bays, or in lines over a large single area.

Car parks consisting of small bays often arise from traditional use, where over the years cars have been parked wherever physically possible, usually destroying the turf and leading to widescale erosion. Such car parks can be formalised by placing barriers around the margins to prevent further spread, and also by placing internal barriers to organise the parking. This can work satisfactorily, and is usually the cheapest solution. Where the area is restricted by scrub, this makes the access from the car parks easier to manage, as people's options are limited, and also hides the cars to some extent. A disadvantage can be that the layout is often confusing to newcomers, leading to problems both in parking and in finding the designated path to the beach. Orderly parking can be more difficult to organise, as well as keeping 'through routes' clear on busy days. Small enclosed bays are also more difficult to police, and can encourage theft from cars and other problems.

Small bay parking can encourage people to stay near their cars, especially on days when the weather is not conducive to being on the beach. Where there is a view from the car park people will come simply to sit in their cars or picnic nearby. This can be an advantage as it reduces the pressure on the paths to the beach, but can also be a disadvantage if it encourages erosion, litter, damage and illegal camping all around the fringes of the car park.

Large 'formal' car parks with rows of cars look intrusive in rural areas, but can have advantages. The simple layout means that the car park can be used to capacity without too many problems. It is easy to check that the cark park is full, and if supervised, further entry can then be stopped. With only one parking area it is possible to clearly sign the access points to the beach, so that unofficial paths are less likely to develop.

Except in quiet seasons, visitors are unlikely to stay by their cars or use the edge of the car park for recreation, and other less desirable activities are also easier to control. The disadvantages can be the initial cost of clearance, improvement of the surface and layout of internal barriers. Large open areas can also encourage some drivers to race around when the car park is quiet, causing danger and damage to the surface.

Tree planting can improve the appearance of car parks, with the shade making it pleasant for users. However, standard trees of a shape suitable for parking under are not typical of dune areas, where most trees are rather low and scrubby in nature due to poor soil and exposure to the sea. In areas where pine has already been planted, a few more for improving a car park may be justifiable. Other species used with varying degrees of success include birch, poplar and willow.

The free draining soils of sand dunes mean that car park surfacing is not too much of a problem, although some areas may flood in wet spells when the water table rises. Any locally available surfacing material such as chippings, gravel or hoggin can be used to fill holes and make a wear-resistant surface.

On some dune systems, such as Murlough NNR, Co. Down, cars are parked on grass. A seasonal pattern of use plus constant management allows the car park to be kept in use throughout the year, with a maximum capacity of 350 cars. Management includes spiking the grass to allow the air and water into the compressed soil, raking to remove dead vegetation, and re-seeding bare patches with fine-leaved grasses. Low levels of fertiliser are also used, with two light applications of NPK grassland fertiliser from spring to early summer, to promote top growth, and an autumn application of potato fertiliser (PK with low N) to promote root growth (Whatmough, J, 1985).

Fencing and signposting

Depending on the location, the surrounding vegetation and the type of use, external fencing may be needed to prevent free range use of the area around the car park, and to encourage use of the designated paths to the beach. Types of fencing used vary from single 'guide' wires, to several strands of wire, stock netting and chestnut paling. Natural barriers of cut brushwood can be very effective, particularly if of thorny hard-to-burn material such as sea buckthorn. New plantings of trees and shrubs are unlikely to survive unless they themselves are fenced. Access control fencing is discussed on page 63.

Clear signing of the start of the paths to the beach is very important: a fractious family arriving for the first time does not want to have to hunt about for the quickest route to the beach. It is easy to become so accustomed to an area that you fail to appreciate how a newcomer may find it confusing. Observe how visitors behave when they first arrive, and act accordingly to make the access clearer. If necessary, erect large raised signs saying 'Path to beach', with arrows as necessary; such signs being probably a lesser evil than the damage done when people fail to find more discrete signs. Visitors are more likely to respect fences around restoration areas and other erosion control measures if they have a hassle-free and welcoming arrival at the site.

Typical Access Problems

Access from roads to beaches through dunes

It is often possible to predict erosion areas even before pressure is intense enough to show up on the ground. The diagram shows a typical case in which people struggle to the beach by the shortest possible route from car park or track. The example is from Lindisfarne NNR, Northumberland, but similar situations occur on many sand dune sites.

The worst affected areas are the 'passes' in the dune ridges. The intervening slack is relatively erosion resistant.

Assuming access in the general area is to be tolerated, two solutions are possible:

a   Fence the eroded areas and other nearby passes in the dune ridges and plant the bare slopes with marram or other sand-trapping vegetation. At the same time, suggest an alternative route. You should site this to minimise wind erosion, signpost it clearly at both ends and restrict it if necessary by fencing or planting along the borders of the path.

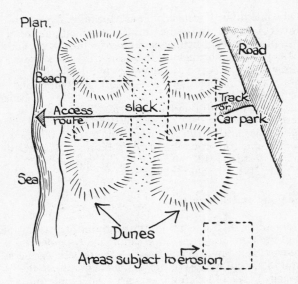

Plan.

Road

Beach

Track or Car park

Access route

slack

Sea

Dunes

Areas subject to erosion

Eventually the new route is likely to develop erosion problems of its own and will have to be replaced in turn. A continuing programme of fencing, restoration and rotation of trampled areas may be required.

b Surface the path through the eroded area so that it can withstand existing and foreseeable peak pressure (see page 55 for types of surfacing). This, perhaps combined with rerouting, may be the only solution where pressure is very high, but the more permanent surfaces are liable to be very expensive to install. Path maintenance is essential or people will abandon the surfaced route for others which are more attractive. Fencing may be necessary alongside.

Dunes as view points and slides

The diagram shows an old track leading into the dunes which invites people to park and clamber up the surrounding dunes for the view.

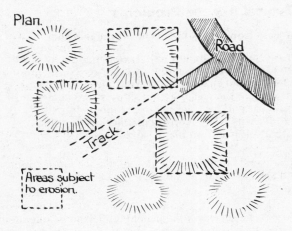

Plan.

Road

Track

Areas subject to erosion.

Unless this de facto car park is to be blocked off entirely, it should be legitimised and restricted by signs and car barriers (p66). If access to a viewpoint dune is unrestricted, trampling will gradually open up well defined trackways to the top. These tend to merge into an enlarging, horseshoe-shaped bare slope which may threaten to reduce the dune to an eroded hummock.

Solutions include:

a Accept the problem, even if it means the destruction of the dune. This is the easiest way out and is suitable where the dune is some way back from the sea in a wide system, as at Braunton Burrows, Devon.

b Fence, signpost and plant the dune to stabilise it. This may be required where the bare slope faces into the dominant wind so that erosion is rapid, but it invites vandalism or transference of pressure to the nearest suitable dune. It has worked well on some sites, though, including Lindisfarne.

c Provide steps up the paths to the summit and install a view platform (p63), and restrict the sliding face to a tolerable area. This can be done by placing dead thorn 'kidding' along the edges of the paths and slope, thatching and planting most of the slope and leaving a small bare area for children to slide on. This is worth doing where the slope is relatively sheltered so that erosion from the reduced opening is not too serious. At Saltfleetby-Theddlethorpe National Nature Reserve, Lincolnshire, such a procedure has led to nearly complete regeneration of the thatched and planted face in a period of five to six years.

Paths

GENERAL POINTS

a The simplest techniques are often the best. In the past, much effort and expense has gone into building boardwalks, which although very successful on some sites, have been costly failures in others, due to poor siting, design or lack of maintenance. A basic rule of thumb suggested from experience of the Sefton Coast Management Scheme is as follows. Where there is no sandblow, a surfaced path of gravel or chippings is suitable. In areas where accretion or erosion is in the range of 25–150mm (1–6″) per year, adjustable boardwalks can be constructed. In areas of greater movement, from 300–900mm (1–3′) per year, a simple mulched walkway provides an inexpensive access route which can be renewed or altered as necessary (see p56).

b Path construction is a time consuming operation, and it is well worth spending the extra money to buy good quality tanalised, or otherwise durable, timber for boardwalks, steps, and edgings to surfaced paths. The extra expense is outweighed by the advantages of having a uniform product which is easy to handle and join, looks good, lasts, and is usually respected by visitors. Cheap offcuts and unpeeled timber are difficult to use because of non-uniform size, they have a short life, and are more likely to be vandalised or used for firewood.

c Existing eroded paths can either be realigned or surfaced. When choosing an approach, remember to include maintenance as well as construction costs. Where a heavily used path is severely eroded, both realignment and surfacing may be necessary.

d   Where you change a path alignment, indicate the new route by signs or fences and fence off or block the entrances to the old route with brushwood or shrubs.

e   Paths which receive moderate or heavy use should be at least 1.2m (4′) wide, and 1.5m (5′) wide, if possible, to allow people to walk side-by-side and to pass. If a path is too narrow for comfort, people will widen it or stray off it unless restricted by fencing.

f   Pony tracks should normally be kept separate from pedestrian accessways. You may be able to restrict riders by signposting alone, but fencing along the length of the track is often necessary to keep horses in bounds. Often all that is needed is a single-strand plain wire fence on either side. The track should form a circuit for added interest.

ALIGNMENT OF PATHS THROUGH DUNES

a   Paths through dunes should normally be angled obliquely to the direction of dominant winds, especially where these are on-shore, to reduce the risk of wind scour and blowout formation. However, on at least one site – Braunton Burrows NNR, Devon – paths are positioned in line with the wind, using slatted, movable duckboards (p59), without erosion occurring. The wind can be used to advantage here to blow the path clear of drifting sand (Roberts and Venner, undated, p11).

b   Where strong winds are not directly on-shore or where the dune system is rapidly prograding, paths should take the shortest possible route. This does not necessarily mean a straight line, since existing unplanned paths often wind slightly to cross firm slacks and to avoid high, steep dunes. The alignment of such paths should not be changed unless there are signs of serious wind funnelling and erosion along the route.

c   Alignment is most critical where paths cut the windward sides of foredune ridges.

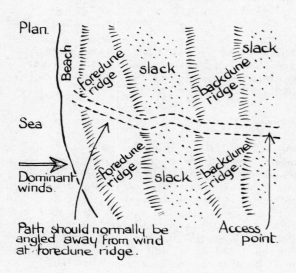

Path should normally be angled away from wind at foredune ridge.

Alignment is less crucial in backdune ridges of wide systems and where paths cross slacks.

d   Paths which are intensively used or which cross

areas where the wind may be strong from various quarters should be taken through the dunes in an irregular zig-zag pattern, with each section no more than about 18m (20yds) long.

e   When choosing a new route through the dunes, there can be advantage in initially just marking the route and requesting people to keep to it, rather than investing straightaway in surfacing or boardwalk construction. The route can be marked with white painted posts, with some temporary post and wire fencing as necessary. This serves a dual purpose, firstly in showing whether the route is direct and attractive enough for people to follow it. Secondly, if people do keep to it they will trample the vegetation and start the process of path formation. Where it is required to keep people to one route, destruction of any vegetation followed by surfacing or boardwalk construction is usually inevitable. Where pressure is lighter, it may be possible to then encourage and maintain a trample-resistant sward by fertilising, seeding and periodic repair.

f   Consider the routes that people may take if they don't find or avoid the start of the path from the car park, as they may find their way to the sea blocked by newly planted areas or fencing. If necessary make linking paths, or mark the main path clearly along its route with white posts so it can easily be seen. Avoid creating the situation where people can only turn back or climb through a fence, as they will almost certainly do the latter (see diagram on page 52).

SURFACING

Choice of materials

a   The best surface is one which is cheap and easy to apply and maintain and which looks in keeping with the surrounding terrain. In erosion-resistant areas such as dune slacks, and where use is so light that erosion is minimal, the existing natural surface is adequate, possibly aided by seeding and fertilising. Where artificial surfacing is necessary, its durability and replacement cost is as important as the initial cost of construction. For a detailed comparison of the use of various surfacing materials on one sand dune site, see Roberts and Venner (undated).

b   Some sites have nearby sources of cheap surfacing material (eg shells) which should be exploited before other materials are brought in, even if only part of the path can be finished in the local product.

c   Surfaced paths must be comfortable to walk on (preferably even for barefoot children) or else people will walk beside rather than along them. People also avoid timber walkways which have tilted due to shifting sand. Paths suitable for disabled people and pram-pushers must be made smooth and firm. But footpaths should not be too inviting to cyclists, for instance, since this makes them hazardous for pedestrians.

d   Erosion or drifting is likely to occur where a hard-surfaced path runs out onto soft sand.

Duckboards, which can be lifted and repositioned as necessary, are often the best choice here. Expanded-metal tracking is another possibility. Stone and other fixed materials are best limited to relatively stable backdune areas.

e   Where permanent paths cross areas of tidal flooding, duckboards or raised boardwalks are necessary. Duckboards must be staked securely to keep them from shifting. Raised boardwalks are preferable since they can be used even at high tide and are less likely to settle unevenly.

Tidal creeks should be avoided where possible and bridged where a crossing is needed. Bridge design is covered in the 'Foothpaths' handbook (Agate, 1983).

f   Consider the environmental effects of surfacing materials before using them on sites of botanical interest. Fertilising and seeding, or the use of mulches, may promote rank grasses or introduce weed seeds along the path. Shells and limestone chippings may increase the alkalinity of the soil and encourage lime-loving plants to invade. Such changes usually affect only the immediate line of the path.

Grass

Natural vegetation, encouraged by fertilising and augmented if necessary by sowing with mixed native grasses, makes an ideal surface for paths through backdunes and slacks and over dune pastures which receive only moderate wear. Foredunes usually are unable to support species which resist trampling and so must be surfaced in other ways. See the chapter on Vegetation Establishment for information on sowing and fertilising.

The path must be closed off long enough for the vegetation to become well established. Where the path soil is compacted, aerate it before treatment using a light spiked roller. Where the soil is loose and dry, mulching is beneficial.

Mulch

On moderately used paths where the existing turf is worn or broken, or on heavily used bare sandy paths, a covering of chopped straw, mown vegetation from slacks, wood chips or bark peelings can be applied as a surface mulch. This helps hold the loose sand in place to make it easier to walk on, increases moisture retention, prevents sand blow, and slowly improves soil fertility to allow vegetation to recover. Note that bark peelings should be chopped and partly composted for this use; fresh, long pieces of bark can be slippery and uncomfortable to walk on. Of the available materials, straw and mown vegetation are best in dry sand because wood chips and peelings make more of a mess if they blow about. Chips and peelings are more useful in wet slacks where they help bind the sand and make walking easier.

Mulching is quick and easy and can be done while the path remains in use. Mulching can be effective for up to six to twelve months, according to exposure, but where use is heavier mulching may need to be done several times each summer as the material breaks down underfoot.

A useful product of modern agriculture is the 'big bale'. These large cylindrical straw bales can be brought as close as possible to the path by tractor, and then rolled along by hand as necessary. Up to six people may be needed to roll a bale uphill. The bale can then be undone, and simply unrolled along the line of the path.

This technique has been used at Formby, Merseyside, on a new access route up and over a dune, totalling an area of about 1000 square metres (1200 sq yds). Two treatments, each using 12 bales, were carried out. The first was done in April, the straw being chopped by spade into the top 100mm (4") or so of sand, to prevent the straw blowing away. This proved sufficient to bind the sand and prevent sand blow, whilst at the same time making it easier to walk on. After a busy early season of use the straw had mainly broken down, so the treatment was repeated in mid June, it being necessary only to trample the straw into the surface. The cost in 1986 was 10p per metre for a four metre width path. The only problem found was the straw path proved an attraction to horseriders, although this use was illegal.

Shells

Shell fragments make a durable surface which blends into the coastal dune environment and which can be added to easily as the need arises. Cockle shells are long lasting but oyster shells and mussel shells (the least durable) can also be used. They all break down into a fairly comfortable surface for walking. Shells should only be spread on bare areas since the aim is to supplement the vegetative cover rather than create an entire new surfacing. Shells increase the lime content of leached backdune soils and any vegetation which grows up during periods of low use may be more resistant to trampling than the original cover.

Shell waste is available virtually for free from shellfisheries. Because of the large amounts needed, it is best to get a lorry load and stockpile it. If shells are being dumped in the vicinity, you may be able to persuade the driver to distribute a load at convenient depots. It is better to have several small caches than one big one since this produces less stench as the shells rot clean and makes for easier distribution later.

Shell paths, like those of stone, can be contained by edging boards if necessary, but they look better and are usually just as effective if left free at the sides to blend with the verges.

Stones

Broken stones (gravel, chippings, quarry scalpings, hoggin or even fly ash or brick fragments) make a durable path in areas free from sand blow, but one which may look out of place depending on the colour and texture of the material used. The main thing is to build up a surface which is comfortable to walk on and not composed of sharp fragments. Ideally, you should grade the path in layers, with the biggest material at the bottom and the smallest on top. Firm each layer by tamping or rolling so that the large stones don't work to the surface with use. The most durable paths are slightly cambered to aid rain runoff. It may be necessary to build up the surface between board edging to prevent it being broken loose at the sides with use.

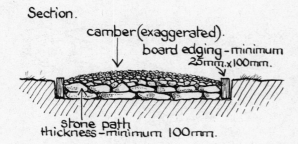

Section.

camber (exaggerated).
board edging - minimum
25mm.x 100mm.

stone path
thickness - minimum 100mm.

Depending on the material used and the care taken, stone paths can last a long time with only minor repair. If some of the fine material is chalk or limestone the surface tends to bind together under pressure like concrete. At Braunton Burrows NNR, Devon, experimental concrete 'stepping stone' paths have been tried, but the results were poor (Roberts and Venner, undated, pp8–9).

Fabric

Various loose-weave fabrics, including fish netting, 'Wyretex', 'Terram' ('Cambrelle' with PRF 140) and 'Broplene' land mesh, have the ability to stabilise sand, support people and vehicles, and allow vegetation to grow through to help bind the fabric in place. 'Wyretex' is supplied by Malcolm, Ogilvie and Company Ltd, Constable Works, 31 Constitution Street, Dundee DD3 6NL; 'Terram' by ICI Fibres Ltd, Pontypool, Gwent; and 'Broplene' by Bridon Fibres and Plastics Ltd, Team Works, Dunston, Gateshead, Tyne and Wear.

Used fish netting may be available cheaply but much of it has too big a weave to be really useful. 'Netlon', a garden netting, has been tried at Braunton Burrows but was found to be too fine and could be dangerous to walkers (Roberts and Venner, undated, p9). All the special-purpose fabrics are expensive, but they are durable, relatively easy to handle, can be cut with shears and are easily staked in place, following manufacturer's instructions where given.

Fabric is best used in fairly flat areas where the turf is vigorous and unbroken so that grass grows up through the netting and anchors it in place. Where the surface is bare, sand tends to shift under the fabric so that it rolls or bunches up, or else the sand drifts over the top, making the path difficult to follow. Where the turf is open and slow growing, the fabric tends to shift slightly when walked on which damages the plants. Staking is important to minimise this problem and to provide a taut surface which conforms to the contours and is safe to walk on. Fish net and 'Broplene' tend to stretch with use, making periodic relaying essential, so that these fabrics cannot be fixed permanently or secured against theft.

Metal tracking

At some sites used for military training, such as Braunton Burrows, Devon, sections of expanded-metal track with bitumen underfelt may be available free or nearly so. The tracking is ugly, and the felt collects rain water, but it lasts indefinitely and makes a wide path (about 3m, 10') which can support vehicles. Sommerfeld tracking, which consists of wire netting reinforced by rods and edging bars, lacks the underfelt but has similar uses. This is available from

Sommerfeld Flexboard Ltd, Doseley Industrial Estate, Frame Lane, Doseley, Telford, Salop. Both types of tracking are normally held in place by 600–900mm (2–3') long metal pickets.

Boardwalks

These include sleeper walkways, duckboards, and fixed boardwalks with handrails. The first two types may be movable. All boardwalks are expensive and time consuming to build, and need some degree of maintenance. Because of this, they should not necessarily be the first solution tried at any particular site. Consider the following points.

a   A boardwalk should not be sited where it will either be undercut or buried as sand levels change. Slight movements of up to 150mm (6") loss or gain can be coped with by using a design which can be lowered or raised. However, this requires frequent supervision as it may need moving several times a year. Boardwalks are not usually suitable for going up and over dunes, nor along the back, where levels can change rapidly. Those along the top of fixed dunes, such as at Holkham, Norfolk, can work extremely well. Other successful boardwalks, through extensive areas of fixed dunes, include those at Ynyslas, Dyfed and Braunton Burrows, Devon.

b   All boardwalks need some degree of maintenance, according to the level and type of use, the incidence of vandalism, the degree of sand movement, and the initial design specification and quality of construction. Badly maintained boardwalks which have tilted, or have missing or broken decking, loose wires and so on are not only dangerous, but will not be effective, as people will avoid using them. They also create an eyesore and a large amount of debris which will need clearing up. The time, labour and cost of maintenance must be taken into account at the outset.

c   The boardwalk must be designed with the use in mind. A route that is used by elderly people or those with pushchairs will need closely spaced or butted decking planks, and gentle slopes, preferably without steps. A handrail may be of assistance. Boardwalks for school parties and field study groups can be more adventurous to use, but need platforms and other points where groups can gather for discussion and study. The examples following give more details on design and width for different uses.

Sleeper and log walkways

Old railway sleepers are still available, at a price of around £5 for first quality sleepers, and £3.75 for second quality (1986 prices). They are thoroughly pressure treated and make a durable surface. Roberts and Venner (undated, p8) estimate a lifetime of ten years for sleepers placed on sloping ground well above the water table. Sleepers are normally 250mm (10") wide, 125mm (5") thick, and from 2.6–3m (8'6"–10') long. The usual sleeper walkway design is shown below.

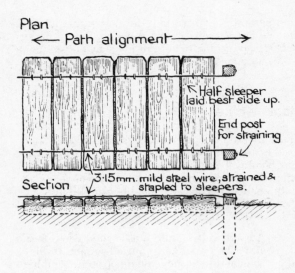

Plan
← Path alignment →

Half sleeper laid best side up.

End post for straining

Section

3·15mm. mild steel wire, strained & stapled to sleepers.

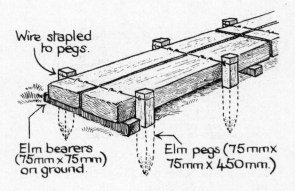

Wire stapled to pegs.

Elm bearers (75mm × 75mm) on ground.

Elm pegs (75 mm × 75mm × 450 mm.)

The wires are secured by stapling around one peg, which is driven in, and then fixing the free end of the wire to a second peg before driving this in to tighten the wire.

Half-round logs may be cheaper than sleepers and may be readily available as thinnings from nearby forestry work. Softwood should be pressure treated or at least peeled and creosoted. The logs should be buried flat-side up and wired together the same as sleepers. A log walkway at Holywell, North Cornwall, uses half round 2m ($6\frac{1}{2}'$) × 125mm (5") timbers set in the sand about 40mm ($1\frac{1}{2}''$) apart, with two wires (3.15mm) stapled to each log, 300mm (12") from the ends. The walkway can be lifted and re-laid as necessary, as sand levels change. The lack of runners underneath allows the walkway to follow contours and curves along the route, so that only minor adjustment and levelling of the sand is needed. Where necessary, steps are made as shown.

Sleepers should normally be used cut in half and laid at right angles to the line of the path as shown. They can also be nailed on top of sleepers which are laid along the line of the path at each side, for extra support and rigidity and for longer life in damp ground. This method uses more materials and is normally not necessary in dry conditions. Where only a narrow path is needed, the sleepers can be laid two or three abreast, in line with the path, and anchored with 600mm (2') pickets or half-round posts hammered into the ground and nailed to the sleepers.

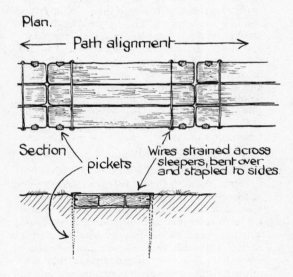

Plan.
← Path alignment →

Section

pickets

Wires strained across sleepers, bent over and stapled to sides.

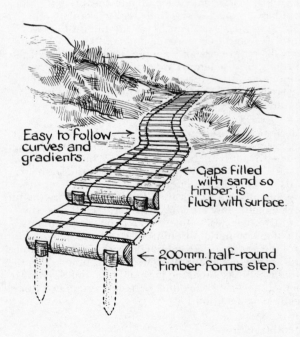

Easy to follow curves and gradients.

← Gaps filled with sand so timber is flush with surface.

← 200mm. half-round timber forms step.

Whichever method is used, it is important to strain plain wire across the tops of the sleepers before stapling to help bring the timbers tightly together and to secure the sleepers against vandals. Where the sleepers run at right angles to the line of the path (the normal design), you can fix the wires most easily and securely by hammering in posts at each end of the section of path to be strained. Strain the wires between the posts and staple. Then staple them to the individual sleepers without driving these staples fully home. Where this method is impractical due to terrain or path design, just hand tension the wires as you lay each sleeper and staple them home.

On the Suffolk Heritage Coast, the sleeper walkway shown below is employed where lightly used footpaths cross marshy ground:

Sleeper and log walkways can be angled around corners by cutting wedge-shaped timbers as shown.

In damp ground, sleeper and log walkways tend to rot out quite quickly and also to swell and pop out of alignment. Sleepers can be laid on top of runners as mentioned above, but logs, which are of varying thickness, cannot readily be secured except by burying them in the ground.

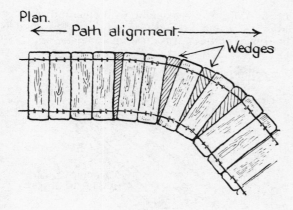

Plan. ← Path alignment. →

Wedges

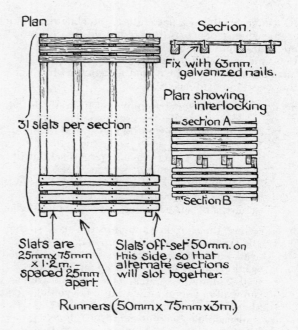

Plan

31 slats per section

Section.

Fix with 63mm. galvanized nails.

Plan showing interlocking

section A

Section B

Slats are 25mm x 75mm x 1·2m. - spaced 25mm apart.

Slats off-set 50mm. on this side, so that alternate sections will slot together.

Runners (50mm x 75mm x 3m.)

Duckboards

Duckboards are slatted wooden walkways made of relatively light, portable sections which can be detached as necessary for adjustment. They are mainly designed for boggy ground but are useful also on soft sand, especially foredune ridges, where they can easily be shifted as the sand surface changes. The seawardmost sections usually should be removed and stored over the winter out of the reach of the high storm tides.

In places where vandalism is a problem, two or more wires should be stapled along the length of the walkway, to discourage removal of sections. Sections can also be wired to buried timber anchors, as shown, so that wire cutters are needed to free them. When the section needs lifting, the wires can be cut and joined so that the anchor can be re-used.

On slopes the sections can be cut as shown below, so that their ends continue to interlock neatly. Staking at the joints is necessary on slopes to hold them steady.

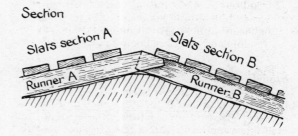

Section

Slats section A

Slats section B

Runner A

Runner B

A slightly different design is used at Holkham NNR, Norfolk. Only three runners are used per section. These are of pressure treated pine, 50 × 100mm × 2.7m (2″ × 4″ × 9′) while slats are 25 × 125mm × 1.2m (1″ × 5″ × 4′) untreated pine. Slats are nailed up to each end of the runners, and sections are bolted together with coach bolts and anchor plates instead of interlocking as in the Braunton Burrows design.

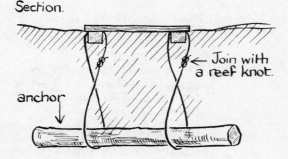

Section.

Join with a reef knot.

anchor

Design and dimensions vary, but it is important in all cases to space the slats close enough so that people with fairly narrow-heeled shoes find them comfortable to walk on. A 25mm (1″) gap is about the maximum. Even so, people may prefer to walk beside rather than on the duckboards, especially if they are pushing prams, and fencing may be necessary to discourage this.

One design, used at Braunton Burrows National Nature Reserve, Devon, is shown below. Each section takes 45 minutes to an hour to build.

The 3m (10′) sections are made on a template with a 50mm (2″) offset to one side so that the sections, when laid alternately, slot together and hold each other in place. Slats with knots may soon break but are easily replaced as necessary. The overall life of the duckboards is five to ten years (Roberts and Venner, undated, p9).

At Braunton Burrows, a narrower duckboard design is used on a path over mobile sand which is relatively lightly used. Each section slots into the next one as shown by the diagram. Sections take less than half an hour to construct, but because there are only two runners the slats must be free of large knots to prevent breakage.

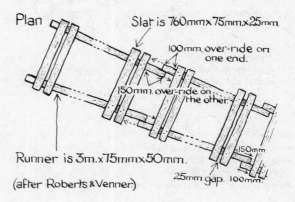

Plan

Slat is 760mm x 75mm x 25mm.

100mm. over-ride on one end.

150mm. over-ride on the other.

Runner is 3m. x 75mm x 50mm.

150mm

25mm gap. 100mm.

(after Roberts & Venner.)

All timber walkways, particularly duckboards, require regular maintenance as the sand builds up or blows out from around them where they transect the foredunes and abut on the beach. Several methods have been tried to reduce the frequency with which they have to be adjusted:

a   Where sand tends to blow out from under the walkway, you can lay brushwood across the path beneath it, extending beyond it to either side, to help trap sand. Stake the walkway sections firmly to reduce tipping if sand drifts away. Sideboards have been used at Ynyslas NNR, Dyfed, nailed along the lower edges of the runners, but these may actually increase scouring because they are hard and clean edged.

b   Where the sand is trapped by the slats, so that the surface tends to build up beneath the walkway, you can occasionally lift the affected sections a few inches and dig out hollows 150–200mm (6–8″) deep below them to act as sumps to contain blown sand. Leave the ends of the sections resting on packed sand. This approach has been used at Holkham NNR, Norfolk. At Braunton Burrows NNR, Devon, by contrast, the aim has been to trap as much sand as possible. Here the duckboards have simply been lifted and repositioned as sand accumulates. Lifting and repositioning may be required several times a season for the first few years, but should be needed much less often as adjacent dune-stabilisation efforts such as fencing and planting begin to take effect.

Murlough track

This is a timber trackway, first designed and used at Murlough NNR, Co Down, with similar designs now used at other sand dune sites. The pressure treated timbers are joined by 4.00mm mild steel wire, spaced with 25mm (1″) pieces of alkathene water pipe. The track is built in 3.6m (12′) sections, so it can be lifted and relaid if necessary. The timbers can be of any size to suit the intended use. At Murlough the timbers are 1.8m (6′) × 100mm (4″) × 75mm (3″), to take upwards of 250,000 people per year, as well as estate and emergency vehicles. Over a mile length has been in use for 15 years, with minimal maintenance.

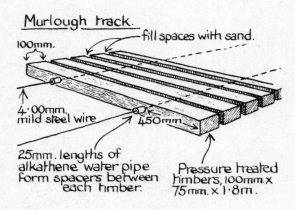

Murlough track.

100mm.

fill spaces with sand.

4·00mm. mild steel wire

450mm

25mm. lengths of alkathene water pipe form spacers between each timber.

Pressure treated timbers, 100mm. × 75mm. × 1·8m.

At Formby, Merseyside, a 'rolling walkway' of similar design uses plastic-covered steel cable, threaded through 900mm (3′) × 75mm (3″) × 50mm (2″) timbers, spaced 25mm (1″) apart. The walkway is made in 6m roll lengths, the ends being finished as

shown. A disadvantage, along with other movable walkways, is that sections can be removed by vandals. The weight of these rolls does act as a deterrent.

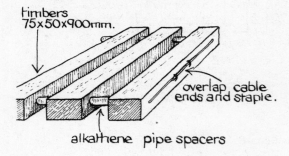

rolling boardwalk.

timbers 75×50×900mm.

overlap cable ends and staple.

alkathene pipe spacers

Boardwalks

Boardwalks built with a permanent, rigid construction can withstand heavy use and provide a comfortable surface to walk on. They are raised above ground level to protect dune, marsh and other easily disturbed surfaces and to reduce the effects of drifting sand. Boardwalks may cost no more than sleeper walkways in terms of materials but they are relatively laborious and painstaking to assemble.

Boardwalks need little maintenance but you should check them each season and tighten bolts, replace occasional slats and treat the timbers as necessary. Very occasionally you may have to dismantle a section and raise or lower it according to sand movements.

The design shown below is in use at Ynyslas National Nature Reserve, Dyfed, where it runs through fixed dunes for about 470m (560yds) from a caravan site to the beach. The timber is tanalised softwood.

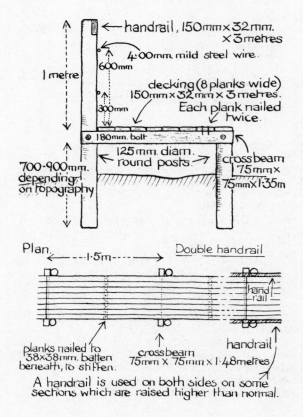

handrail, 150mm × 32mm. × 3 metres

4·00mm. mild steel wire.

600mm

1 metre

decking (8 planks wide) 150mm × 32mm × 3 metres. Each plank nailed twice.

300mm

180mm. bolt

125mm. diam. round posts.

cross beam 75mm × 75mm × 1·35m

700–900mm. depending on topography

Plan.

1·5m

Double handrail

hand rail

planks nailed to 38×38mm. batten beneath, to stiffen.

cross beam 75mm × 75mm × 1·48 metres

handrail

A handrail is used on both sides on some sections which are raised higher than normal.

Both the design and route of the boardwalk have been very successful, with few problems over many years of use. Sections have been replaced, as time and wear have caused deterioration of the timbers. One design weakness which has emerged is that the posts have tended to rot at the point where they are cut to take the handrail. Rotting could be reduced by screwing the handrails direct to the posts, without cutting a rebate in the post, and by weathering the top of the post to a slope so that water runs off quickly.

On the Suffolk Heritage Coast, a simple design is used to take footpaths across marshy areas where the boardwalks may occasionally be covered by tides.

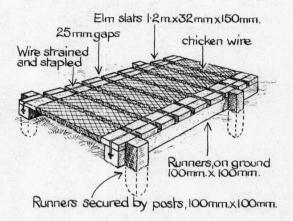

Elm slats 1·2m.x32mm x150mm.
25mm gaps
chicken wire
Wire strained and stapled
Runners, on ground 100mm. x 100mm.
Runners secured by posts, 100mm. x 100mm.

Elm has proved to be durable in these conditions and is used throughout. The chicken wire stapled to the tops of the slats provides a better footing than the boards alone.

RAMPS AND STEPS

Ramps

Raised boardwalks should have ramps rather than steps at their ends to make them easier to use by elderly and disabled people and those pushing prams. A simple design of ramp is shown below:

Where possible, ramps should have a slope not greater than 1:12.

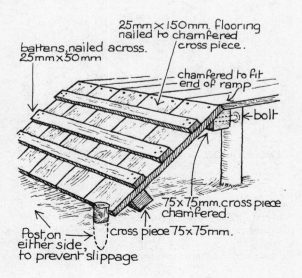

25mm X 150mm. flooring nailed to chamfered cross piece.
battens, nailed across. 25mm x 50mm
chamfered to fit end of ramp
bolt
75 x 75mm. cross piece chamfered.
Post, on either side, to prevent slippage
cross piece 75x75mm.

Steps

Ramps are not always feasible or necessary, eg where a path ascends the steep slope of a dune face or cliff or where it leads to a view platform off the main route. In these situations steps may be easier to build and more secure.

Step designs must be adjusted to fit the situation. A few points are basic:

a   When possible, position steps a uniform distance apart. Otherwise people may find them difficult to use. Spacing should allow a comfortable descent, and there should be a 100–200mm (4–8″) rise between steps. The steps must be clearly visible when approached from the top end or people may just walk down the slope at the side.

b   Normally it is best to build an interlocking flight of steps, for strength and stability. Where the steps are subject to erosion (eg by tides, or soil slippage on soft cliffs) it is better to secure the steps independently to posts driven into the ground. This way damage to one step does not affect adjacent steps.

c   Where handrails are necessary for safety, make them an integral part of the step construction. The posts which support the steps should form the uprights for the handrails, and the handrails should be bolted to the insides of the posts. Where the steps traverse a cliff or ascend a gulley, it may be better to fix the rails directly into the cliff.

The simple step design below uses logs or sleepers with oak or tanalised softwood stakes.

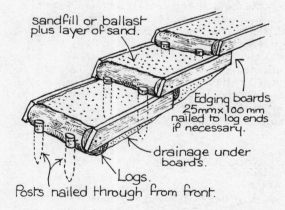

sandfill or ballast plus layer of sand.
Edging boards 25mm x 100mm nailed to log ends if necessary.
drainage under boards.
Logs.
Posts nailed through from front.

A problem with sand-filled steps is that people tend to loosen and push the sand downhill. Also the steps are easily undermined by wind, unless the steps are built at a gradual slope. To reduce these problems, it is best to bed the logs in ballast 25–50mm, (1–2″ gravel or 'crusher run' stone) with about an inch of coarse sand on top. Drive the stakes in front of each riser and nail them to the risers before placing the fill. If the steps are in a cutting, earth over the ends of the logs. This helps secure the logs and prevents the fill washing out around the ends. Where this is difficult, use edging boards as shown.

The box steps shown below can either be filled with packed sand and topped with 12mm ($\frac{1}{2}$″) of gravel, or decked with timber slats.

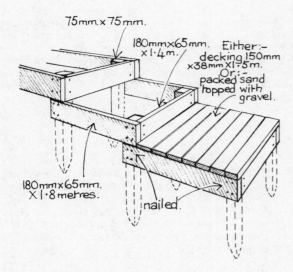

75mm × 75mm.

180mm × 65mm × 1·4m. Either:- decking 150mm × 38mm × 1·75m. Or:- packed sand topped with gravel.

180mm × 65mm. × 1·8 metres.

nailed.

The design below is used at Hayle, Cornwall, to provide access from a car park to the beach through sections of fixed dune. The steps link to sections of boardwalk.

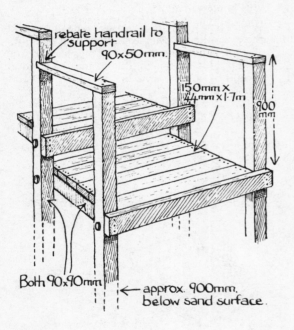

rebate handrail to support 90 × 50mm.

150mm × 44mm × 1·7m

900 mm

Both 90 × 90mm

approx. 900mm. below sand surface.

Sand ladders

These originated in Holland, and have recently been used at Crantock, North Cornwall and Giltar Point, Dyfed. The design is similar to a large steel or rope ladder, which is anchored at the top of steep sandy slopes that are otherwise difficult to climb and liable to erode.

At Crantock, a ladder has been placed up a steep narrow dune between a car park and beach, to reduce the amount of sand pushed down as people climb up and down the slope. Such sand movement encroaches on the car park. The angle of slope is very steep, and although most people have no trouble climbing up the ladder, some find it easier to scramble down the bare slope rather than balance on the ladder when going downhill. However, even partial use has made a noticeable decrease in the amount of sand displaced. As sand movement leaves the ladder 'proud' of the

surface, every few weeks it is necessary to swing it to one side or other, to keep it stable. Two or three times a season the anchoring timber at the top is dug out, and the whole ladder is moved 10 metres or so along the ridge. It is removed for safe storage in the winter.

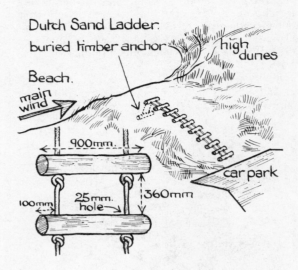

Dutch Sand Ladder.

buried timber anchor

high dunes

Beach.

main wind

car park

900mm

25mm hole

100mm

360mm

The design uses a rope rather than a steel cable. The rungs are 75mm (3″) diameter tanalised timbers, 900mm (3′) long, with 25mm (1″) holes drilled as shown. The ropes are threaded through and knotted beneath each rung. The top is anchored by a 3m (10′) by 150mm (6″) timber, buried 600mm (2′) down.

At Giltar Point, Dyfed, a 30m length of sand ladder is used on a busy two-way stretch of the coast path, where it follows an eroded sandy gully. This ladder is of the original 'Dutch' design, using an 8mm ($\frac{1}{3}$″) steel cable threaded through the rungs, which are held in place by cable grips. On flatter sections of the path grips are used both above and below each rung. To keep the ladder in position, the cable is stapled to stakes driven in at 3m intervals. When the ladder becomes buried with sand, it is lifted and replaced along the same route.

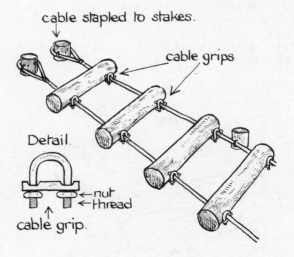

cable stapled to stakes.

cable grips

Detail.

nut

thread

cable grip.

In conclusion, sand ladders are useful in particular circumstances, where access is limited to a narrow corridor of unstable sand or sandy soil. They are less suitable for areas where there is general access over a wide area of dunes, as people are unlikely to use the ladder when there are other options. They also need fairly frequent checking and lifting to keep them effective.

VIEW PLATFORMS

View platforms should be restricted to backdune areas and other sites where wind erosion around the installation is not too severe. The design should be adapted to the site and should be big enough to accommodate any large groups using the path. Routes to and from the platform must be clearly marked. It may be necessary to provide fencing or thorny barriers around the perimeter, especially to keep children from jumping off the platform and eroding the surrounding slopes.

The design below is from Saltfleetby-Theddlethorpe. The material is untreated softwood, which lasts well in the well-drained soil of the dune top. In wetter soil, joists should be tanalised and stakes should be tanalised or of oak. The stakes do not support the platform but simply anchor the flooring until plants can grow up around the edges.

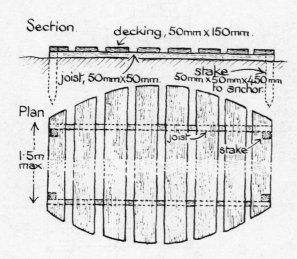

Fences and Other Barriers

FENCES

Sand-trapping fences are discussed in the previous chapter. Many of these fences are suitable also for access control.

Around car parks, buildings and along path edges where you want to avoid sand build-up, post and wire fencing is the cheapest and most suitable. Strong straining posts must be constructed. For short lengths, post and rail or chestnut paling may be preferable, as these do not need straining posts.

For details of wire and methods of fastening, see page 44. Full details are given in 'Fencing' (BTCV, 1986). Note that high tensile wire has advantages in use, provided adequate straining posts can be constructed. For short lengths of post and wire fencing, say up to 50m in length, mild steel wire may be sufficient, although radisseurs or other adjustable devices will be needed to keep the wires taut.

The following types of strainers have been developed by Cornwall County Council for straining high tensile wire fencing in sand dunes.

a   The A frame shown below is strong enough to support three lines of 3.15mm high tensile wire. These strainers are very effective, but are cumbersome in materials and time consuming to erect.

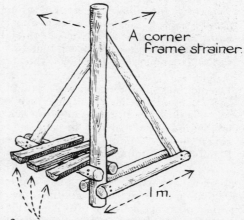

Strainer 2·1m x 150mm. diameter.
struts(2) 1·9m x 100mm. diam.
cross pieces (2) 1·5m x 100 m.diam.
nailed with 100mm. galv. nails.

The A frame can be adapted as shown for straining at corners, or for turning posts, at which the wire is not fastened off, but is run on to the next straining post.

driftwood, or other timber, can be laid across, for added stability.

b   This is an adaptation of the New Zealand style 'box strainer' (see Fencing, BTCV, 1986), where the strain of the fence is taken by the brace and the angled wire. This adaptation has been designed specifically to take up to five high tensile wires in soft sand. The strainer can be pre-fabricated in a workshop and then assembled on site.

To assemble, first dig three holes at the required spacing using a shuv-holer. Nail on the timber 'feet', and set the posts in the holes, but do not backfill until the brace has been fitted. Finally, staple on the angled wire, making sure it is taut.

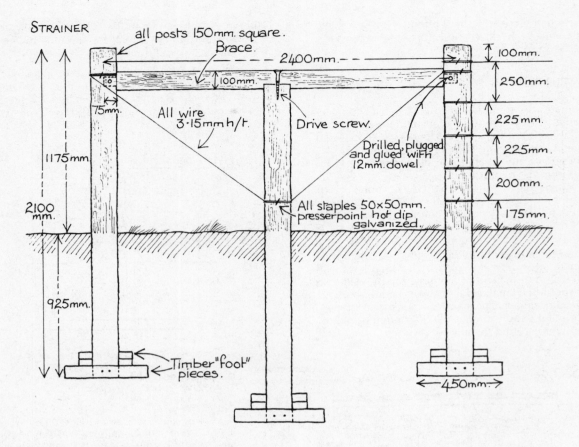

STRAINER

all posts 150mm. square.
Brace.
2400mm
100mm.
75mm
All wire 3·15mm h/t.
Drive screw.
Drilled, plugged and glued with 12mm. dowel.
1175mm
2100 mm
All staples 50×50mm. presserpoint hot dip galvanized.
925mm.
Timber "foot" pieces.
100mm.
250mm.
225mm.
225mm.
200mm.
175mm.
450mm

The fence wires can either be stapled to the post, or attached with spiral fence connectors (see p45).

At corners, the following design of turning post should be used. The fence wires are not terminated at the post, but are run on to the next straining post. Like the strainer, this should be prefabricated in a workshop.

To erect, dig out a trench at least 1.15m long and 1.025m depth. Nail the timber baulks to the posts, and lift the structure into the trench, taking care not to dislodge the sand as you do so. Fit the brace and then backfill the trench. Finally staple on the angled wire.

Where high tensile fences cross undulating ground, special attention must be paid to holding down the intermediate posts at the base of dips and hollows. This should be done by nailing cross pieces about 1m long at the base of the post, and then cover by piling large rocks on top.

Some further designs which have been used on sand dunes are shown below. The first design is used by the National Trust at Formby, Merseyside. The high tensile 3.15mm wires are terminated at the 'A' frame straining posts with spiral fence connectors (see p45). Where there is particularly heavy public pressure on the fences, the top wire is replaced by a tanalised rail of round timber. Barbed staples are used to hold the wires where the fence follows an inside curve.

Two other designs are shown, the three wire fence being suitable for average use, and the six wire fence for sites where a greater deterrent is needed. Sometimes it is better to choose a design which allows

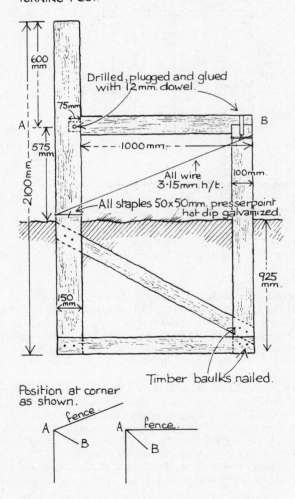

TURNING POST.

600 mm
Drilled, plugged and glued with 12mm. dowel.
75mm
A
575mm
1000mm
2100 mm
All wire 3·15mm. h/t.
100mm
All staples 50×50mm. presserpoint hot dip galvanized.
925 mm
150 mm
B
Timber baulks nailed.

Position at corner as shown.

fence
A
B

fence
A
B

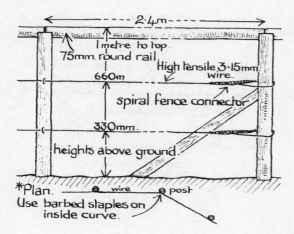

Plan.
Use barbed staples on inside curve.

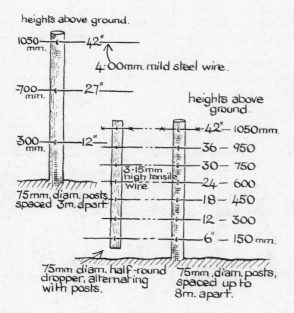

people to climb through if necessary, particularly for fences around recreational areas, where balls, kites and so on need to be retrieved. This saves on the damage which would otherwise be done to more secure fences.

Where you need to combine access control and sand build-up, 1.2m (4′) chestnut paling fixed to posts is usually adequate. See page 48 for methods of stapling to posts. An alternative method of erecting chestnut paling is to fasten it to strained wires. This is more expensive and time consuming, because of the need to erect straining posts, and should not be necessary where sand is likely to rapidly build up. It probably is worth doing for access control chestnut paling around car parks and along pathways, where a permanent fence is needed. The paling should be attached to the 3.15mm mild steel wires with gordian rings or netting rings (available from major fencing suppliers), spaced about every 450mm (18″). Twists of baling wire can also be used.

A method used at Morffa Dyffryn NNR, Gwynedd, where chestnut paling is used for access control alongside a boardwalk, is to erect the paling with a gap of about 200mm (8″) beneath. This prevents sand building up against the fence and over the boardwalk, but allows it to blow underneath to be trapped by brushwood fences beyond. The paling is attached to a

strained wire fence, in order to prevent it sagging. Some of the posts need supporting with struts, as the extra height makes the fence more vulnerable to wind damage.

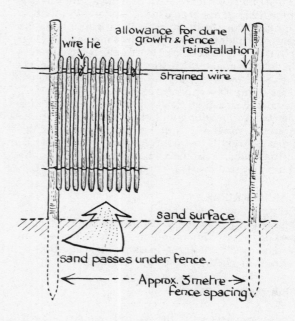

'Psychological' fences are often as effective as other types and are cheap and easy to place. They are worth trying where you have to enclose a number of small areas such as dune stabilisation sites or experimental plots. All you need for such fencing are posts about 900mm (3′) high, with a single strand of plain wire hand-tensioned and stapled at the top, and small explanatory signs if the purpose of the fence is not obvious.

Pathways may be fenced on one or both sides to keep people from straying. Often it is best to fence just one side at a time, since this antagonises people less and vandalism is less likely. A single fence with explanatory signposting conveys the erosion-control message adequately to most people. The fence should be shifted from one side to the other every few years, or when it needs replacing, to equalise wear on the two sides. A boardwalk handrail makes an effective fence, because people tend not to realise that this safety device is also being used to restrict their access.

PLANTINGS AND CUTTINGS

Fencing is obtrusive at best and often acts as a focus of vandalism. In some places live vegetation or deadwood cuttings can be used cheaply to replace access control fences. Sea buckthorn (*Hippophae rhamnoides*) is the obvious choice on sites where it already flourishes. Rather than plant more of this invasive species, it may be best to cut out pathways through dense sea buckthorn thickets and so effectively channel people. Where this is not possible, 'kidding' (cut stems) can be pushed into the sand to form dead hedges about 1m (3′) high and 300mm (1′) thick. This has been done extensively at Gullane, East Lothian, and on a smaller scale at Gibraltar point, Lincolnshire. Dead buckthorn is even tougher and scratchier than the living plant and such hedges should remain effective for about five years, although they may need bulking out where occasional breaks occur. Check such hedges the year after 'planting' and cut out any stems which have survived to take root.

Where sea buckthorn is not already present it is best to use other species. Burnet or Scotch rose (*Rosa spinosissima*) has been used at Longniddry, East Lothian. This shrub grows to about 1m (3') and may be propagated by cuttings in the same way as elder (p77). At Ynyslas Dunes, Dyfed, efforts have been made to transplant this shrub but without success. Gorse (*Ulex europaeus*) has been planted along path sides in the Gower peninsula (Trew, 1973, p47). At Camber, East Sussex, several species have been used for walkway planting including blackthorn (*Prunus spinosa*), hawthorn (*Crataegus monogyna*) and the Duke of Argyll's tea-plant (*Lycium halimifolium*), an introduced species which flourishes mainly on the south and east coasts (Pizzey, 1975, p281).

CAR BARRIERS

These may be needed to control the limits of car parking within dunes and on beaches. Barriers can also be used to delineate parking lines and bays within car parks.

Spur posts

These are posts set in the ground, and spaced just sufficiently to prevent cars passing between them. The posts should be 1.2–1.5m (4–5') long, and set in the ground with about 450mm ($1\frac{1}{2}'$) projecting. They should be spaced no more than 1.5m (5') apart. Normally tanalised timber about 125mm (5") diameter should be used.

On sandy sites, it is important to nail a 300mm (1') cross piece to the bottom of the post to make it harder to pull up. Make sure the big end of the post is downward. If you have to install posts where the water table is high, use three people, two each with shuv-holers to scoop out the sand, and the third to quickly drop the post in before the hole collapses. Posts in these conditions on backshores need fairly frequent maintenance, as they tend to be forced upwards by the water table and loosened by wave action.

Spur posts are effective and economical in terms of materials, but they are laborious to install. Because they can cause real damage to cars, they are sometimes attacked in retaliation. It may help to paint the tops white to make them more obvious. At Braunton Burrows, Devon, ex-MOD corkscrew-shape metal pickets have been found equally effective and easier to install. They look fierce but cause little damage if accidentally run into, so they are seldom pulled up in return. They are sometimes joined by a string 'fence' to mark out newly seeded areas next to car parks. Old concrete fence posts have also been used at this site, as wooden posts tend to get vandalised and burnt.

Log barriers

Large tree trunks, about 3m (10') long and at least 250mm (10") diameter, or old telegraph poles, make effective barriers if dug part way into the ground or set on posts. Where the logs are big enough, it is easiest to dig them in, but they are likely to be rolled aside unless bolted to posts or anchored to buried concrete blocks by chains. Smaller timbers of about 150mm

(6") are best set across short supporting posts as shown below. Softwoods should be pressure treated.

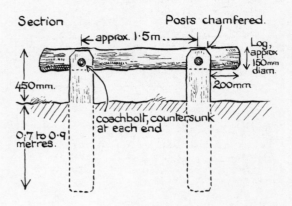

This method of fixing reduces the problems of rotting and weakness associated with notch-type joints. Although this sort of raised-log barrier is fairly easily vandalised, it has the advantage of being usable as a seat and play-rail for children. Sets of posts can be placed with 1m (3') gaps between them to mark out car parking bays — a continuous barrier is needed only if you want to keep motorcycles from getting through.

Barriers can either be set along a straight line, or staggered as shown, to indicate individual parking spaces.

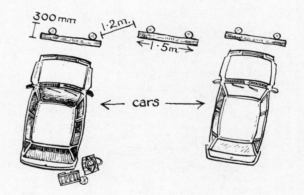

Turf banks

Car parks and trackways can be defined by peripheral banks and ditches. The ditches provide spoil for the banks and, if positioned on the side of the banks towards the cars, increase the effective height of the barrier.

When you dig the ditch, first cut out turfs at least 50mm (2") thick and lay them aside. After building the bank nearly to the required height (600mm, 2' minimum, to accommodate settling), place the turfs along the inner (ditched) face as shown and tamp them well down. If possible, water the new bank to promote the survival of the turfs and the spread of vegetation.

Turf banks are much less obtrusive than other sorts of barriers but they are relatively easily broken through. They are most useful where the out-of-bounds area is only moderate attractive for parking or holds only a few cars. The ditches do tend to collect litter and may

66

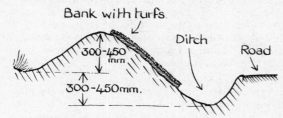

Section.

Bank with turfs.

Ditch

Road

300-450 mm

300-450mm.

speed erosion if dug near a cliff edge or in soft sandy soil.

Signposting

For details of signposting in the countryside, see Brown (1974), Agate (1983) and the Countryside Commission leaflet on waymarking public rights of way (1985). A few points should be kept in mind to make signposting effective:

a Signs with a positive, explanatory emphasis usually work better than those that simply prohibit.

b Dune restoration works should be explained in detail by signs at major access points and by small, briefly worded 'reminder' signs fixed every 20 metres or so along perimeter fences around planted or seeded areas.

c Signs restricting access should be as inconspicuous as possible, given the need to convey the message. For example, at Holkham National Nature Reserve, Norfolk, small signs are placed on short posts in backdune hollows where people tend to picnic. The signs say 'Please dig on the beach and not on the dunes as this causes erosion. Thank you'. Only the people who use the hollows need see the signs. At Ainsdale Sand Dunes NNR, Merseyside, discreet 'No Entry' signs on 600mm (2') posts are placed along footpaths and beside gates in the dune woodlands, but some way back so that only people who stray from permitted paths come across them. This negative signposting is balanced by positive routemarking along the paths themselves.

d Many site managers feel that cheap-looking, mass-produced signs are more likely to be vandalised than carefully hand-routed signs in materials such as pine, which are sympathetic to the local environment. But any signs may become damaged, and it is always important to consider the number of signs involved and to weigh up the time and cost of replacement when choosing between different materials. Where it is not possible to give each sign the hand-made touch, it helps to have pasted-on maps etc which can be easily and cheaply replaced when ripped off. Whatever the material, good design is essential to provide a readable sign which is in keeping with the setting.

One system which is used on Merseyside and elsewhere is to make up blank signs as shown. A selection of sticky-backed signs with wording such as "Dune Restoration – please keep out" can then be attached as necessary. Such printed signs cost only about 50p each in quantity, and the wooden backing and posts about £2 (1986 prices).

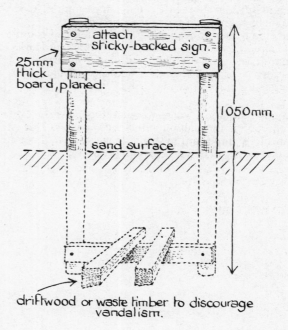

attach sticky-backed sign.

25mm thick board, planed.

1050mm.

sand surface

driftwood or waste timber to discourage vandalism.

e In tern nesting sites it is important to post explanatory signs near the zones of heaviest traffic, eg along the tide mark. If signs are posted for example at the foot of sand dunes behind the nesting beach, people may walk straight through the nest area to read the signs, completely unaware of the damage they are causing.

WAYMARKING

On many dune sites waymarking of both public rights of way and other paths such as nature trails is most important. Dunes can be very confusing areas to walk in, one dune looking very much like another to those not familiar with the area. Waymarking must be done consistently and given regular maintenance, so that visitors have confidence in following the marked route and are not tempted to make their own way. It can be important that people are kept to the path to avoid erosion or damage to restoration work, and to minimise disturbance to ecologically sensitive areas.

The usual technique is to use posts, with the tops painted the appropriate waymarking colour of yellow for footpaths, blue for bridlepaths and red for byways. Alternatively, colour coding may be used in conjunction with nature trails and interpretative material. Space the posts according to the topography, normally so that there is one always in view. Well worn or surfaced paths may not need such frequent spacing. Posts should be of tanalised timber, set at least 600mm (2') in the ground, with cross pieces to prevent them being pulled out. Make them just tall enough to be easily visible.

At Walney Island, Cumbria, very short posts are used, protruding only about 300mm above ground. This saves on materials, and is sufficient on this site where the vegetation is cropped short by cattle. The posts are also less vulnerable to being used as rubbing posts by the cattle, although the posts still need to be set in dug holes and wedged in with rocks, to hold them firm. On this site it is vital that no visitors stray from the path, as an entire gull colony can be disturbed by a single intruder. Posts are set at a maximum distance of 50 metres. Frequent posts are also a good encouragement to walkers to keep going and complete the circuit, especially on sections where landmarks to aim for are few. Low signs, with black lettering on a white background are also used, large enough to be visible but not to intrude.

Another situation where waymarking is very important is through dune restoration areas. This is especially important in the early stages, when fencing and planting may not be complete, and it is not immediately obvious, even to sympathetic visitors, which is the designated route. It saves much antagonism if you can avert trouble by clearly waymarking the route and informing the public. White painted posts and a temporary sign may be sufficient initially, with more permanent signs as necessary once the scheme is completed.

Also remember to mark paths at their seaward end. Having walked some way along a beach, it is often difficult to re-find the place where you emerged through the dunes. Use tall posts, painted white, on the seaward edge of the foredune, or put in several in a row down toward high water mark, so the point is easily visible. If there are several exits, use different colours.

7 Vegetation Establishment

This chapter describes the main dune grass species which form the pioneer vegetation of the foredunes. An important part of any dune stabilisation work is the transplanting of grasses, usually marram, to reduce wind blow at the surface (see p9), and create a living system of dune growth and stabilisation. Fertilising, turfing and transplanting of shrubs are also described.

Transplanting Grasses

GENERAL POINTS

Uses

Dune grasses may be used to:

a   Trap sand at the eroding windward faces of dunes and so help maintain their positions

b   Reduce the scouring effect of wind in blowouts and at the same time trap sand to help fill them in

c   Consolidate areas of loose sand including blowout deposition areas, embryo dunes, newly contoured dune faces and zones of accretion along fencelines. Fencing without planting does nothing to stabilise the sand surface.

Other considerations

a   Transplanting is at present the cheapest and most effective way to establish species of dune-building grasses.

b   Mixed dune grassland species may be transplanted by turfing (p76) but this must usually be augmented by sowing (p78).

c   Transplanting is usually most effective when done in conjunction with fencing or thatching. Transplanting is often benefited by mulching or binding, and in some situations fertilising may help. Thatching should normally be done before or at the same time as planting, rather than afterwards which may damage the plants.

d   Protective fencing is often required around planted areas to prevent public access while the plants become established. It may be possible to limit fencing to the tops or crests of dunes and ridges. People tend to avoid climbing dunes which are vegetated and closed off at the top, provided convenient paths are made available in less vulnerable areas.

SPECIES

The most useful species to plant on bare sand and to initiate new dune development are the three natural dune-forming perennial grasses: sand couchgrass, sea lyme grass and marram. Marram is most widely used but the others may be preferable in certain circumstances. All have the ability to slow the wind and trap sand without causing scour. They maintain their effectiveness (within limits) by growing out and up through new deposits.

Sand couchgrass

Sand couchgrass or sand twitch (*Elymus farctus* syn. *Agropyron junceiforme*) is almost universal around the coasts of the British Isles wherever there is moderate sand blow. It is the usual pioneer of embryo dunes since even as a seedling it stands salt and can grow within reach of the high spring tides. Its extensive rhizomes creep through the sand and send up new aerial shoots when buried, as long as the annual sand accretion is under about 300mm (1'). If sand blows out from around the plant it continues to grow on the surface, protecting it from further erosion by a network of rootlets and shoots. The shoots and rhizomes tend to get tangled up when the plant is lifted, which can cause problems when transplanting. Sand couchgrass shoots are bluish-green and form loose clusters. The leaves are 100–350mm (4"–14") long with upper surfaces which have close parallel ribs and many rows of short hairs. The leaves curl inward in dry conditions.

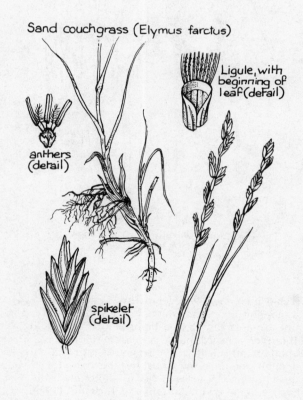

Sand couchgrass (*Elymus farctus*)

anthers (detail)

Ligule, with beginning of leaf (detail)

spikelet (detail)

Sand couch rhizomes grow almost without limit horizontally but not vertically. The plant prefers mixed sand and shingle to pure sand. These factors mean that sand couch dunes are characteristically low and broadly domed. Such dunes resist wind erosion well, but where more height is required sea lyme grass or marram must enter the community to continue the dune-building process.

Sea lyme grass

Sea lyme grass or lyme grass (*Leymus arenarius* syn. *Elymus arenarius*) is widespread around the coasts of Britain but is most common in the North and East, where it may be locally abundant. Elsewhere it is likely to be in short supply compared to the other two dune-forming grasses. This restricts its availability for transplanting, but if sowing methods improve it may be used more widely in the future (p78).

Sea lyme has a high salt tolerance. It usually forms a fairly narrow strip above the pioneering couchgrass on the windward side of foredunes. Its tolerance to sand burial is similar to that of sand couch, but it is a much sturdier species in appearance, with stout rhizomes which produce clusters of large, sword-like bluish-green leaves 600mm–1.5m (2'–5') high. The upper leaf surfaces are rough due to slightly raised parallel veins while the under surfaces are smooth. The stems are stiff, upright and smooth.

Lyme grass (Leymus arenarius).

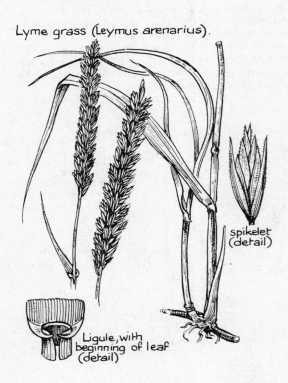

spikelet (detail)

Ligule, with beginning of leaf (detail)

Sea lyme grass spreads vegetatively via horizontal rhizomes and, like sand couch, it tends to form broad humpbacked dunes. Once established, it can extend itself farther seaward than can marram but it is distinctly wind sensitive and so flourishes mainly in moderately sheltered locations. For this reason, and because in winter it loses its leaves and offers little resistance to the wind, Adriani and Terwindt (1974, p48) recommend that it be planted between other dune-building grasses rather than alone. They also report that it is very prone to rabbit attack (an observation borne out on a number of British sites) and conclude, 'one wonders whether it is in fact suitable for use in coastal management at all'. On the other hand, Ritchie (1975, p2580) says that it has spread spontaneously and rapidly under natural conditions in many parts of Scotland where it seems as disease resistant as marram and more effective at the seaward edge of dunes. Transplanting experience on the East Lothian coast and on Anglesey bears this out, while in Northumberland it has been found to have a much faster initial growth rate than marram in favourable locations. In view of these mixed results, it is best initially to use sea lyme grass in fairly small

quantities, in sheltered places on the seaward side of dunes, preferably interplanted with marram to give some protection from rabbits and to insure some cover if the sea lyme grass fails.

Marram grass

Marram (*Ammophila arenaria*) is the major dune-building plant in Britain, as it or the closely-related *A breviligulata* is throughout the world where conditions are suitable for really high coastal dunes. In certain localities, a hybrid occurs between marram and wood small-reed (bush grass, *Calamagrostis epigejos*). This is Baltic marram grass (*Ammocalam – agrostis baltica*), which is even more vigorous than marram but is completely sterile and so can only be propagated vegetatively. At the present, planting stock are limited, although it was planted extensively on the coast of Norfolk and Suffolk after the 1953 floods (Boorman, 1977).

Another vigorous cultivar, American beachgrass *Ammophila brevigulata* cv Hatteras, has been tried at Newborough Warren, but has not proved superior to native marram, and is susceptible to fungus disease (Ranwell and Boar, 1986).

No other plants have the ability to grow without limit not only horizontally but also upward through blown sand (Ranwell, 1972, p140). In fact, marram positively requires blown sand to thrive. Once it is sheltered from further sand accumulation, it gradually dies back and reduces its flowering. The reasons are not fully understood, but it does seem that marram roots are fairly short-lived so the plants may depend on frequent new root formation to survive (Boorman, 1977, p165). Unlike sand couchgrass, marram prefers to spread its rhizomes in pure sand, sending clusters of roots downward while the young shoots grow straight up. As sand accumulates around the shoots, marram forms adventitious roots at higher and higher levels, thus continuing to dominate the dune and make it higher. Ranwell (1958, p96) reports that at Newborough Warren, marram just withstands burial by up to 900mm (3') of sand in a year provided its leaves are no more than half buried in any gale period and that there is time for the leaves and growing points to reach the new sand level between gales. On the East Lothian coast, local experience is that marram survives up to 1.2m (4') burial at any one time. This is clearly a critical factor in its success when transplanted in areas of loose sand. In any case, its density declines rapidly if very high levels of sand blow persist, as is likely on the higher lee slopes of dunes where marram establishment may be more difficult than elsewhere. To some extent the system is self-regulating, as once marram is buried nothing remains to cause further sand accumulation, until the marram starts to grow through again.

Marram has parallel-veined, light yellow-green leaves, 600–900mm (2'–3') long, which remain tightly rolled except in very wet weather. It can be confused with sand couchgrass when young, or with sea lyme grass when well developed, but unlike these it has a particularly long ligule, 10–30mm ($\frac{1}{2}$–$1\frac{1}{4}$") in length, at the inner junction of the leaf-sheath and the blade. This can be seen at all stages of growth.

Marram tolerates at most 1% salinity, according to Adriani and Terwindt (1974, p13), so it only grows in

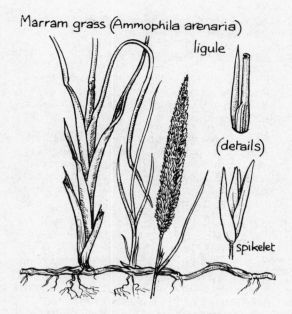

Marram grass (Ammophila arenaria)

ligule

(details)

spikelet

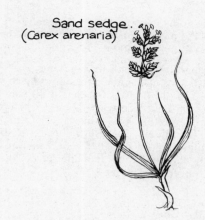

Sand sedge.
(Carex arenaria)

areas out of reach of the tides. Once established, it is very drought resistant. In the initial colonising phase of its growth it produces few flower spikes, but when well established, it flowers freely and its clusters may spread until they occupy ten or twenty times the original volume of sand. In favourable conditions, it takes about eight years for the grass clumps to gradually coalesce to form a continuous open sward (Hewett, 1970, p664). In the postoptimal phase, when fresh sand supplies are cut off, it may persist for many years but gradually gives way to other plant species as it dies back.

Marram dunes tend to become steeper and higher than those of sand couchgrass or sea lyme. Where the forward face becomes too steep it may be undercut by the wind so that clumps of grass slide to the bottom of the slope. Often the clumbs re-establish themselves, but meanwhile much loose sand drifts onto the lee slope so that the dune tends to move slowly downwind. This process is accentuated by the fact that individual clumps of marram trap more sand in their lee than among the shoots themselves, and that new shoots grow up most vigorously in this heavily sanded 'shadow', so that individual clumps and their minature dunelets also tend to grow downwind. Because of this, marram plantations seldom remain fixed unless fences are used to act as fixed points of sand buildup.

Sand sedge

Sand sedge (*Carex arenaria*), has a similar growth form to dune grasses, although not a grass itself. In some places, eg Braunton Burrows, Devon, it helps to stabilise very gritty sea-facing eroding slopes where it withstands the battering of blown grit better than marram. Usually, it grows in dry slacks, where it spreads over the surface via straight runners to form a loose network, occasionally colonising the sand slopes to either side. Although it only grows a few inches high, it might prove useful for stabilisation work provided it could be successfully transplanted.

WORK SEASON AND STORAGE OF PLANTS

Sand-trapping grasses are remarkably tolerant and often survive transplanting even under seemingly

adverse conditions. There are a few seasonal considerations which, if followed, allow the greatest success rate:

a   Take and transplant offsets during cool weather. If the average maximum air temperature rises above 55°F (15°C) during the first three days after planting, few offsets are likely to survive (Hewett, 1973, p58). If possible, carry out transplanting in the season of relative dormancy. This means, broadly speaking, September to April (November to April in the South West).

In general, planting is most successful in early March. At this time it is also easy to distinguish the living stems of grass by their green colour, so that these rather than dead stems are gathered.

b   Success in other seasons varies greatly in different parts of the country, depending on rainfall. Planting in summer is not successful in the dry east or warmer southern locations, but may be possible in the north-west. On stable and sheltered sites, planting is possible from November to February, but is not worth doing where wind erosion, burial by sand or grazing is going to damage the offsets before they have a chance to establish. The following summary is from 'Dune Grass Planting' (CCS, 1985). The greater number of stars indicates greater success rate.

Oct–Jan	***	Avoid if grazing, burial or erosion is likely in winter.
February	****	Conditions often too severe for planting comfort. Avoid frosts.
March	*****	By far the best for all sites.
Apr–May	**	Dependent on cool spring weather.
June–Sept	*	Avoid on east coast; moderate success on north or north-west coasts.

c   Mid-summer planting may succeed given a spell of cool weather, provided that the work is done carefully. The usual advice is to dig and transplant offsets on the same day. If there is any delay, keep the plants covered in moist sand during the interval before setting out and be sure to plant deep enough so that living roots reach moist sand. Try to avoid disturbing the sand more than necessary since this allows it to dry to deeper levels than would otherwise occur. If you thatch the planted area at the same time as transplanting, the brushwood helps shade the plants and reduces drying of the sand in hot summer weather.

d   Experience on the Northumberland coast suggests that marram can be stored up to six months in plastic bags (eg clean fertiliser sacks opened at their narrow end), and that storage for three months causes the nodes of the plants to swell and develop, resulting in faster growth after planting (Bacon, 1975, p8). Pack the bags loosely and keep them in a cool place, sheltered from the sun, for storage.

SOURCES OF SUPPLY

a   The supply site should be as near as possible to the work area, especially if transport is by hand over the tops of dunes. If transport is by trailer or lorry-load, driving time is as important as distance. Choose an area where plants are abundant so that offsets can be collected efficiently. If you have to find a source away from the planting site, look for areas of accreting duneland in fairly sheltered locations, eg around small estuaries (Bacon, 1974, p2).

b   Do not gather plants from exposed shorelines or windward dune faces, even those which lie well back of the coastline, unless the turf contains other well established plants and the dune-building species are dying back. It is important to maintain the stability of the supply site as well as to improve that of the planting site.

c   The best place to gather marram is on the lee side of a back dune ridge where the stand is still dense and vigorous but where it is entering the postoptimal phase of its development. Such a site is fairly erosion resistant provided that you dig selectively, to thin rather than open up the stand, and that you transport the marram in a way which does not create gullies and other focal points for wind scour. Thinning may even restore the remaining marram to vigour. Where the supply site is sheltered, you can experiment with removing up to 90% of the marram in small areas. This can result in very good new growth, as has been found in East Lothian.

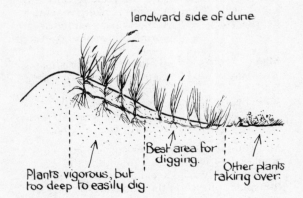

landward side of dune

Plants vigorous, but too deep to easily dig.

Best area for digging.

Other plants taking over.

d   Other 'donor' sites for marram include postoptimal areas such as fixed dune ridges and dune grassland. The problem here is that extra time and effort may be involved in gathering the more scattered plants and in carrying them to

the planting site. Avoid collecting very poor quality plants.

e   Gather sand couchgrass and sea lyme grass from relatively sheltered seafronts where further dune growth is unlikely. Supplies are often limited because these species generally grow in easily eroded foredune situations which should not be disturbed.

f   You can sometimes dig dune-building grasses from the foreshore where they are colonising areas of bare beach sand. Supplies from this source are usually meagre. Be careful not to over-collect since this prevents the formation of new embryo dunes.

g   In Cornwall, it has been found that growth of marram in newly planted fenced plots can be so rapid that it is possible to use the plots as a 'nursery'. Within 12–18 months planted clumps are thinned by one third, by pulling the new, vigorous growth. This is easy to pull and quick to collect, being in planted rows and concentrated in a small area. Such pulling invigorates the 'mother' plants which keep growing fast. Here, and elsewhere, it is reckoned that any plants which are too old to pull are too old to transplant, and that in general, digging is unnecessary (see p74).

h   Another situation where plants are usually growing rapidly are alongside any narrow paths which wind through the back of the dunes. Plants can be quickly dug or pulled all the way along the path edge, thus making collection a rapid process. The remaining plants regrow quickly to repair the path edge.

WORK RATES

Work rates vary greatly, from under 200 to almost 2,000 offsets dug, transported and planted per person per day.

The low figure, based on BTCV tasks at Lindisfarne National Nature Reserve, Northumberland, is for work in difficult terrain with transport involving frequent Land Rover runs of 1 mile (1.6km) between the digging and planting sites with a considerable hand carry at each end.

The high figure is derived from estimates given by Nash (1962, p9) for work on flat areas of the Outer Banks of North Carolina, USA. This is a maximum output for teams of experienced paid workers who can dig all the offsets for the day's work in the morning, load them into a truck and drive them to the afternoon's planting site. Average output under these conditions is about 1,200 plants per day but for inexperienced workers or in poor weather it can drop as low as about 450 plants per person per day.

An intermediate figure, of about 700 plants per person per day, is derived from East Lothian County Council (1970, p7) for the digging and transplanting of sea lyme grass by three-man teams of paid workers.

At an average spacing of 450mm ($1\frac{1}{2}'$), the above work rates result in 16 square metres (20 sq yds) to 200 square metres (240 sq yds) planted per person per day. In conditions where marram can be tractor-planted work rates may be five to ten times faster.

LOCATION AND SPACING OF PLANTING

Location

a   Do not plant marram within 2–3m (6'–10') vertical distance of mean high tide level on the seaward face of foredunes. If you plant it lower than this, it may be damaged by salt water. Use sand couchgrass or sea lyme grass on the lowest levels of shifting coastal dunes.

b   Whatever species you use, it is important to plant an entire slope from crest to bottom. If you plant only the upper slope the dune will develop too steep a face and become more prone to erosion.

c   Suitable slopes for planting marram range up to 27° (1:2). Although offsets will survive on steeper slopes, the slopes are likely to remain unstable and should, if possible, be contoured to a lesser angle prior to planting.

d   Where you cannot regrade a very steep slope, and erosion appears to be a natural and continuing situation, it may be best to just plant the lee side of the dune crest provided sand buildup is within tolerable limits. As the crest is undercut, marram clumps will tumble onto the forward face and may take root. Meanwhile the planted marram on the lee slope should keep the sand from blowing farther back.

You can plant steep slopes more easily and with greater success if you thatch or mulch them before planting.

e   Before planting backdunes, check for evidence of adequate sand supply (eg natural recolonisation by marram). If there seems to be too little blown sand for the dune-building grasses to thrive, sow mixed grasses instead, using a fertiliser and binder as necessary.

Spacing

a   Plant offsets in any convenient pattern, normally spaced from 300–900mm (1'–3') apart.

b   Site conditions, the amount of grass available and the area to be covered by the work party in the given period all affect the spacing. Close spacing is best where the surface is actively eroding and likely to suffer further wind blow in the months after planting. Where supplies and labour are plentiful, spacings of as little as 150mm (6") between plants in a row and 225mm (9") between rows have been used with success at Balmedie Beach, Aberdeenshire. Close spacing has also worked well at Lindisfarne, Northumberland. Usually it is better to plant up the entire area at a slightly wider spacing than to leave some of it unplanted and open to erosion. On steep slopes, 300mm (1') between plants and 450mm (1½') between rows is often easier than closer spacing of rows.

c   The most common pattern is quincunx ('domino 5') with about 450mm (1½') between plants on average.

Adriani and Terwindt (1974, p48) recommend planting marram and sand couchgrass in this

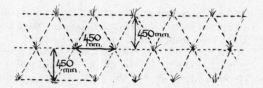

pattern at 500mm (1'8") spacings with an interplanting of sea lyme grass at 250mm (10") spacings.

d   Plant in staggered rows to limit any problem of wind-scour between the rows and to encourage the even spread of new growth into the intervening spaces. Staggered-row planting also makes it easy to see where you have finished. 'Random' planting may look more 'natural' at first but it can result in uneven coverage. Staggered plantings soon blend with their surroundings as some plants die and others send up new shoots and spread.

TRANSPLANTING METHODS AND WORK ORGANISATION

Arrange details of work organisation according to the site, size of working party and supply of plants. Aim to supply offsets at a steady rate for planting. In some situations, eg where plants must be transported some distance by road or where a mechanical planter is being used, it may be best to have all volunteers dig until the supply vehicle is loaded, then have the same people plant until supplies are exhausted.

Generally, digging the offsets is quicker than planting them. Where the digging and planting site are within easy walking distance, a typical way to organise the task is to have four people digging and loading the plants into containers, two people carrying them between the digging and planting sites and six people planting. It is often easiest if diggers work in pairs to fill containers, so that four diggers use two containers. Planting can be done singly or by teams depending on the site and the inclination of volunteers.

Digging and transporting

a   The aim is to extract plants with at least 150mm (6") of healthy root or rhizome, with two or three nodes from which the new roots or shoots will grow. A longer length of rhizome, of 300mm (1') or more, is not necessary for successful establishment, and makes planting more awkward.

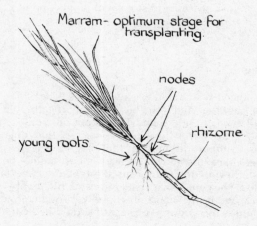

Marram – optimum stage for transplanting.

nodes

rhizome

young roots

73

The usual method is to dig, and then pull on the plant so that enough rhizome breaks away from the tangle of roots deep in the sand. The point at which it breaks will depend on the vigour of the plant, the depth you dig and the depth and dryness of the sand. In damp sand, which anchors the rhizomes, you may need to dig deeper to get a sufficient length, as pulling will break the rhizome off short.

b   When using a spade or fork, cut out a block of turf and lever it up so you can lift the offsets.

Where the root mat is dense you may have to cut the block on all four sides to lift it. Otherwise just cut two sides. You can usually do this without shifting your position.

Leaving the spade or fork in place to minimise disturbance to the soil, reach down and pull apart bundles of offsets. Shake most of the sand loose from the rhizomes so that it falls back into the hole. This lightens the load when transporting and gives a higher proportion of offsets to sand. Lay the offsets to one side or place them directly into the container. After the block is completely separated and removed, pull out the spade or fork and heel in the remaining sand in the hole.

c   Move a few feet away to dig up another block of grass. Leave plenty of grass in proportion to dug-up ground, to minimise the risk of erosion.

d   Gather the offsets and pack them closely into the transporting container. There should be plenty of living stems with succulent white rhizomes and root hairs but don't bother separating out dead plants unless they form a very high proportion of the total.

For hand carrying by one or two people, polythene bags (eg old fertiliser sacks) are ideal. These keep the plants moist, but should be kept shaded so that the plants don't overheat. Coil the plants into the bags to minimise tangling. You can also pack plants into old fish boxes or buckets, although these are more cumbersome. For transporting large quantities of grass in a Land Rover or lorry, use old fish nets folded into long thin rectangles. Lay the plants on the folded netting and roll up the nets to form bundles.

e   If you have to store the offsets for more than a few hours, cover them with damp sand and keep this moist. This is especially important when planting in hot dry weather. See also 'Work season and storage of plants', point c (p71).

Pulling

Experienced workers in Cornwall and Merseyside have found that much the best method of gathering transplants is to pull them. This is not only quick and easy, but it disturbs the sand surface less than digging, and most importantly means that the plants are at just the right stage for transplanting. If plants cannot be pulled, they are too old for rapid establishment. Plants should be less than two years old, with plenty of fibrous root. If the shoots are a pinky-purple colour, the plant is too young. The sheath should be dry and yellowing, with the whole plant forming a 'funnel' shape.

The only problem is that it does require experience to recognize when plants are at just the right stage. Inexperienced workers can waste time and plant material by pulling plants that do not have sufficient roots on them, or damaging plants that are too old. Digging is a safer method in this case, as it ensures that some viable root is obtained from each plant.

Planting by hand

a   It is essential to plant deep enough, so that the active growing point at the leaf base is 50–100mm (2–4″) below the sand surface. This normally means planting about 100mm (4″) deeper than the plant was when lifted. The reason is that the plant is adapted to increasing in vigour by developing new roots and shoots as it grows upwards through the sand. If the growing point is put at the sand surface, the plant stagnates (CCS, 1985).

The number of plants put in each planting hole will depend on the size of the plants. Normally, two large, three to four medium or five to six small plants will be needed, making a bundle of about 38mm (1½″) diameter, which can be held with the thumb and forefinger touching. Do not bother separating the live stems from dead litter or other species which may be intermixed. Dead material helps trap sand, and probably protects the live stems and provides a mulch when it breaks down. If other species survive along with the grasses, so much the better.

Overall success rates for transplanted marram are usually in the order of 60–70%, so it is wise to include at least two living stems per hole and as many as can be managed, given the available supply and the time and area to be planted.

Heel in each bundle using the foot or palm of the hand. Check them for firmness. They should withstand a gentle tug.

b   When planting a slope or blowout, start at the top and work downward to reduce the amount of trampling as you work.

If thatching is being done (p81), do this as you plant. You can use thorn-free brushwood to stand on as you work. On very steep slopes, stake straw bales in parallel lines from bottom to top, spaced a few metres apart. By using these as access routes, you disturb the slope much less than if you climb on the unprotected sand face. The stakes can be tricky to hammer in, so work with care and stand on brushwood to keep from sliding. Leave the bales in place after use to help trap sand and to gradually break down and form a mulch.

c   You can plant offsets using a spade, a dibber or with your bare hands, depending on soil conditions and personal preference. Many people like to use a garden spade, especially when planting in firm ground. In hard or stony ground, a pointed spade such as a Schlich planting spade or a trenching spade is easiest. Working from a standing position, make a notch to take the offset.

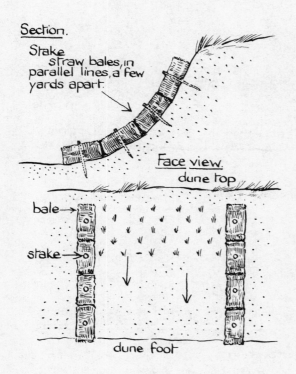

Section.

Stake straw bales, in parallel lines, a few yards apart.

Face view.
dune top

bale →

stake →

dune foot

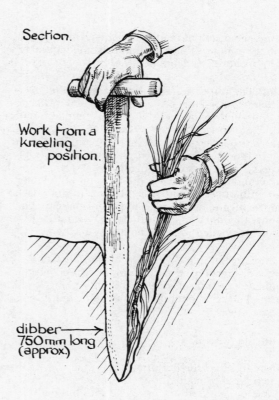

Section.

Work from a kneeling position.

dibber 750 mm long (approx.)

Some people favour using a long, narrow spade held 'back to front', as the blade makes a concave face for planting against, and leaves the handle nearer the hand, which is quicker and less tiring.

If the hole tends to fill in too quickly, work the spade around to enlarge it and slide the plant down the blade with the blade in the ground. Push the rhizomes well down in the hole as you lift the spade free. This gets the rhizomes deeper than if you pull the spade out first.

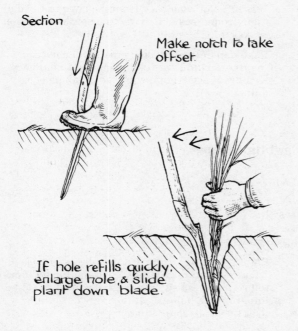

Section

Make notch to take offset.

If hole refills quickly, enlarge hole & slide plant down blade.

In soft sand you can make a hole with a broken, sharpened spade handle, used like a dibber. Garden dibbers are too short to be effective. In firmer sand use a small crowbar.

In very soft sand, use your bare hands to scoop out a hole. You may have to make it extra large

so that it stays open long enough to place the offset.

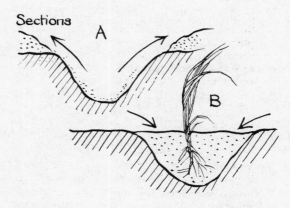

Sections

A

B

d   Always start planting up against any boundary, so the planters are not confined as work reaches completion. Normally it is efficient for each pair to work along a line of about 10–15m length so that teams do not get in one another's way, whilst remaining close enough to their own supply point (CCS, 1985).

e   Two-person planting is best done with a spade. One person should stand to make a notch with the spade while the other kneeling, places the offset.

Where the soil is firm it may be easiest for the person who cuts the notches to work slightly in advance of the planter. He may be able to keep two people busy planting if he works quickly.

f   Transplants may benefit from fertilising at the time of planting (see below).

Planting by machine

Agricultural planting machinery can be adapted to transplant offsets of marram. This is only worth doing where a large area of relatively flat terrain is to be planted up, but in this situation it is much quicker and less laborious than hand planting.

Nash (1952, p9) says that a root planter pulled by a small crawler tractor improves man-day outputs by five times and reduces costs by 80% compared with a paid labour force. The best system is for a team of five workers to gather offsets all morning and then plant them in the afternoon. When planting, the work party consists of one person driving the tractor, three on the planter and one who keeps the trays on the planter filled with offsets and drives the lorry full of offsets from the digging to the planting site. Where digging and planting are done simultaneously, another five people are needed to keep the lorry supplied.

On the East Lothian coast a tractor-pulled cabbage planter has been used with similar success, but ten people were required to supply it with plants and the marram had to be chopped before being fed through the machine.

Fertilising transplants

Transplants of dune-building grasses may be fertilised at the time of transplanting. The value of this is variable on exposed or unstable dunes but may improve growth considerably on areas less subject to rapid sand movement. See page 79 for details. When fertilising transplants, it is best to incorporate the first treatment directly into the planting hole, and follow this by periodic top dressings as for sown grasses.

Turfing Eroded Machairs

Machair restoration work at Achmelvich, Sutherland, and at some other sites involves covering areas of eroded machair edge with turfs to mark out areas for sowing and to encourage the spread of vegetation. At Achmelvich the procedure used is as follows

1   Cut turfs from the top of the machair 'cliff' and let them slide down the face to the beach. Turfs should be rectangular, about 600mm (2′) wide and of any convenient length. Cut them about 200mm (8″) thick. Some of the excess soil falls from them as they slide downhill but enough should be left to prevent them drying out before re-use.

2   Stack the turfs along the cliff bottom, not too close or they will get in the way of contouring.

3   Regrade steep sections of the machair edge by cutting it back at the top and shifting sand to the bottom or into blowouts and gullies. Aim to produce a final slope of 30°–45° and a rolling profile at the cliff's top and bottom.

4   Dig in a line of turfs at the base of the contoured slope.

5   Where the slope is more than a few feet high, put another row of turfs along it about half way up and place occasional rows running up and down to divide the slope into a series of rectangles.

The horizontal rows reduce sand slip and provide the basis for vegetation to spread over the bare surface. The vertical rows aid this and

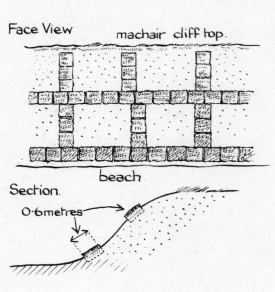

Section.

Turfs, cut and stacked. Final profile Original profile

Face View   machair cliff top.

beach.

Section.

0·6 metres

also mark the slope into convenient areas for sowing.

If you don't have enough turf to create horizontal and vertical rows, you may be able to cut turfs from sheltered areas of the machair surface some way back from the edge or to take them from areas which are to be surfaced for car parks etc.

6   Rake remaining unturfed areas and stabilise them by sowing, fertilising and binding. Fence to prevent access by people and grazing animals.

Planting Shrubs

GENERAL POINTS

Uses

Shrubs may be used on dunes to:

a   Protect eroding windward sand faces in areas where the sand is too steep and mobile for grass to take. In these situations the shrubs tend to be undermined, but even if they die and topple over they trap some sand.

b   Check sand drift and slow the rate of accretion on the lee slopes of dunes

c   Supply cuttings for use in thatching and brushwood fences

d   Form barriers, shelterbelts etc for amenity use and access control

Other considerations

a   Shrubs change the dune ecosystem more radically than do grasses and should only be used on sites where they already occur or where the need to retain open dune habitats is less important than the need to fix shifting sand.

b   Most sand-trapping shrubs spread horizontally by suckers, but the rate of spread is much slower than their upward or oblique growth through moderate sand burial. For this reason, shrubs maintain a fairly tight form which creates rather steep-sided hummocky dunes which are less erosion resistant in exposed conditions than dunes built by grasses.

c   Shrubs should be planted in the period September to April, with February and March being best (Adriani and Terwindt, 1974, p56). This gives the plants time to root before the onset of summer droughts.

d   Plant shrubs in groups rather than individually, to give them mutual support and increased overall wind resistance. Where the aim is not to create dense thickets but to provide stability for a variety of herbaceous plants, plant them at about 10m (30') intervals to allow room for other plants in between (Adriani and Terwindt, 1974, p48).

SPECIES

Sea buckthorn

Sea buckthorn (*Hippophae rhamnoides*) is rampant on many sites where it occurs naturally or has been introduced, and it is controlled more often than it is fostered where the aim is to promote diverse plant communities. Introduction in such areas is obviously counterproductive. There may be other species native to the site which may be substituted, although with care an all-male colony can be established which is easier to manage than a mixed one since it spreads only by suckering. See page 89 for more on the ecology and management of this species.

Sea buckthorn survives both in dry and damp locations, although growth is poor in soils deficient in lime. On the East Lothian coast older specimens continue to grow even when successively buried by 4.5m (15') of sand with only about 600mm (2') of the shoots remaining exposed (Ranwell, 1972a, p18). As with many shrubs, the buried portion dies but the shoots which remain above the sand root again to form new plants at a higher level.

Adriani and Terwindt (1974, p49) recommend planting sea buckthorn suckers or seedlings only where a good cover of grass has already been established. Suckers should have a good root system and should be dug up and planted out on the same day. The roots should be placed 250–400mm (10–16") deep according to the dampness of the soil.

Sow sea buckthorn in sheltered places having little if any sand disturbance, where it germinates readily, and in areas with too much sand for transplanting. Soil salinity must be below 0.05% (Adriani and Terwindt, 1974, p48). One trouble with sowing is that you can't ensure an all-male population which will not spread further by self-seeding.

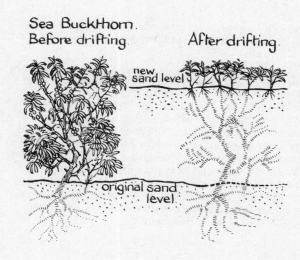

Sea Buckthorn. Before drifting. After drifting.

Creeping willow

Creeping willow (*Salix repens*) is a widespread shrub of moist dune slacks. In areas which are drying out, it often persists and becomes deep rooted.

Creeping Willow.

This is a dwarf species which grows up to 1m (3') high. Like sea buckthorn, creeping willow has spread rapidly on many sites since the 1950s when myxomatosis reduced the rabbit population and grazing restraints lessened. As yet, control does not seem to have been required. Where it becomes firmly established it acts as a good sand stabiliser, provided accretion is not over about 400mm (16") per year (Ranwell, 1958, p96). Creeping willow should be established by transplanting seedlings or suckers in the same way as sea buckthorn.

Other species

A few other shrub species may be of use in restricted situations:

a   Elder (*Sambucus nigra*) often invades the landward side of shifting dunes, inland fixed dunes and the borderline between dunes and woodlands. It prefers a relatively rich soil, eg where fresh organic material such as bird droppings decompose rapidly. In such places it often invades and shades out stands of sea buckthorn. It is normally 2–4.5m (6'–15') high, but under conditions of wind pruning and sand burial it suckers from buried shoots to form low thickets of upright shoots which trap sand efficiently. At Ynyslas Dunes (Dyfi NNR), Dyfed, it has survived well where this has occurred to plants growing on the edges of blowouts.

To propagate elder, take cuttings about 1m (3′) long and force them well down into moist sand with 300–450mm (12–18″) of stem projecting.

b   Tamarisk (*Tamarix* spp) is an introduced evergreen shrub from southern Europe which survives along the south coast of England and in places as far north as Lincolnshire. It withstands sea wind and occasional flooding by salt water and makes a useful coastal hedging plant. Tamarisk spreads by suckering and grows 2–3m (6′–10′) high. As a non-native it should not be planted on nature reserves and other sites of scientific interest.

c   Tree lupin (*Lupinus arboreus*) is an evergreen shrub which grows to 3m (10′) high. It is an exotic species (from California) which has been successfully interplanted with marram at Dawlish Warren, South Devon and has been used to screen car parks on the Suffolk Heritage Coast. It does best where there is not much sand accretion. It is much favoured by rabbits and may require fencing to survive.

d   Common, field or English elm (*Ulmus procera*) has formed dense thickets of suckers in part of the dunes at Holkham, Norfolk, where it is very effective in blocking access and stabilising sand through its mat of surface roots. It is, however, very subject to rabbit attack when young. It may be propagated by transplanting suckers.

e   Privet (*Ligustrum vulgare*), a plant which is widespread but most common in the South, is a useful sand stabiliser on calcareous dunes where its thickets form an effective barrier and its dense, fibrous root system holds the sand. It can be propagated from seeds, cuttings or suckers.

f   Shrubby seablite (*Suaeda fruticosa*) has been used in attempts to stabilise mobile shingle (not sand) at Blakeney, Norfolk, around 1953 (Jane and White, 1971, p29).

According to Frank Metson, who has had many years of experience with the Anglian Water Authority, the plants were only able to survive in sheltered places. He concludes that similar plantings along stone revetments in Essex have been worse than useless from a stabilisation viewpoint, since storm waves have tended to pull loose any plants which have rooted, along with a large amount of shingle or stonework.

On more stable shingle this plant can be valuable as a shelter for wildlife and for scenic amenity. It can be transplanted by uprooting existing plants and laying them in at a 45° angle, with the roots well buried.

Sowing

GENERAL CONSIDERATIONS

a   Sowing can be used to establish a vegetative cover in areas where transplanting is impractical, eg where there is very little blown sand, where there is insufficient transplant material or where a large area must be treated quickly.

b   Dunes are poor in several important nutrients, so fertiliser applications are usually required at the time of sowing and often afterwards also. Mulching, thatching or binding also aids seedling establishment.

Nature reserves and other sites of scientific interest should be sown with native dune species only and fertilisation should be kept to the minimum.

c   Do not sow exposed windward faces of foredunes unless these can be stabilised with binders or by other methods. Seeds of dune-building grasses take at least six months to germinate and are easily blown away by high winds during this period. Other seeds germinate more quickly but seedlings are unlikely to survive in unstable soils. Sowing is also likely to fail where there is significant sand drift or flooding with salt water.

DUNE GRASSES

Native dune-building grasses have a poor rate of seedling regeneration in the wild. Marram, for instance, has a maximum germination capacity of only about 15% (Pizzey, 1975, p287). Attempts to sow them have met with only limited success, although further experimentation may improve techniques.

Adriani and Terwindt (1974) give further information on harvesting, processing and pre-treating seeds to improve germination and facilitate mechanical sowing. These are suitable, on the whole, only for very large planting schemes or they do not produce significantly better results than simple hand sowing. In the present 'state of the art', it seems best only to sow dune grasses to supplement transplanting and to use simple hand methods to harvest and broadcast seeds even though coverage may be uneven and results sporadic.

Commercial supplies of marram grass are limited, but according to availability, may be obtainable from W W Johnson and Sons Ltd, London Road, Boston, Lincolnshire, or British Seed Houses Ltd, Bewsey Industrial Estate, Pitt Street, Warrington WA5 5LE. Any supplies will be listed in their seed catalogues, available annually. In 1986, W W Johnson were able to supply marram seed at £6 per 100g. There should be about 300 seeds per gram, to be sown at the rate of 100 seeds per square metre. All marram seed is from native stock.

Harvesting and storing seeds

a   Harvest seeds of sand couchgrass, sea lyme grass and marram between mid July and mid August. Test that the seed is mature by picking a handful of flower spikes and beating them across the hand. Sand couchgrass seeds cling to the spikes but the spikes become brittle when ripe and should break into pieces. With the other two grasses, some seeds should fall out of the beaten flower spikes. Don't wait too long after the seeds ripen to harvest them or they will be dispersed by the wind or eaten by mice and voles.

b   Cut off flower spikes with a knife and collect them in baskets or sacks. Allow them to dry in a well ventilated room. Crumble or chop the spikes fairly finely, since if you sow large pieces they may be blown away by the wind (but see point c under 'Sowing', below).

c   Sea lyme grass seeds can be stored air dry at room temperature (68°F, 20°C) for a year and probably longer without losing viability. Marram seeds actually improve in viability with a year's storage. Seaton (1968) reports good germination of sand couchgrass after one year, so it is likely that this species also benefits from storage.

Sowing

a   Sowing may be done in autumn or spring, but in either case, you should sow as early in the season as possible to allow seedlings to become established before winter frosts or summer drought. Ideally, sowing rates should be based on germination tests. In the absence of these, assume 10% fertility or less and sow to get 100 fertile seeds per square metre. If you sow too densely, many seedlings will die from overcrowding.

b   If the ground is hard, hoe or rake it before sowing. Where possible, roll it to compact it (eg by Land Rover) and then rake it, seed it and roll it again. Obviously this cannot be done on soft slopes, in which case a binder is especially useful. On bare sand, the use of a mulch, with or without binder, is essential to keep the seeds from drying out and to promote adequate germination.

Two suitable mulches are seaweed, and where locally available, bog peat. The peat should be spread in a layer of about 20mm ($\frac{3}{4}$"), and then the seed sown and raked into the sand/peat surface. If using seaweed, first rake the seed into the sand, to avoid direct contact with the seaweed. Then spread a 50mm (2") layer of wet, 'fresh' seaweed, which will dry out to a layer about 10mm ($\frac{1}{2}$") thick.

For large-scale programmes you can combine mulch, seeds and binder and spray the mixture over the surface using a mechanical crop sprayer (Countryside Commission for Scotland, 1977, 1978). If a mulch is not used, apply a fertiliser (p79) either as a base dressing (raked into the topsoil before seeding) or as a top dressing after the grass has become established.

c   Another method, which has worked well with marram at Scolt Head Island, Norfolk, is to 'plant' whole flower spikes in late summer and autumn. Cut spikes off the seeding marram in an area of vigorous growth and put them into sacks for transport. Stick the seed heads into the sand at about 3m (10') intervals or, if the seed is easily shed, broadcast it directly.

OTHER GRASSES AND HERBACEOUS PLANTS

Mixtures of meadow and other grasses and herbaceous species have been used with success to seed bare backdune areas which are not normally prone to wind erosion. They have also been used to stabilise eroded machair surfaces and, at Camber, East Sussex, to treat accreting dunes – sites where agricultural and amenity factors justify the widespread use of mixed non-dune species.

Seed mixes may be 'off-the-shelf' sports turf mixes or they may be specially formulated for dune use, with drought- and winter-resistant cultivars. Each site differs, so it is best to seed experimental trial plots first before going ahead with a large-scale programme.

The Countryside Commission for Scotland (CCS, 1980) recommend a basic seed mix of 60% slender creeping red fescue, 30% perennial ryegrass, 5% smooth-stalked meadow grass, and 5% white clover. The slender creeping red fescue group of cultivars are salt tolerant, spread by running roots, and can be heavily grazed or trampled. Two especially salt-resistant cultivars are 'Dawson' and 'Oasis'. The ryegrass gives a rapid initial cover, dying out as the drought resistant and slower-growing fescue takes over. The white clover is important as it fixes nitrogen from the air, so increasing the soil fertility. For further details, see the Countryside Commission for Scotland leaflet 'Reseeding of dune grass pastures'.

Commercial mixes may include small proportions of common bent (*Agrostis tenuis*), smooth-stalked meadowgrass (*Poa pratensis*), broom (*Sarothamnus scoparius*) and white clover (*Trifolium repens*), but in general the simplest mix is best so long as it provides surface stabilisation. This allows other dune species to invade and diversify the sown area more quickly. On nature reserves it may be important to use only species native to the site. Where you are sowing the seaward side of dunes, it may be worth adding marram seed to the mix at the rate of about 25% marram to 75% mix.

For simple seeding direct onto sand, the Countryside Commission for Scotland recommend raking the seed of grass species about 35mm ($1\frac{1}{2}$") deep, to avoid desiccation. Small seeds such as clover should not be sown deeper than 10mm ($\frac{1}{2}$"). In practice it is impossible to be this accurate, and it is best to use a higher than normal seeding rate, and accept some losses. Sow at 30g/m², and apply a binder (see p84) to the surface to stop wind blow. With a mulch of peat or seaweed, used as described above, the rate can be lowered to 25g/m².

Otherwise, sow at the rate recommended by the manufacturer or, if using your own mix, establish the optimum sowing rate experimentally on trial plots. Fertilising should be delayed until after germination, as fertiliser salts can inhibit germination and young growth.

Ritchie (1975, p2576) reports that mixed grasses may be mown about a year after seeding so that they tiller and produce a denser cover. Other aftercare may include periodic fertilising, but this must be decided on a site-to-site basis and should normally be avoided where you want the turf to develop along relatively natural lines. At machair edge restoration sites, it is important to turf (p76) as well as seed, since seeded areas tend to remain sparse until colonised by plants which spread from the turfs (Countryside Commission for Scotland, 1978, p11).

Fertilising

GENERAL CONSIDERATIONS

a   Dune-building grasses are adapted to growing in nutrient-poor soils, so transplanted offsets usually survive quite well without the benefit of extra nutrients. But where a quick 'take' is essential, it may be worth fertilising transplanted grasses to increase their vigour and rate of tillering. Fertilising is much more important where an area has been seeded. It can also be useful to promote the growth of established vegetation in partly stabilised areas. On machair sites, fertilising does not always do much good and it may be that plant growth here is limited by a trace element deficiency in addition to, or instead of, a lack of major nutrients (Countryside Commission for Scotland, 1978, p10).

b   Where fertilisers are used on unstable soils, it helps to apply a sand binder or mulch to reduce soil movement and ensure that the fertiliser remains available to the plants. Note that some organic mulches (p82) are rich in nutrients and their use may make other fertilisers unnecessary.

c   Because leaching is rapid through porous soils, most dune fertilisation programmes use a slow-release formulation such as 'Enmag'. However, some researchers have had equally good results from straight agricultural fertilisers (see below), which are cheaper. On dune grasslands or machair surfaces not subject to very rapid leaching, there seems to be little advantage in using slow-release fertilisers.

d   Fertilising dune soils increases the density and luxuriance of grasses at the expense of lower-growing herbs and bryophytes. This may not be desirable on nature reserves. Where possible, restrict fertiliser applications to the minimum necessary to maintain the typical flora for the site. For example, less fertiliser is needed to maintain an open marram-dominated community on mobile dunes than a mowable sward on backdune pastures (see the suggested rates below).

'ENMAG'

'Enmag' slow-release fertiliser, produced by Scottish Agricultural Industries PLC, Firth Road, Houstovn Industrial Estate, Livingston, West Lothian (tel: 0506 39281) has seen widespread use on open marram dunes. It contains 5% nitrogen, 24% phosphate, 10% potash and 10% magnesium in an inorganic, granular formulation which is slowly soluble but has variable particle sizes to give a prolonged, steady release. 'Enmag' costs £17.27 plus VAT per 25kg sack (1986 price), and is available from the above address and from distributors nationwide. Charlton (1970, p43) reports good results on marram grass, compared to unfertilised controls and straight agricultural fertilisers, but a slow effect on sea lyme grass. The manufacturers recommend a rate of 10–15g per plant applied around the base, or spread at 70g per square metre, which is 700kg per hectare. For newly planted or seeded areas, repeat this treatment three times in the first year (eg at the time of autumn sowing, in spring and in mid-summer).

OTHER FERTILISERS

Research by Paul Johnson and Professor A D Bradshaw of the University of Liverpool suggests that nitrogen is the crucial nutrient in short supply in marram dunes, and that application of a straight nitrogen fertiliser such as ammonium nitrate is sufficient to promote plant vigour and increase the rate of tillering by up to four times over unfertilised controls. Ammonium nitrate is relatively cheap (prices vary greatly depending on the amount purchased and the supplier, so shop around) and concentrated, and for most volunteer-type projects it can be carried in buckets and hand broadcast at the rate of 50kg per hectare (44lb per acre) per treatment with two treatments per year for the best results. This can be reduced to 25kg per hectare (22lb per acre) each time for economy but in either case the first application should be a week or two after planting to give the plants time to root.

For fertilising transplanted marram grass, the Countryside Commission for Scotland (CCS, 1985) recommend a top dressing in April, June and August of the first year, and again in April of the second year. Apply 30g per square metre of 'Nitram', 'Nitrashell' or 'Nitro-top' agricultural fertilisers. Alternatively, all-nitrogen fertilisers can be used at a rate of 10g per square metre.

Leave newly-seeded areas until about a month after sowing, and then apply fertiliser in about mid-April, mid-June and mid-August. Supplement the first application with superphosphate. Expressed at g/m^2 of N:P:K:, the initial dressing should be 4:10:10 and subsequent dressings 4:2:2. For further details see 'Reseeding of Dune Pastures' (CCS, 1980).

On machairs straight agricultural fertilisers are likely to be as effective as slow-release formulations (Countryside Commission for Scotland, 1977). Formulations used in various trials have differed so that it is not possible to give a standard rate or frequency of application (for details, see Adriani and Terwindt, 1974, pp34–44, Seaton, 1962 and Nash, 1962). Prices also vary according to formulation and amount purchased. The usual first-dose fertiliser is granulated superphosphate (NPK), applied at a rate of between 300kg per hectare (265lb per acre) and 450kg per hectare (400lb per acre) either all at once at the time of sowing or divided into two equal applications in spring and early summer. Spring-sown areas usually need a further application of nitrogen at 112–200kg per hectare (100–170lb per acre) in August or September.

Thatching, Mulching and Binding

GENERAL POINTS

Uses

Thatching, mulching and binding can be used separately or in combination to:

a   Protect exposed or steep dune slopes from wind erosion. Mulches can also be applied to help stabilise path surfaces (p56). Straw bales, which break down to form a mulch, can be used to aid marram planting on steep slopes (p75).

b   Encourage better growth of newly planted or seeded vegetation by providing organic matter and improving the heat- and moisture-retaining capacity of the soil.

Other considerations

a   Thatching, mulching and binding are seldom worth doing except in conjunction with planting or sowing, although thatching can be used alone or with fences to fill in small blowouts and to protect dune cliffs from tidal erosion.

b   Wherever suitable material is available, thatching, mulching and binding are worth including in a planting programme even where the plants may survive without them, because they markedly improve growing conditions. However, thatching does modify the typical marram-dominated open dune habitat by providing suitable conditions for fixed dune species to invade, especially away from the foredune ridge.

THATCHING

Thatching is the covering of exposed sand faces with cuttings (brashings, trimmings, lop and top, broust) from scrub thickets or forestry plantations. It is a traditional method of stabilising sand, and was used for example at the end of the 19th century to stabilise large areas of sand blow at Culbin in Moray (CCS, 1981). Thatching should prevent further erosion by the wind, act as a sand trap and discourage people from trampling.

Thatching can be used in combination with planting on difficult sites, to increase the chance of transplant success. Such sites include dune crests, irregular slopes where turbulence is caused, gullies which funnel the wind, and areas likely to be trampled by people or stock. Do not thatch areas of rapid sand build-up, as it may be buried before grasses are established. Where brushwood is in good supply, thatching is quicker than mulching or binding. It is however slower and more expensive if the brushwood has to be gathered and transported some distance. Leafy material can be used on backshore sites, followed by seeding once the thatching is buried. The decaying material improves seeding success.

If you have a choice, use the species recommended on page 45 for brushwood fencing. Conifer brashings, which are the lower branches trimmed off commercial trees, are better than conifer tops. This is because they are fan shaped, and thus easier to transport and lie flat on the sand, giving good coverage. It is estimated that a 10 tonne open lorry should be able to carry sufficient brushwood to cover 100–150m^2 (CCS, 1981). Note that conifer brashings are more combustible than deciduous material, and more likely to be set alight by vandals.

Thatching cannot in itself anchor over-steepened sand slopes, although it helps provide a mat for workers to stand on when planting. Normally it is best to lay thatching before or at the same time as planting a steep face or blowout, unless a thorny species is used when obviously planting should be done first. One problem with thatching after planting is that it tends to damage the newly planted grass.

Procedure

a   Lay the brashings at a density such that about 20–30% of the sand surface is covered

(excluding any needles or leaves that will drop off). If the brashings are fan shaped, lay the concave side downwards.

b   Where public pressure is low, you can protect the thatched areas by pushing in brash at a 45° angle around the boundaries. Elsewhere, it is usually necessary to fence the path edges to keep people off the thatch unless you have used a thorny species. Where public pressure is intense, it is worth tying the thatch down with old fencing or baling wire (2mm diameter) to keep people from using it for firewood. Run the wire out in parallel lines, about 2m apart, and staple or tie at 3m intervals to short stakes, driven down into the sand to secure. Baler twine can also be used which although not as strong, is less of a hazard when partly buried. This technique is also worth using for sites very exposed to the wind, to stop the brashings being blown about.

c   When thatching a slope, work from the top down. Place the first (topmost) row of branches with their upper twigs just level with or below the top of the dune ridge. If they project higher, wind damage will occur. Turn the branches so that they curve into the slope as shown below.

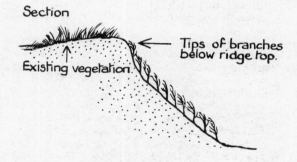

If turned outwards, the wind is liable to twist them loose. Follow the contours closely.

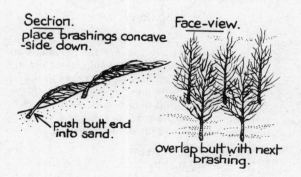

On very shallow slopes, angle the branches at about 45° to discourage people from walking on top of or between them.

d   Where both sides of a ridge require treatment, thatch the lee face first and then the windward face, which should overtop the lee thatching to protect it from the wind. When thatching the top of a rounded dune, angle the branches nearly horizontally, with their tips at an even height and intertwined to protect against variable winds. On sharply peaked dunes, you may have to start thatching a few feet below the summit and allow the top to be eroded to the level of the thatching.

e   Place small branches with their butt ends 225–375mm (9–15″) apart and larger brash 375–760mm (15–30″) apart. Mix any branches over 1.2m (4′) in with smaller branches or save them for use on flat expanses.

Push all branches well into the sand: at least 75mm (3″) for 600mm (2′) long branches, 150–225mm (6–9″) for 1.2m (4′) long branches and 300mm (1′) or more for longer branches.

f   On gentle slopes not exposed to strong winds, you can limit thatching to a border around the edge of the area, with strips of brushwood placed across the enclosure at right angles to the prevailing winds. Make the border at least one yard wide. If necessary, you can extend the inner strips to form a complete 'maze'. Mulch open areas between brashings to give some protection against wind while grass becomes established.

g   When thatching a large conical blowout, place cuttings around the periphery and work down in concentric rings, with the brushy ends of the branches sticking outward to discourage people from walking over them. Leave an exit at the front of the blowout while you work. Then block this off with a line of brushwood pointing outward.

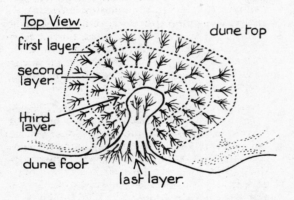

It is usually necessary to fence the perimeter of thatched blowouts where the area is subject to access pressure. You may have to extend the fence along the dune crest or around the entire ridge if you find that people concentrate their trampling just to the sides of the fenced blowout and start to create new gulleys.

h   When thatching extensive areas, it may be wise to leave occasional paths through the thatched area, so that people are less tempted to disturb the thatch. Be sure to align and surface the paths as necessary to prevent them eroding (see next chapter).

Work rate

Bacon (1975) suggests that thatching at the density suggested above (his 'open work' method), plus planting, takes from 139 to 232 man-hours per acre (348–579 hours per hectare). This includes 59 to 112 hours per acre (148–279 hours per hectare) bundling and transporting the cuttings and gathering the grass offsets, and 80 to 120 hours per acre (200–300 hours

per hectare) planting the grass and placing the thatching.

Rooting thatching

Some thatching material, such as poplar, may resprout if set in the sand over the winter. This can be an advantage in badly eroded areas around car parks, for example, as it stabilises the surface, gets something growing, and keeps people off. Use only species which are native to the area, and do not try this technique on areas where spread of scrub would be undesirable.

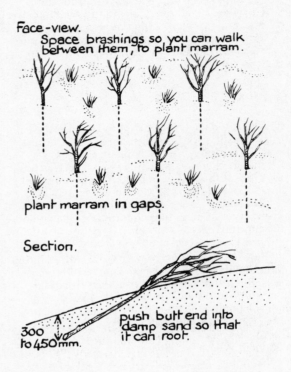

MULCHING

Mulching can be used to reduce erosion, keep the ground surface moist and gradually fertilise the soil as the mulch breaks down.

Mulching may be done by hand or machine. The latter is most efficient where a large area is to be covered. Access for machinery is often difficult in soft sand but mulches can be pumped in the form of slurry up to 180m (200 yds) (Kirk, 1970, p43). If this is to be done, seeds can be added to the mulch to combine sowing and seeding in one operation. Where a binder is used, this can be added to the mix if necessary, although it may be more effective to spray on the binder afterwards (p84).

Note that on nature reserves it may not be desirable to use mulches such as straw, topsoil or manure since these contain seeds of plants which may be alien to the reserve.

Mulches which can be used for dune stabilisation work include:

a   Chopped straw, forked into the sand prior to planting or seeding or spread on afterwards. This provides a very small amount of surface roughness and is useful where it is important to reduce sand blow from the treated surface (as at

Camber, East Sussex). Adriani and Terwindt (1974, pp45–55) suggest mulching with straw at a rate of 5–6 tonnes per hectare (2–2.5 tons per acre). Bacon (1975, p6) recommends wheat or oat straw in preference to barley, which decays more quickly. Wheat and oat straw remain effective for two or three months before rotting, when spread at a density of one bale per 33–50 sq m (40– 60 sq yds). You may be able to get old straw bales free from farmers in March and April.

b   Peat. This is particularly useful for machair restoration work, when peat may be dug from inland bogs, broken up on site and spread by hand to an average thickness of about 10mm ($\frac{1}{2}$″) before raking in grass seed. Despite the tendency of the wet, cohesive peat to dry into uneven, patchy lumps, germination is faster and more consistent than in the alternative method of hydraumatic seeding. In the hydraumatic method, granulated peat is mixed with seed and binder and sprayed over the surface to an overall thickness of about 1–2mm ($\frac{1}{16}$″). Both methods achieve a much higher germination rate than if the seeds are raked into pure sand (Countryside Commission for Scotland, 1978, p10).

c   'Horizons' of topsoil or leaf litter, dumped and spread on dune faces to provide a stable sill 50–100 mm (2–4″) thick. In pipeline restoration work in Aberdeenshire, overburden from a nearly access road was used for this purpose (Ritchie, 1975). At Calgary Bay on the Island of Mull, volunteers have used leaf litter and humus from nearby woodlands to help fill machair-edge erosion.

d   Reed, cut grass or other coarse herbaceous vegetation, which combines the features of thatching and mulching. If possible, harvest the material when seeds are nearly ripe and take it to the restoration site as soon as possible to avoid loss of seed. Germinating plants help bind the sand and form a turf under the planted dune-building grasses.

e   Seaweed and other storm litter. This can be used to repair minor dune damage and to promote the growth of embryo dunes if it is collected and spread above high water mark. It is especially useful for treating heavily trampled beaches and foredunes.

On parts of the Sefton coast, the local council clear the beach each winter of rubbish and rotting seaweed. To encourage foredune formation, the Sefton Coast Management Scheme asked them to dump the material at the back of the beach, where it was then graded with a bulldozer. By early April a mass of seedling plants had emerged from the seed contained within the debris. The dilemma is that councils are expected to keep recreational beaches tidy and odour-free, but the rubbish in fact helps prevent sand blow. The most visually unattractive beaches are often the most ecologically sound. In the Outer Hebrides, seaweed is collected on a large scale in the winter to spread on machair blowouts and to top-dress farmland. It is applied at a rate of 6 tonnes per hectare (15 tons per acre) (Seaton, 1968).

At Ynyslas National Nature Reserve, Dyfed, volunteers have collected dead *Spartina* from the strandline and used it to form a layer about 150mm (6″) deep between concrete blocks placed as foundations for new dunes (the concrete is from old road and military works on site). The *Spartina* is gathered with garden forks and loaded into a trailer for transport. Pebbles, collected from below high water mark, are then scattered on the mulch to hold it down.

f   Wood pulp. At Northam Burrows, Devon, wood pulp has been applied to about 4 hectares (10 acres). It successfully promotes vegetation and lasts about as long as straw mulch, but less long than bitumen binders in extreme maritime conditions (Hewett and Lamerton, 1970, p29). Pulp, chipped bark or peelings from fence posts may be cheaply available from sawmills. Peelings are unpleasant to walk on, which can be advantageous, and free of weed seeds.

Sawdust is not recommended, because it is unpleasant to handle, tends to blow away and may actually reduce soil nutrient levels as it rots.

g   Farmyard manure. This has been used, at 6 tonnes per hectare (15 tons per acre), to maintain machair surfaces. It can also be spread on dune faces. Unless well rotted, it supplies weed seeds to help colonise the dune.

h   Sewage sludge. This is recommended for use on dunes by Paul Johnson and Professor A D Bradshaw of the University of Liverpool, who have conducted trials including a major erosion control programme near Prestatyn, Clwyd. Merseyside County Council have used sewage sludge on a large dune protection scheme at Formby.

Sludge can be obtained very cheaply, often for nothing, from local sewage works – but avoid works which receive industrial effluent because sludge from these sources may contain heavy metals and other toxic substances. The sludge can be poured over the sand to coat eroding hollows or spread in two or three thin coats to adhere to gentle slopes. The total thickness should be about 25mm (1″). It dries to a stiff crust which stabilises the surface, acts as a slow-release fertiliser of comparable value to artificial fertilisers and catches blown plant seeds so that the surface is quickly colonised by native plants. Sewage sludge also has self-fencing qualities: most people avoid walking on it!

MATTING

A new matting material has been used experimentally at Ainsdale NNR, Merseyside, to stabilise an eroding foredune on its windward face. The material is made of a straw filling sandwiched between two layers of netting. It is laid direct onto the sand surface and pegged down with metal pegs. Holes are then made in it, using a crowbar, and marram transplants set in. It is important that corners are well anchored, so that the wind cannot lift it. The surface can be disguised with sand to discourage pyromaniacs. Trials so far have been promising. A similar material called Geojute 500 is now being marketed by Ardon International Ltd, PO Box 111, Tunbridge Wells, Kent TN4 9NW.

BINDERS

The following information is based on the laboratory and field tests carried out by the Countryside Commission for Scotland, the results of which are detailed in the leaflet 'Sand Stabilisation by Spraying' (CCS, 1982).

Binders are chemical glues which are used to prevent wind erosion of areas which have been planted or seeded. They create a 'skin', which helps to hold the sand surface together, particularly on slopes, and reduces surface drying. The improved vegetation growth which it provides more than makes up for the loss of sand-trapping capacity of the dune itself, which is made rather smoother by the use of the binder. Where the sand slips, it moves under the skin which should remain intact.

Binders can be used in the following situations:

a   in combination with marram planting on active dunes. Normally the foliage of the transplants is sufficient to reduce wind erosion during the establishment phase but on exposed locations, such as dune crests and gullies, a binder will help stabilise the surface. A binder with a life of one to three years should be used.

b   for reseeding of dune pastures or machair, where the site is exposed and organic matter is absent from the surface. The binder should be needed for only six to eight weeks, while the seedlings establish.

The binders described below were developed for use in hydraulic seeding, in which seed, fertiliser and binder are applied in one operation. This method is not satisfactory on sand, as the seed is only sown in the surface layer and does not then root deeply enough to withstand surface drought. The binder should therefore be used after the seed has been raked or harrowed into the sand.

Binders form a layer only a few millimetres thick, which can be damaged by trampling. Sprayed areas must therefore be fenced. It is important that the type of binder used forms a flexible layer, so that changes in level as sand settles can be accommodated, without the layer fracturing. Binders can be used in combination with some of the mulches described on page 00, but in most cases are more effective on their own. The Countryside Commission for Scotland have found the following products to be satisfactory.

The first two are recommended for use on dunes after planting with grasses. Both should last one to three years.

'Dunebond'

Supplier:
Dunlop Irrigation Services Ltd, Box 1, Thame Park Road, Thame, Oxon OX9 3RQ Tel: (084421) 5411
This has good flexibility with reasonable strength. The cost per square metre for materials and labour is about 17p (1982 price), making it the most expensive of the products listed.

'Bitumuls Stable'

Supplier:
Colas (Scotland) Ltd, Imperial Works, Douglas Park Road, Hamilton ML3 ODF Tel: (0698) 282522
This has good strength and flexibility, but is less permeable to water than 'Dunebond'. This may cause run-off and gullying at the base of slopes where it is applied. The cost per square metre of materials and labour is about 15p (1982 price).

The following three products are recommended for use on dune pastures after seeding. All have a life of three to twelve months.

'Huls 801'

Supplier:
Huls UK Ltd, Byrom House, Quay Street, Manchester M3 3HQ Tel: (061) 832 7715
This is strong and permeable, but is rather brittle and should not be used on areas which are liable to settle. The cost per square metre of materials and labour is about 10p (1982 price).

'Curasol AE'

Supplier:
Hoechst UK Ltd, Salisbury Road, Hounslow, Middlesex TW6 3JM Tel: (01) 570 7712
This has good flexibility with fair strength and water permeability. It can adversely affect seed germination if the seed comes into contact with it. The cost per square metre of materials and labour is about 6p (1982 price).

'Vinamul 3277'

Supplier:
Vinyl Products, Mill Lane, Carshalton, Surrey SM5 2JU Tel: (01) 669 4422
This has good strength and permeability with fair flexibility. At about 5p per square metre (1982 price), it is the cheapest of the products listed.

Procedural points

a   Depending on the area to be treated, you can spray diluted binders using a watering can, knapsack sprayer or – most practical for many stabilisation programmes, although beyond the scope of most volunteer projects – a small motorised crop sprayer equipped with a hand lance and having a high volume output. For more on knapsack sprayers, see page 45.

If you use a motorised sprayer, wear a protective face mask to prevent irritation from fine droplets of oil and resins. Whatever the method used, stand upwind of the area which you are treating when possible. When treating small areas with a watering can, you may have to enlarge the holes of a metal rose to reduce clogging. Plastic roses are less likely to clog.

b   Apply the binder immediately after sowing, fertilising and covering with sand.

c   Binders come in drums which are too big to pour out of easily. It is worth buying and fitting a reusable tap (cheap plastic taps are readily available). Follow manufacturers' mixing instructions. When mixing directly in the sprayer reservoir, it is important to put in the water first and the chemical second to get a good mix and avoid clogging.

d   Spray the sand in parallel strips, 600mm–1.2m (2–4') wide depending on the spray apparatus. Start at the top of a slope and move down. The spray should sink into the top layer of sand. If it remains on the surface you may be spraying too heavily or using too concentrated a mix. But if the spray fails to bind with the surface sand, the mix may be too dilute. Experiment on trial plots first before mixing a large quantity of spray solution.

Use marker poles or some other means of identifying areas sprayed with light-coloured binders such as latex, otherwise you may have trouble telling sprayed from unsprayed sand until the binder hardens and darkens.

e   Refill sprayers before they are completely empty, and clean them out immediately if you are finished for the day. If you let them sit around they get gummed up.

f   Avoid working in strong winds, which will make even application difficult.

8 Vegetation Management

Factors to Consider

a   The management of vegetation in natural and semi-natural habitats is always problematical, and in the naturally unstable and changing communities of sand dune systems, it is even more difficult. Decisions about the need to intervene require careful study and analysis of the existing vegetation, as well as knowledge of historical changes, both natural and man-made.

b   The general aim is usually to maintain the greatest diversity of plant communities naturally found within the dunes. However, problems can arise when man-made communities such as conifer plantations support their own community of interesting plant and animal species.

c   The types of intervention most commonly made on duneland areas are management of existing woodland, clearance of scrub, and maintenance of grassland areas by mowing, grazing or burning. These are discussed further below. The transplanting of marram and other erosion-control measures, described in detail in chapter 7, are normally urgent tasks for which the need is clear-cut.

Woodland Management

Many dune systems, including Holkham NNR, Newborough Warren, and Ainsdale NNR have substantial areas of conifer plantation. These were planted originally to stabilise the dunes, but are now mainly also managed for timber production. Not only do these plantations represent a loss in terms of area of duneland, but mature trees can cause problems by seeding into adjacent areas of open duneland and slack. Corsican Pine, for example, does not usually produce a heavy cone crop until it is 25–30 years old, but once this stage is reached, prolific regeneration can occur.

At Ainsdale, woods of Austrian pine (*Pinus nigra*), maritime pine (*Pinus pinaster*), Scots pine (*Pinus sylvestris*) and beach pine (*Pinus contorta*) surround many of the interesting slacks. These shelter the slacks, and provide a seed source, which together cause rapid invasion of the slacks. An approach to the problem suggested by Rothwell (in Doody, 1985) includes:

a   removal of main seeding trees surrounding the slack

b   removal of seedlings and saplings from the slacks by either spraying, cutting or pulling, or by scraping the vegetation off using a low ground-pressure bulldozer.

Although removal of seed trees will reduce the spread, continual management is likely to be needed to keep areas clear. In some cases, removal of seed source may be impossible, so removal of seedling invaders is the only solution.

Total clearance of forest is a major operation, as all stumps have to be removed before they rot and increase the nutrient status of the soil. The accumulated leaf litter will have caused the top layer of soil to become acidified, thus removal of this layer may also be necessary.

When planning felling operations, keep the following points in mind:

a   The amount of felling and thinning which a given site can tolerate must be found by experimentation. When in doubt, it is best to underthin. Overthinning opens up the area to wind erosion and leaves the remaining trees subject to wind-throw.

b   At all stages, the seaward edge of the plantation must present an oblique face to the wind. If it runs at right angles to storm winds, the front rows of trees are very liable to undermining and wind-throw. You should also thin so that the seaward face is not uniformly dense, otherwise you will create a too-solid barrier against which the wind can push.

c   When thinning and felling, avoid creating paths aligned with dominant winds. Even in the centre of an afforested area these are subject to wind-throw. The same applies to regularly mown firebreaks within the plantation.

d   Build as few fires as possible to dispose of trimmings.

e   'Landscaping' may also be needed, to recreate dunes and slacks within the cleared areas, with the aim of 'remobilising' the dunes.

Besides the slacks within the forest, other areas which may develop their own ecological value are the rides and firebreaks. For example, in the forest at Newborough, the firebreaks support an interesting plant community including unusual winter-flowering annuals. Rotovation should therefore be done before the main period of autumn germination.

The need for any removal of woodland should be publicised locally, especially where public access is allowed, as any removal of trees is likely to cause adverse public reaction.

Instead of clear-felling, another approach is to slowly diversify conifer woods by planting species such as oak, birch, willow, alder and holly. This maintains the shelter and landscape feature of the woodland, while making it ecologically more interesting.

Scrub Control

One of the most troublesome species on sand dunes is sea buckthorn (*Hippophae rhamnoides*), especially where it is introduced into west coast dune systems. Sea buckthorn is considered separately below. Other introduced species which may spread include turkey oak and rhododendron, with native birch, privet, sallow, gorse and creeping willow also becoming a nuisance in some areas.

Scrub has benefits to offer, and the need to control has to be assessed by careful study of each site. Such advantages include:

a   Stabilisation of the dunes. This can be useful in areas of public pressure and erosion damage.

b   Control of access by keeping people to paths and excluding them from certain areas.

c   Shelter and nesting sites for birds, shelter for invertebrates and mammals.

Young seedlings of many species can be pulled by hand, but older plants will need cutting, and any regrowth spraying. The herbicide currently favoured for use on woody growth is Garlon 2, described on page 92. To aid thorough treatment, a red dye can be mixed with the herbicide to colour areas which have been sprayed. The dye is supplied in powder form, and is simply sprinkled in to give the required colour. It is available from Hortichem, 14 Edison Road, Churchfields Industrial Estate, Salisbury, Wiltshire SP2 7NU.

At Braunton Burrows, clearance is carried out of areas of sallow carr, hawthorn and privet. The method used is to first fell trees and larger shrubs using a chain saw, followed by a clearing saw to take the tops off the remaining growth. Volunteers then come in to clear and burn the debris. This procedure avoids volunteers having to work with the noise and danger of machinery. All clearance is done in December and January to minimise the disturbance to birds. A tractor can be used to grub up hawthorn growing in the drier part of the reserve, but sallow indicates wetter areas where a tractor is liable to get stuck. Any regrowth is sprayed with glyphosate in late May, with a re-spray in July if necessary. The aim is to spray when regrowth is about 500mm high, as any higher than this requires excessive expense on herbicide. After-treatment can be a problem, as the rotting stumps add nutrient to the soil, and it is reckoned to take at least 10 years for nutrients to leach out. The stumps also make it difficult to bring in machines to mow the resulting vegetation. On this site, wartime rubbish, ant-hills and other hazards make machinery use awkward.

Where gorse occurs on dune heathland, some clearance may be needed to reduce fire risk. At Studland NNR, firebreaks have been cut through large stands of gorse. Once cut to ground level, rabbits nibble the soft young growth, so further cutting is not needed, provided rabbits are present in sufficient numbers.

Creeping willow supports a large number of invertebrates but, due to myxomatosis reducing rabbit grazing, has become invasive of some wet areas. Experimental cutting with an Allenscythe seems to give promising results, provided the clippings are removed to prevent them resprouting. Grazing by cattle over a period of 10 years or more has also been successful in maintaining an excellent species mix in an area which would otherwise be entirely comprised of creeping willow.

In general, grazing is not effective as a method of reducing scrub growth, as animals merely move away from those areas to more palatable vegetation. Grazing is better used as a method of management following mechanical clearance. This is clearly shown by photos of Braunton Burrows in 'Sand Dunes and their

Management' (Hope-Simpson, J, in Doody, 1985). These show how the rabbit-free years from 1954 to the early 70s allowed shrubs to invade. When rabbit population picked up again in the 70s, these individual plants were above rabbit-damage height, and have since increased greatly in area. However, no new individual plants have appeared, due to the rabbits destroying the seedlings.

According to Oosterveld (in Doody, 1985), increased stocking rates in autumn can retard shrub development, when other fodder is becoming short in supply. Browsing and bark damage by sheep can destroy young trees. At Newborough Warren, hawthorn and birch up to 2m high were killed by sheep damaging the bark, but blackthorn were only browsed, and were thus not destroyed. Creeping willow was also only browsed, which encouraged shooting from ground level, so overall cover was not reduced (Hewett, 1985). Blackthorn can be as invasive as sea buckthorn, spreading in similar fashion from underground shoots, and similar control measures may be necessary.

Dune Grasslands

The general picture is of a loss of these species-rich grasslands, due to the invasion of scrub from lack of rabbit and stock grazing, the spread of introduced scrub species, and the loss of vegetation cover from trampling, erosion and over-grazing. Much area has also been permanently lost to urban development, agricultural improvement and military and recreational use (see chapter 2).

Where intervention is decided to be appropriate, it may take one of the following forms:

a   Except in areas of mobile dune, follow-up management of the vegetation resulting from scrub clearance will be needed. As well as spraying or cutting of regrowth, as described above, grazing or mowing will be needed to encourage the return of short-sward species.

b   At the stage before dune grassland succeeds to scrub, grazing, mowing or burning can be used to reduce the amount of coarse grasses and prevent scrub encroachment.

c   Restoration may be needed where over-grazing, trampling or erosion has caused loss of turf. The first stage is to tackle the problem at source, by reducing grazing levels or fencing to keep stock and rabbits out, and by taking measures to control access. Measures to hasten recovery of vegetation cover, by seeding, fertilising and mulching are described in chapter 7.

Restoration after clearance

Few records have been made of the recolonisation of dune vegetation following scrub removal; a gap now being tackled by analysis of the recovery of dune vegetation at Murlough NNR, following sea buckthorn clearance (Ellis, edit. 1983).

Any after-treatment is made very much easier if stumps are removed, both so nutrient enrichment does not occur, and so that mowing or cutting machines have easy access.

Burning does not necessarily enrich the soil. Allen (1964) showed loss of nitrogen up to 45kg/ha, and losses of other nutrients which form volatile compounds when heather is burnt. However, input from rainfall can more than make up for the losses. At bonfire sites on sandy soils the nutrients remaining in the ash are likely to be quickly leached, therefore removal of ash is not necessary. At Whitford Burrows, bonfire sites do not show enrichment, but are recolonised first by mosses. Burning of vegetation is an important way of reducing fertility on a site.

Grazing is likely to be needed at quite high levels initially, to knock back the flush of growth after clearance. Cattle or horses are more useful than sheep in grazing rough and lush vegetation.

If cutting or mowing is used, this needs to be done two or three times in the first season, with all cuttings removed to reduce nutrient enrichment, and to prevent the material suppressing the germination and growth of more desirable species. Any management by grazing or mowing must be maintained, or coarser vegetation will rapidly spread back.

Grazing and mowing

Experimental work with mowing and grazing by sheep is being carried out at Newborough Warren NNR, and the results of many years work in the Netherlands are reviewed by Oosterveld (in Doody, 1985).

In general, cutting results in a short vegetation sward, tending towards uniformity. Conversely, grazing introduces diversification, due to uneven trampling, dunging and grazing, with palatable species being selected preferentially.

According to Oosterveld, the most important factor in grazing is that no improvement should be made by way of fertilising, draining or levelling of the land. Slight overgrazing seems to do little harm, so long as it is not to the level that can only be supported by supplementary feeding of hay or silage. Damage of this type has occurred at South Walney, Cumbria, where the Cumbria Trust for Nature Conservation who manage the site have no control over the numbers of cattle being grazed, and in winter silage is fed to support a high stocking level. It is feared that permanent damage will occur, as in places the vegetation is being completely destroyed, with subsequent erosion. Some of the most vulnerable areas, and those used for shade and shelter and thus most heavily trampled, are being protected by fencing.

Oosterveld has demonstrated a non-random use of grazing areas by stock, due to such factors as shade and water. He has shown that cattle and horses prefer to graze facing away from the sun, which in large grazing areas results in a daily clockwise pattern of herd movement. During the middle part of the day, most animals will be in the northern part of the area, moving towards the south eastern part to sleep. Where grazing plots are being established, it can be arranged that the most vulnerable vegetation types are not situated at the border of the area, especially in the northern and south-eastern parts.

Overgrazing of dune-heathland can cause conversion to grassland, which is usually less desirable. Stocking levels will vary greatly with the area, but an example is given below of levels suggested by the NCC for the management of dune-heath at Earlshall Muir SSSI, Fife (Doody, 1985).

The recommendation is that there should be no grazing on the frontal dunes, due to vulnerability to erosion. The main area of dune-heath, which had been lightly grazed in the previous 20 years, should also be mainly not grazed, apart from some winter/spring grazing at the rate of 0.5 ewes per hectare in years when the rabbit population is low. Cattle should not be grazed, because of the damage done by heavy trampling to lichen-rich heath. On the areas which are mainly grassland, grazing should be continued at 0.15 beef cattle per hectare, or sheep equivalent.

Oosterveld, writing about the Netherlands, gives figures of 1 horse or cow per hectare or 3 sheep per hectare for seasonal grazing. For year round grazing without additional winter feed, only very low rates are possible, at 1 horse or cow per 10 hectares or 1 sheep per 5 hectares. Horses are more suitable for year round grazing as they can compensate for low quality fodder by eating greater quantities.

The grazing experiments at Newborough Warren use the equivalent of 1 or 2 sheep per 0.3 hectare, grazed for either one third, two-thirds or the whole year. For management reasons, flocks of 4 and 8 sheep are used. The mean number of plant species recorded as a result of grazing were highest for plots grazed for $\frac{2}{3}$ of the year by 2 sheep. The highest grazing level, of 2 sheep per 0.3 hectare all year was too high for optimum numbers of species (Hewett, 1985).

Experience at Braunton Burrows has indicated that it is not worth burning areas unless follow-up management by grazing can be done. Without it, areas quickly return to their previous condition. Here, as in other areas, the topography and wartime hazards make mowing a difficult job, although small areas have been cut with hand machines, on an experimental basis.

Since the introduction of myxomatosis in the 1950s, and the great reduction in the rabbit population during that and the following decade, numbers have been building back up again in some parts of the country. Fluctuations of population occur due to further local outbreaks of the disease. The problem with this is that during times of low rabbit numbers, the vegetation grows taller, with coarser grasses becoming dominant, that are less palatable to rabbits. Under a sustained moderate level of grazing, the more interesting, attractive and palatable species are retained. In the past, this moderate level was probably sustained by cropping.

Work at Holy Island (Garson, in Doody, 1985) suggests that forage is in short supply from November/December to April/May. During the summer, some of the slacks are heavily grazed, reducing flowering and seeding in years when the population is high. The summer grazing period is important in determining the success of that year's juveniles. It was found that by fencing a slack against rabbits, flowering and seeding was improved. However, it is also suggested that such exclosure reduces the numbers of juveniles surviving in that year, due to forage shortage, so such exclosures may provide a way of keeping populations at a moderate level. If this forage shortage is allowed to develop naturally through high population increase, it is likely that grazing would be at too high a level to maintain an interesting sward. Following further experiments at Holy Island, Garson recommends using temporary electric netting (see 'Fencing', Agate, 1986) as a cheap and effective alternative to permanent galvanised netting. This need not be formed into an exclosure, but can simply be run out along a line barring the routes from burrows to slack.

Practicalities

The following section is contributed by David Hewett.

The preceding paragraphs give an indication of the grazing regimes that can be applied to dune grassland. However, there are considerations concerning grazing which do not apply to the management of vegetation by machines. A tractor or mower can be stored in a shed, and requires limited maintenance, whereas responsibility for animals is a 24 hour/day, all year job. This will fall largely on the owner of the animals, but the land manager has a certain responsibility. If grazing is let, then the manager specifies the conditions, such as the number of animals and the time of year during which the land is grazed. It will be essential to ensure that conditions are followed, and careful records kept.

As a general rule, land cannot be grazed without fencing to contain the stock. The type and height of fencing will vary with the stock (see 'Fencing', Agate, 1986). It may even be possible to maintain a population of rabbits, but they must be kept out of neighbouring farmland.

For the health and well-being of the animals, an annual programme of care must be followed. This is likely to include dosing, vaccination, care of hooves, as well as statutory requirements such as dipping of sheep and treatment for warble fly in cattle. An example routine for sheep management is given in the MAFF leaflet 'The Lowland Ewe – Shepherd's Calendar'. Management of flock or herd numbers by breeding, buying, selling and slaughtering must also be considered. The whole exercise needs to be thought through carefully before any animals are brought onto the site.

In addition to fixed equipment such as fences, pens and dips, a truck or trailer for transporting animals may also be needed. It may be necessary to move animals elsewhere for certain periods, for example to allow summer flowering plants to seed, or when food is short. Supplementary feeding of hay and concentrates is not usually desirable where land management is primarily for conservation, as alien seed can be introduced. When fodder is in such short supply, damage to the vegetation and soil surface is also likely to occur.

Sea Buckthorn Control

Much of the information in this section is based on Ranwell (1972a), Venner (1977), and Ellis (edit. 1983).

Sea buckthorn is a very thorny shrub, growing usually as a bush up to 3m (10') tall, but occasionally found as a tree up to 6m (20') tall.

Its spiny branches and narrow, linear leaves, greyish-green on the upper surfaces and silvery below, are unmistakable.

Sea buckthorn is dioecious, ie male and female flowers are borne on separate plants. This difference is easiest to see on older plants in winter, as the flower buds of male plants are large while those of females are small. The females bear pale yellow to bright orange berry-like fruits which tend to hang on the branches through the winter.

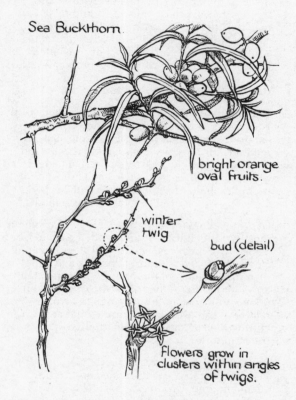

Sea Buckthorn.

bright orange oval fruits.

winter twig

bud (detail)

Flowers grow in clusters within angles of twigs.

Pollen records suggest that sea buckthorn was formerly widespread in Britain on nutrient-rich soils exposed at the end of the last glaciation, but with the spread of forests it was pushed to a few isolated dry sandy sites on the east coast of Britain between Kent and East Lothian. It may possibly be native to a few west coast sites as well. Starting in the mid-18th century it was introduced for erosion control purposes on many sites around the coasts of Great Britain and Ireland as well as inland. Although it has since died out in some places, it has continued to spread in others and has colonised new sites from bird-sown seeds. Since the early 1950s sea buckthorn populations have exploded due to the virtual end of rabbit grazing, possibly aided by increasing soil nutrient levels due to fallout from air pollution.

REASONS FOR CONTROL

Sea buckthorn may be controlled in order to:

a   Prevent it invading open and fixed sand dune communities, where it suppresses other lower-growing plants and leads to permanent changes in dune habitats

b   Restrict or eliminate it on sites of scientific interest where it is not native but has been introduced deliberately or accidentally in the past, in order to maintain or restore more truly natural conditions.

FACTORS TO CONSIDER

a   Sea buckthorn appears well suited to most semi-natural dune habitats other than permanently flooded hollows, dune heaths and the arctic-alpine conditions of the northernmost British dunes. Wherever it invades, it is liable to replace existing plant communities. Because of this, the Hippophae Study Group recommended that while it be allowed to develop to maturity in its most natural and interesting east coast sites, it should be managed to provide greater diversity of shrub species on most of its altered west coast sites and that it be eliminated from or prevented from establishing itself on most other sites. (See Ranwell, 1972a, pp46–9, for management recommendations for individual sites.)

b   Sea buckthorn has a number of positive uses in addition to consolidating and protecting exposed sandy areas (see page 77 for planting methods). It provides material for brushwood fencing, thatching and dead and live hedges. It can be planted as an aid to dune afforestation. It provides shelter for picnic sites and car parks and can also be used to reclaim waste land.

c   Dense sea buckthorn stands have little value for most wildlife but they do provide nest sites for a variety of birds (especially warblers in young stands) and cover for foxes, rabbits and small mammals. They are important winter feeding areas for fieldfares and other thrushes. Where other scrub species are lacking, it is worth retaining some sea buckthorn habitat and cutting the stands in rotation to diversify their age structure.

d   Sea buckthorn tolerates a variety of soils but it is most prolific on well-drained soils with adequate lime. On lime-poor soils it grows poorly and is prone to insect attack. Seedlings germinate only where the soil salinity is under 0.05%. Mature plants are more salt tolerant but they cannot penetrate the dune-salt marsh transition zone. Sea buckthorn is a nitrogen-fixing species which can colonise nitrogen-poor soils. The decaying roots of cut plants release the nitrogen in a form which can be used by nettles (Urtica dioica) and other nitrogen-demanding species, so the plant community which results from sea buckthorn clearance is unlikely to be the same as that which precedes it. The dense leaf litter can also have an adverse effect on the germination of duneland species.

e   Sea buckthorn is light demanding and is killed soon after being overshadowed by taller trees or fast-growers such as elder (Sambucus nigra). Sea buckthorn seedlings cannot survive the shade of the parent plants and mature specimens tend to become bare underneath from overshadowing branches. In some places old (eg twenty years or more) stands seem to be dying of their own accord. It seems likely that other species, protected from winds and grazing animals by the sea buckthorn, may invade and diversify many unmanaged stands and lead eventually to the development of woodland conditions.

f   It is possible to restrict the spread of newly introduced sea buckthorn by insuring that only individuals of one sex are planted. It is best to use all males, since if females are used there is some danger of fertilisation from self-seeded male plants or pollen blown into the area from outside. At Holkham NNR, Norfolk, it has been found that old female bushes occasionally develop fertile seed even when the flowers are carefully isolated from pollination. Sexes of young plants are hard to distinguish, so it is important to weed out any plants of the wrong sex as soon as you notice them.

g   Even single-sex stands spread vigorously by suckering around the periphery, unless controlled. At Braunton Burrows, Devon, plants have been known to spread 2.1m (7') in every direction in a single year and at Yellowcraig, East Lothian, vegetative spread is estimated to be as much as 4.3m (5 yds) per year (East Lothian County Council, 1970, p22).

h   Once plants of both sexes are present over a large area, the only answer to their continued spread is total eradication. In the long run this is less laborious and more effective than any attempt to restrict the spread and multiplication of colonies or to selectively cut female plants to stop seed production (Venner, 1977).

i   Sea buckthorn clearance is a job for cold weather and experienced, well-equipped workers. Protective clothing is essential. See the list on page 30. Heavy-duty hedging gauntlets and a safety helmet with visor and ear protectors, or at least a hat and goggles, are especially important. Anyone felling or spraying should also wear a tough jacket such as a 'Barbour' jacket and heavy leather 'chaps' (trousers cannot turn the thorns). Wear the jacket over the saw harness, when using a scrub cutter, to stop branches catching in the straps. Wear leather boots, not wellies which are liable to puncture. Resist the temptation to strip off and hope for the best – you are likely to end up at hospital with a thorn in too deep for d-i-y removal.

If you can't afford full equipment for the entire work group, be sure at least that the power tool user is properly clad. Volunteers who are helping to clear up behind the power tool user should take great care and work slowly to reduce the risk from thorns.

CONTROL METHODS

A variety of control methods may be used on sea buckthorn, depending on the age and density of plants, the size of the stand and problems of regrowth. On many sites a varied programme is most effective. For example, at Braunton Burrows, the yearly programme, now mainly completed, involved cutting in winter, burning felled material in spring, and spraying regrowth and stands of first year seedlings in late summer and autumn. Scattered first-year seedlings are sprayed or are pulled up by hand as the opportunity allows. However, the effectiveness of treatments varies greatly from one part of the country to another. On a few sites, such as Whitford NNR, Gower, regrowth is nil and a straightforward cutting programme has been enough to virtually eliminate the plant. By contrast, at Murlough NNR, Co. Down, neither cutting nor spraying have been found effective, and large areas have had to be grubbed up (see below).

Where you combine winter cutting with summer-autumn foliar spraying, be sure to fell only as big an area as you can later treat by spraying. Otherwise unsprayed regrowth may get out of hand and have to be cut a second time.

Cutting

Advantages:

a   Cutting is selective and thorough.

b   Cutting is the easiest way to get rid of large plants where a mower or bulldozer is unavailable or site access is difficult.

Disadvantages:

a   Cutting is labour intensive and may be costly.

b   On sites where sea buckthorn regrows after cutting, stumps or regrowth must be treated with herbicide. This adds to the costs and overall work commitment. Old plants (eg 3m, 10' high) are often killed by cutting, especially in damp conditions. But regrowth is likely from plants 1–2m (3'–6') high, while smaller plants tend to sucker profusely after cutting.

c   Clumps which are cut may regenerate rapidly around the edges. The peripheral stolons are stimulated by the cutting of the older part of the plant.

Procedural points:

a   Use a bow saw or power chain saw on large plants which have lost their lower branches and a scrub cutter on plants with stems under about 100mm (4") diameter which are well furnished with low branches and are hard to get at using other tools. Cut small, whippy stems with pruning shears or dig them up by the roots.

b   Cut sea buckthorn near ground level unless the stumps are to be grubbed up afterwards, in which case stems should be cut off at about 1m (3') level so they can be more easily pulled or winched out.

c   When using the scrub cutter, cut with a scythe-like motion to fell the small stems of young colonies and the margins of the main stands. Once you have opened up a 'face', work around the stand in an anti-clockwise direction (if the scrub-cutter blade turns anti-clockwise), cutting uphill on steep slopes or round and round on level ground. Hold the cutter in front and to your left and advance along the 'face' to the right so that the cut stems fall clear of you after you have passed. Cut with the part of the blade between 12 o'clock and 3 o'clock as you view it. Rest after each swath, or let someone else take over cutting for a while. It is dangerous to work too long without a break.

After finishing a swath, throw or fork the cuttings clear to leave a space at least as wide as the height of the next shrubs to be cut. This insures an unimpeded work area when cutting the next swath. Where the sea buckthorn has been bent by the wind or is tangled with brambles or climbers, work slowly, cutting each stem into lengths and pulling it out from the face by hand. Anyone helping to clear up while

the scrub cutter is in use should stay *at least* 5m (15') away from the operator.

Carry 8 or 10 sharp scrub cutter blades with you each day, since they can dull in as little as half an hour in sandy conditions. It is not practical to sharpen these blades in the field, and a dull blade is tiring and dangerous to use.

d   You can reduce the extent of suckering from cut stands by chopping through the horizontal roots at the margins of the stand with a spade.

e   Dispose of cuttings by piling them in windrows for burning or to rot down or by re-using them elsewhere for dune stabilisation or access control purposes. It is essential to clear up the cuttings if you plan a follow-up spraying programme. A bulldozer can be used to pile up the cuttings quickly and safely. On ground too steep for the 'dozer', volunteers can pitchfork the cuttings downhill to the machine.

Leave cuttings for several weeks to dry out. It is best to cut the oldest stands first to give them the longest time to season. They will then burn easily without sparking and leave only a small line of ash. Avoid burning on a very windy day. Cuttings also need to season if they are 'planted' in dead hedges, to insure that the replanted stems do not root. Finish burning by the end of March, otherwise the brush piles will be occupied by nesting birds.

Grubbing-up

Advantages:

a   Grubbing-up, if done with care, largely prevents problems of regrowth although spot-treatment is often necessary for surviving suckers.

b   Grubbing-up can be done by hand or machine depending on the size of the problem.

Disadvantages:

a   Grubbing-up by hand is slow.

b   Uprooting by machine is unselective and can damage the soil and produce erosion. However, this may be balanced by the benefit gained from disturbing the seed bank buried within the soil.

Procedural points:

a   First-year seedlings are soft and spineless and can be pulled up by hand. With older seedlings and suckers you need a spade, garden fork or mattock to get up the roots, which regrow into new plants if they are left in the ground.

For small, shallow-rooted plants one person should dig around the root-plate while another pulls on the stem. Larger plants may need to be hauled free using a hand winch.

b   The root system may extend up to 2m (6') beyond the visible margin of the clump. Regrowth from the periphery is vigorous, so care must be taken to remove as much as possible. This is not easy however, as the roots are slender and brittle.

c   Shake as much of the soil as possible from stumps and roots so that it falls back in the hole. This makes the plant material lighter and easier to burn and also reduces soil disturbance.

d   A bulldozer or tractor with front plate can push over stems of almost any size. The machine must have a closed cab to protect the operator, who should push the material into windrows or leave it in place for volunteers to cut and drag away. At Ainsdale NNR, a low ground pressure bulldozer has been used successfully to uproot bushes and push them into a pile for burning. This method has proved quick and cheap, with good recovery of desirable dune species, and has been the standard method for some years.

e   At Murlough NNR, a tractor-mounted 'grubber' was used, which could clear the roots down to their normal maximum depth of 500mm (18"). Large stumps, or those on steep slopes, were removed with tractor and chain. Inaccessible areas were cleared by hand using mattocks.

f   Dispose of grubbed-up material in the same way as with cuttings.

Burning standing material

Advantages:

a   Where live sea buckthorn can be burnt it is a low-cost method of disposal.

b   Burning can clear sizeable areas quickly.

Disadvantages:

a   Burning is hazardous and must be done with great care to prevent it getting out of hand.

b   Burning is very destructive to wildlife, especially ground flora and fauna. If at all possible, burning should be done in winter or early spring (by the end of March at the latest), before the main flowering and nesting season. This is also usually required by stubble-burning (swaling) regulations. But at this season live sea buckthorn is much harder to set alight than in dry periods. If summer burning is essential, it may be possible to get the permission of the County Agricultural Executive Committee.

c   Dead, unsightly stems are likely to remain standing after a burn and should be cleared if amenity is an important consideration.

d   Regeneration can occur from burnt and apparently dead stems.

Procedural points:

a   Carry out burning only in a very light breeze. The burn should run into the wind for control.

b   Station people around the are with fire beaters to make sure that the fire does not get out of hand.

c   Burn only a small area (eg 1 acre, 0.4 hectare) at any one time, for safety and to minimise destruction of wildlife.

Herbicides

Advantages:

a   Herbicidal treatment can be effective in controlling growth. However, for complete eradication, repeated spraying of regrowth over many years may be needed, as the plant may continue to sprout from underground stems.

b   Treatment can be done by one or two people.

Disadvantages:

a   The effects of herbicides on the environment are not fully understood and some herbicides may be hazardous to the operator. It is essential to take great care, especially when handling and mixing concentrates. If a volunteer group cannot equip itself with adequate protective clothing and insure a high degree of safety awareness, it should not use herbicides.

b   Chemicals and spray equipment are fairly costly.

c   Dead material remains standing and is unsightly unless cut down. Small stems of young plants may be left standing to form a windbreak which can reduce soil erosion on dunes.

Procedural points:

a   Before its ban by many authorities, 2,4,5-T was formerly used effectively on some dune sites to control buckthorn. However, at Murlough NNR, it was found that stump application appeared to encourage the plant to spread more rapidly around the periphery of the clump, and use was therefore abandoned.

b   Results from experimental work at Saltfleetby NNR (Marrs, in Doody, 1985) have indicated that Garlon 2 is likely to be the most effective herbicide available at present for controlling sea buckthorn. Garlon 2 has been used successfully at Ainsdale NNR, to spot-spray bushes in May and June. Treatment is used to kill regrowth from cut stumps, and to control the spread of clumps where it is desirable to keep the older central part for nesting birds and passerines. Further details on Garlon 2 are available from ICI Plant Protection, Woolmead House, Bear Lane, Farnham, Surrey GU9 7UB.

c   Glyphosate, a translocated non-selective herbicide, has been tried at Murlough NNR. It was found that unless every leaf was sprayed, the effect was patchy, as the herbicide did not appear to be translocated throughout the plant.

d   Ultra-low volume sprayers are not generally recommended, as although these save on transporting large volumes of water to possibly inaccessible areas, their small droplet size means they can only be safely used on very still days.

e   Ammonium sulphamate may be used on larger plants where foliar treatment is impractical. It comes in crystal form and is distributed as 'Amcide' by Battle, Hayward and Bower Ltd, Victoria Chemical Works, Allenby Road Industrial Estate, Lincoln LN3 4NP. Frill-girdle standing stems near ground level and apply the neat chemical to the cut area. You can also use ammonium sulphamate on cut stumps, either neat or diluted in water, within forty-eight hours of cutting. Dilution should be at a rate of 4lb of chemical per gallon of water (0.4kg/l). A wetting agent (eg household detergent) may be added to aid penetration. Wet the stumps thoroughly down to the ground and either mark them with a dye or frill them with a billhook to show that they have been treated.

Ammonium sulphamate is highly corrosive to most metals. Use a plastic bucket to carry the neat chemical or diluted herbicide for painting on stumps, or pour the solution out of an all-plastic watering can with a plastic rose.

Mowing

Advantages:

a   Mowing is quick and efficient.

b   Mowing is suitable for a wide range of plant sizes, depending on the available machinery.

c   In most cases, mown material can be left in place to rot down.

Disadvantages:

a   Regrowth is likely except from old plants or on sites where sea buckthorn does not flourish. The effect of mowing may be to produce a 'carpet' of suckers the next year. Even annual mowing may not eradicate the suckers and new seedlings will rapidly invade the area unless rank grasses grow up which choke them out.

b   Mowing is relatively unselective.

c   Mowing machines cannot be used on very steep terrain. Heavy-duty machines may cause unacceptable erosion on fragile dune soils, even on slopes where they would otherwise be able to operate.

Procedural points:

a   For control of young suckers and seedlings, an ordinary rotary mower is suitable on regular, firm ground while a 'Flymo' is better on rougher ground.

b   Where large areas are to be mown or where the stems are too big for a small mower, a tractor-mounted flail or reciprocating mower-arm works well. See 'Hedging' (BTCV, 1975) for details.

c   Even trees up to 3.6m (12′) tall can be cut up with a tractor-mounted heavy-duty rotary mower such as a 'Bush-hog', provided the tractor has a front plate and can push the tree over first. The tractor must have a closed cab to protect the operator. For details, see Wittering (1974).

Treatment after clearance

It is most important that efforts are made to encourage the return of typical duneland species after the clearance of sea buckthorn, and also that vigilance is maintained in clearing regrowth and seedlings of buckthorn.

a   Rake up and burn as much as possible of the leaf litter formed over the years by the buckthorn.

b   At Murlough NNR, it has been found that by ploughing the surface of the dune, the dormant seed bank of duneland species is activated. A good response from winter annual plants has occurred by clearing buckthorn in the summer, so allowing the newly ripened seed to germinate quickly. The seed of winter annuals appears to have a short period of viability in the soil.

c   By the September following a winter of clearance at Murlough NNR, 79 species of flowering plants were recorded in the 2½ hectare area previously dominated by buckthorn. Growth of many species was luxuriant, due to the high nitrogen status of the soil. Among the many interesting species were several normally found only on the strand line. Some 'weed' species also occurred, a few being new to the reserve. In the spring and summer of the following year there was a spectacular display of flowers in the cleared areas. Flowering dune annuals dominated, with only a few 'weed' species surviving from the previous year.

d   Regeneration of dune vegetation was poorest in the areas where the sea buckthorn had been over 15 years old. This may be due to the thick leaf litter producing acids which destroyed the buried seeds. On the less altered soils cleared of younger buckthorn, the recolonising vegetation is developing towards the typical community of nutrient-deficient soils. For a full account, see Ellis (edit. 1983).

e   Ranwell (1972) states that mowing and removal of clippings is necessary on restored areas to reduce the nutrient levels.

9 Dune Wildlife

This chapter describes some of the management work carried out on sand dunes to encourage various types of wildlife.

Amphibians and Reptiles

Of the six species of amphibians and six reptiles indigenous to Britain, one of each, the natterjack toad and the sand lizard, have major strongholds in coastal dune systems. Both these species are now local in occurrence and declining, and are protected under the Wild Creatures and Wild Plants Act 1975. They should not be removed or even handled by anyone without a licence to do so from the Nature Conservancy Council.

THE NATTERJACK TOAD

The natterjack (*Bufo calamita*) is a small, relatively agile toad which runs rather than hops on its stumpy legs. Although found in a variety of habitats in Western Europe generally, in Britain it is limited to sandy soils where it can burrow easily. Although it was known until recently at a number of inland sites, notably the heaths of the Weald and East Anglia, it appears to be extinct or virtually so at all these places and is confined now to a few coastal areas. The most important of these are in Merseyside between Southport and Altcar and on the north side of the Solway, with smaller colonies around the Cumbria coast. A small colony survives on the Cheshire coast while in the East the natterjack persists at Saltfleetby, Lincolnshire, and at Holkham and Winterton Dunes, Norfolk (Prestt, Cooke and Corbett, 1974, p233).

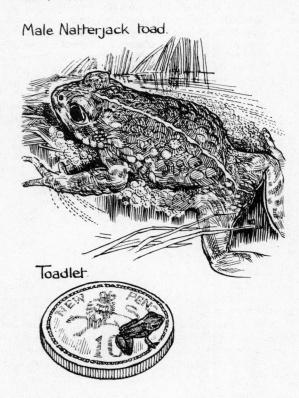

Male Natterjack toad.

Toadlet

Like all amphibians, the natterjack depends on suitable freshwater habitats in which to breed and to pass the early stages of its life history. The major cause of its decline is loss of breeding habitat and, to a lesser extent, an increase in man-made barriers to migration and dispersal.

This century, over 80% of natterjack breeding sites in Britain have been lost. The toads are relatively defenceless against predators, especially in the breeding period, so that small colonies may be wiped out by birds, voles and snakes.

The main way to improve conditions for the natterjack besides protecting its remaining sites, is to create or maintain suitable breeding pools, ponds or ditches. Its natural spawning places are shallow pools. It is thought that adults can survive up to fifteen years of drought. But climatic changes and the lowering of water tables due to increased demands of agriculture and housing may have disastrous consequences on breeding success, since the tadpoles are killed if their ponds dry out before metamorphosis is complete.

At Ainsdale Sand Dunes in Merseyside, Saltfleetby in Lincolnshire and Winterton Dunes and Holkham in Norfolk, the Nature Conservancy Council have dug a number of natterjack breeding pools and shallow scrapes. Small pools can be dug by hand, but it is usually cheaper to get an adequately big and deep pool dug by machine. Experience at Ainsdale indicates that the best equipment is a low-ground-pressure bulldozer, which can make smooth scrapes and grade the spoil into the surrounding landscape. The depth required depends on local conditions but it is important to have at least parts of some pools hold water through mid-summer. On the other hand, pools should not be dug too deep or they will not favour natterjack development and may even be infiltrated by salt water which underlies the fresh water table of sand dunes near the sea. At Ainsdale, the scrapes are designed to dry out in August or September during average summers, since the tadpoles have metamorphosed by this time. Where a mechanical excavator is used, pools should be designed and located to minimise movement of equipment over the fragile surfaces of slacks. Further points include:

a   Natterjack pools or scrapes should be kidney shaped, where possible, with the convex side facing south and the 'peninsular' side to the north.

b   Shallow margins are essential, since natterjacks drown easily and may not even attempt to breed in steep-sided ditches. The sides should be as smooth as possible, otherwise tadpoles may gather in small depressions and be left high and dry as the water level drops. Spoil from the excavation can be placed along one or more sides to provide a burrowing and hibernating place for adults and young toads.

c   Tadpoles need warm water to develop – generally above 20°C (68°F) and optimally above 25°C (73°F). Deep water and shade from trees may keep the water too cool. Also in deep, shaded pools natterjack spawn and tadpoles tend to be at a competitive disadvantage with frogs and common toads (*Bufo bufo*) and are more likely to fall prey to newts, carnivorous insects and other predators which thrive in these conditions. There is also some evidence that common toads and frogs exert an inhibitory influence on natterjacks, causing the tadpoles to develop more slowly than normal.

d   Aquatic vegetation, or at least a few sods or one or more tree trunks on the bottom of the pool, helps the survival of tadpoles, especially for protection from ducks, waders and other birds. Natterjacks must have bare sand areas around the pool in which to burrow.

e   Management work should be carried out from late August to mid October to reduce the chance of destroying tadpoles or hibernating adults. Although their life history varies from site to site, natterjacks generally hibernate from late October to March or April. Their short, powerful limbs are adapted for burrowing into sandy soil, in which they can go as deep as 3m (10'). The mating and spawning period is mid-April to the end of June and tadpoles leave the water between early June and mid-August (Smith, 1951). The natterjack develops through all the stages from spawn to young toad in four to eight weeks, compared with ten to twelve weeks for the common toad and frog. In some years, the tadpoles may emerge in two broods, due to a cool spell of weather occurring mid-season between early and late warm weather.

f   At Formby, Merseyside, new pools are dug to about 1m (3') depth in October, and fenced immediately after (see below). It is difficult to get the pool to just the right depth, so that it is shallow enough to warm up, but deep enough that it does not dry out in July. 'Emergency' digging, when the tadpoles are hatched, is not very successful. Apart from the disturbance caused, the tadpoles are reluctant to move into the newly dug and cooler areas. In the first year after digging, pools are usually satisfactory in terms of water level, but have few toads using them. The second year is normally the best, with a good hatching of tadpoles and toadlets. In the third year, vegetation starts to come in, shading the water and keeping it cooler, and so less suitable for metamorphosis.

g   The toadlets metamorphose in the water, and can find the walk up the dry sand difficult. They tend to stay in the water until it rains, when they can more easily get a footing. The toadlets crawl into cracks in the sand, and can easily be squashed by people walking around the edge of the pond. At Ainsdale NNR, pine brashings are put down in a 2m (6') strip around the pond. These provide protection for the toadlets. The brashings are put down in July, as if done any earlier there is more time for children to disturb them.

h   An alternative method in areas of public access is to fence around each pool. At Formby, 1.1m (3½') chestnut paling is used, encircling the pond about 2m (6') from its edges. Explanatory notices discourage people from climbing in. These notices and other publicity have increased public awareness to such an extent that complaints are made if the pools are allowed to fill in, even though this may be part of the natural cycle.

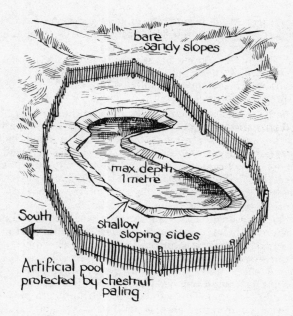

Artificial pool protected by chestnut paling

THE SAND LIZARD

The sand lizard (*Lacerta agilis*) is confined in Britain to mature lowland dry heaths and sand dunes in the southern half of the country. These habitats provide the subsoil warmth necessary for the hatching of eggs and they are only slowly overgrown by vegetation. The sand lizard was once present over a scattering of sites but is now confined to four general areas: the Merseyside coastal dunes; the heaths of Surrey, northeast Hampshire, southeast Berkshire and northwest Sussex; the southwest Hampshire heaths; and the heaths and coastal dunes of southeast Dorset. All four areas have experienced severe declines in this century, and on its coastal sites the Merseyside population is down to perhaps individuals although the Dorset population is considerably larger. The Merseyside lizards are probably a distinct race which have been isolated from those of other sites for at least 2,000 years (Prestt, Cooke and Corbett, 1974). Merseyside is the northern edge of their range.

Sand Lizard

Because sand lizards are highly colonial and stray only a short distance from their basking and nesting sites, local road or housing developments can destroy entire colonies. Collecting (mainly by children) is still a problem and may finish off remaining individuals, especially the males which are a vivid bright green (in Lancashire, yellow-green) in the breeding season. Fires are also a major threat, while magpies and stoats take their toll.

In general, protection and creation of habitat is difficult, as sand lizards, like natterjack toads, are adapted to an unstable habitat. In the case of the natterjack, it is the interface of sand and water which is crucial, whereas the sand lizard needs the changing conditions where bare sand is slowly colonised by vegetation. A suitable site may only remain so for a few years, so the job of managing a threatened population is a constant one.

The British Herpetological Society and the Nature Conservancy Council have constructed vivaria in parts of the country where sand lizards occur, to breed them for release into suitable habitats. This is a specialised operation and no one should attempt it without advice from the BHS and a permit from the NCC to keep lizards.

In areas of heathland, such as in Dorset, habitat can be improved by clearing sandy patches on gently south facing slopes, for basking and egg-laying. Clearance is done by simply pulling or digging out the heather to leave a bare sandy patch about 2 × 3m. In one such project, about 14 patches were cleared in an area of about 60 × 40m. This can be done virtually any time of year on ground where no sand lizards yet occur. A mechanical rotovator has also been used to keep the patches clear of vegetation in subsequent years. This must be done in May or June, after the adults emerge, but before the eggs are laid. For the same reason, May and June is also the time chosen for ploughing the firebreaks to keep them clear of vegetation. This is done every other year.

The Merseyside population of sand lizards is distributed amongst about 20 breeding sites, some of which are completely isolated by urban development, golf courses and so on, and thus it is difficult for the lizards to spread. Normally, lizards will move only about 100m from their nesting and basking sites, although exceptionally they may move up to a maximum of about 700m. Great effort is put into protecting the remaining population and sites, including the release of individuals bred in vivaria. These are released on sites where numbers are low, on those where sand lizards were known to exist in the past, and onto new sites which have suitable vegetation and aspect.

The natural development from marram grass to a suitable mix of vegetation can take 15 to 20 years, so short cuts have to be taken to create new habitats. The technique being tried is to transplant turfs of 'fixed dune' vegetation, from an area where marram is dying off and is being replaced by sand sedge. The transplanting is done in April. Individual plants of marram are also dug or pulled in the normal way (see p73), as these are too deep rooted to be transplanted successfully as turfs. The turfs are laid on the chosen new site, cleared bare of any existing unsuitable vegetation such as shrubs or non-native species, to leave about 10% bare sand. The clumps of marram are planted amongst them. On steep banks, simple steps or paths are helpful so that the progress of the new colony can be checked.

turf cut from south facing slope.

Another technique used is to cut turfs as shown, to create small bare patches for basking and egg-laying. This was done about every 15–20 metres along a suitable south facing bank.

Invertebrates

The mosaic of habitats that comprise a sand dune system can support a large and varied population of invertebrates. For example, over 2,000 species were found in the dunes and salt marshes of Spurn Head, Yorkshire, amounting to between 20 and 25% of the total British invertebrate fauna (Ranwell, 1972, p169).

There is little done in the way of specific management, beyond the general aim of maintaining and improving on the diversity of habitats within the dunes. On some sites, such as Braunton Burrows, Devon, ponds have been excavated to encourage a variety of wildlife, such as frogs, newts and grass snakes, as well as dragonflies and other invertebrates. Each pond is dug to a variety of depths from 2m (6') up to zero, to give the maximum diversity whilst maintaining some water even in very dry summers. Here the water table can vary by up to 1.4m (4½') each year. Willows are left around the edge of the ponds to strengthen the banks, and areas are left overgrown to restrict public access. Care is taken not to use herbicides anywhere near the ponds to avoid pollution.

Birds

The British coasts are especially noted for their bird life. Tidal sand and mud flats provide feeding and roosting sites for wildfowl and waders, both resident breeding species and wintering birds which breed in the arctic and sub-arctic. Migrant warblers, thrushes and finches use coastal scrub for feeding and resting. Seabirds such as guillemots, razorbills, kittiwakes, shags, fulmars and gannets congregate in dense populations on coastal cliffs to nest. Dunes and salt marshes provide undisturbed nesting and feeding areas for many terrestrial species such as meadow pipits and skylarks, stonechats and whinchats. Even shingle beaches are important as nesting areas for terns and ringed plovers. The breeding habitats and nesting seasons of a number of coastal bird species are tabulated in the BTCV handbook 'Waterways and Wetlands' (Brooks, 1976).

PROTECTION OF SHORE NEST SITES

The major problem for birds which nest on coastal sites is disturbance from humans. Cliff-nesting birds are on the whole protected by inaccessibility, but beach- and dune-nesters are highly vulnerable. Terns, which nest just above the tide-line on sand and shingle beaches, are easily disturbed by people and their dogs, and when adult birds are off the nest the eggs and chicks fall easy prey to gulls, crows and kestrels. They are also preyed upon by foxes. Unseasonable storms and high tides make breeding success even more precarious.

Protection of shore-nesting birds has focused on the little tern (*Sterna albifrons*), one of the rarest breeding seabirds in Britain. Unlike the other terns, which usually nest in extensive colonies, little terns occur in small scattered groups of from five to twenty-five pairs on beaches very close to the high tide mark. Breeding begins late in April and the young are usually fledged by early August. Voluntary wardening schemes at a number of sites have failed to give adequate protection, particularly against serious egg collectors. In 1975 the RSPB, Nature Conservancy Council, North Wales Naturalists' Trust and local ornithological societies in Clwyd and Gwynedd banded together to appoint full-time summer wardens at three little tern colonies. The wardens, backed by voluntary assistants, have kept a continuous watch on nests and conducted an intensive education campaign among beach users. These measures, plus fencing and signposting around the perimeter of colonies, have significantly cut down human disturbance. Electric fences about 250mm (10″) high, inside the perimeter fences, have proved a deterrent to foxes (Thomas and Richards, 1977, pp60–1).

Little terns which choose to nest in compact groups have more success than those in scattered groupings, since they are able to mob potential predators more effectively. Once the young chicks are out of the nest, about mid-June, they are more likely to survive where they can scatter into nearby sand dunes when predators threaten or the tide is high. However, disturbance from the dune tops is more disruptive than that from the beach because the tops form the skyline from which the terns expect predators to appear (Mason, 1974). Where terns nest below the spring tide mark, or where tide tables and long-range weather forecasts predict exceptionally high tides, wardens can protect nests from flooding by moving them up the beach a few inches a day. This is done by making a new scrape adjacent to the old one, transferring the eggs and obliterating the old nest. Nest moving should only be considered as a last resort since it increases disturbance of the breeding sites.

On some RSPB reserves, control of breeding gulls has been necessary to reduce competition with terns and other rare breeders and predation on young birds. Thomas (1971) gives results of trials and management suggestions. Often it is not enough just to provide other birds with more nest sites, since an expanding gull population may appropriate these when their own preferred sites are full. At Havergate, Suffolk, gulls have been harassed and their breeding success reduced by the removal of nests and eggs. This forces the gulls to recommence breeding activities, often at a distance from the original nest site. At several reserves, including Dungeness in Kent, the control method is to kill and preserve eggs by injection with formalin, so that the gulls continue to incubate the eggs for many weeks. Direct control of adult birds is seldom practised because it often entails disturbance of other nesting birds.

TREATMENT OF OILED BIRDS

Oil spills claim an increasing number of birds at sea and to a lesser extent in rivers, lakes and estuaries. Most seriously affected are seabirds, especially those attempting to nest and feed near industrial areas and shipping lanes. As Ranwell and Hewett (1964, p195) note, 'oil is not a normal part of a bird's habitat and birds do not appear to have developed any capacity to avoid it or to recognise polluted from unpolluted areas'. Where a spill occurs in a confined area it might be possible to set up buoys with bang-type scarers but otherwise there is little that can be done except to try to limit the amount of oil spilled in the first place.

Oiled birds preen vigorously in an attempt to clean their feathers. The oil swallowed slowly poisons them, while the remaining external oil destroys the waterproofing of the plumage so that the birds become wet and cold and easily die of exposure. Once beached, oiled birds starve or are killed by predators.

It is difficult to treat oiled birds and the success rate is low. Brief notes are given in the leaflet 'Oiled Seabirds First Aid' while details are contained in the booklet, 'Recommended Treatment of Oiled Seabirds'. Both publications are available from the Nature Conservancy Council and the Royal Society for the Protection of Birds. The following points are basic:

a   When approaching or handling an oiled bird, disturb it as little as possible. Approach it from the seaward side, whether it is on the beach or floating in the water. Avoid chasing it, if possible. Use a wide net attached to a pole to aid capture.

b   Hold the caught bird to keep the wings from flapping. Wipe the bill clean and enclose the body in a cloth with head and feet projecting. An old piece of sheet about 200–300mm (9–12″) square with a 50mm (2″) hole in the middle for the head is ideal. This helps immobilise the bird and keeps it from taking in more oil by preening.

c   Place the wrapped bird in a cardboard box at least 450mm (18″) on a side, well lined with newspaper and/or rags for warmth. Never use a straw lining. Keep the flaps down so the bird is in the dark, but make holes or leave gaps for ventilation. Treat the bird gently and calmly.

d   Cleaning should only be attempted after the bird has excreted oil it has taken internally and its general condition has clearly improved. Take the bird as soon as possible to the local RSPCA Inspector (listed in the telephone book) or someone else with experience in treating oiled birds. If three hours or more pass from the time of capture, feed the bird uncooked filleted white fish in finger-sized strips. Give it no other food or medicine. Force-feeding may be required and this should be done with great care: one person should hold the bird and open its bill while another inserts the fish: the bill should be held nearly upright and the throat gently stroked to prevent regurgitation.

Conservation and the Volunteer Worker

The British Trust for Conservation Volunteers aims to promote the use of volunteers on conservation tasks. In addition to organising work projects it is able, through its affiliation and group schemes, to offer advice and help with insurance cover, tool purchase and practical technical training.

To ensure the success of any conservation task it is important that the requesting person or agency, the volunteer and the leader all understand their particular responsibilites and roles. All voluntary work should be undertaken in the spirit of the Universal Charter of Volunteer Service, drawn up by the UNESCO Coordinating Committee for International Voluntary Service. Three of its most important points are:

1   'The work to be done should be a real need in its proper context and be directly related to a broad framework of development'. In terms of conservation, this means that tasks should be undertaken as integral parts of site management plans, not as isolated exercises. Work should never be undertaken solely for the benefit of the volunteer. Necessary follow-up work after tasks should be planned beforehand to ensure that volunteer effort is not wasted.

2   'The task should be a suitable assignment for a volunteer'. Volunteers cannot successfully tackle all types of work and they should not be used where there is a risk of serious accident or injury, where a financial profit will be made from their labours, where the job is so large that their efforts will have little overall effect, where the skills required are beyond their capabilities so that a bad job results and they become dispirited, or where machines can do the same job more efficiently and for a lower cost.

3   'Voluntary services should not replace paid local labour'. It should complement such work, not supplant it. Employers should make sure in advance that the position of volunteers and paid workers is clear with respect to any relevant labour unions. Further advice may be found in 'Guidelines for the relationships between volunteers and paid non-professional workers', published by the Volunteer Centre, 29 Lower King's Road, Berkhamstead, Hertfordshire HP4 2AB.

Volunteers are rarely 'free labour'. Someone has to pay for transport, materials, tools, insurance, refreshments and any accommodation charges. Before each party makes a commitment to a project it should be clear who is to pay for what. While volunteers may willingly fund their own work, 'user bodies' should be prepared to contribute and should not assume that all volunteers, who are already giving their time and effort, will be able to meet other expenses out of their own pockets. Several grant-aiding bodies may help pay the cost of environmental and conservation projects, notably the Nature Conservancy Council, the World Wildlife Fund and the Countryside Commissions. Details may be found in 'A guide to grants by the Department of the Environment and associated bodies for which voluntary organisations may be eligible', available from The Department of the Environment, Room C15/11, 2 Marsham Street, London SW1P 3EB.

It is important that volunteer workers be covered by some sort of public liability insurance for any damage or injury they may cause to property or to the public. Cover up to £250,000 is recommended. Volunteers should also be covered against personal accident.

The volunteer group organiser should visit the work site well before the task, to check that the project is suitable and that volunteers will not be exploited and to plan the best size of working party and the proper tools and equipment. Volunteers should be advised in advance on suitable clothing for the expected conditions. They should be physically fit and come prepared for work and they should genuinely want to volunteer – those 'pressganged' into service are likely to work poorly, may do more harm than good and may be put off a good cause for life! Young volunteers need more supervision and are best suited to less strenuous jobs where achievements are clearly visible, and it is recommended that where they are involved the task should emphasise education. Note that the Agriculture (Avoidance of Accidents to Children) Regulations, 1958, legally restrict the riding on and driving of agricultural machines, vehicles or implements by children under 13 years.

Volunteer group organisers and 'user bodies' both should keep records of the work undertaken: the date of the project, jobs done, techniques used, number of volunteers and details of any notable events including accidents, unusual 'finds', publicity etc. Such information makes it easier to handle problems or queries which may arise after the task. It also provides a background on the task site for future visits, supplies practical data by which the site management plan can be evaluated and allows an assessment to be made of the volunteer effort.

Site Studies and Surveys

Maritime habitats are ideal subjects for ecological study. They are comparatively simple and some are distinctly zoned. Their controlling environmental factors can usually be defined and isolated. The dynamics of their plant and animal communities can be observed more easily than those of many other habitats. Yonge (1949) provides a good basic text for the study of inter-tidal and sub-littoral areas while Ranwell (1972) suggests many topics of importance to the understanding of salt marshes and sand dunes which require further research. Although much can be done through the simple identification of species, many site studies require long-term work using equipment and statistical methods beyond the scope of this Handbook. Watkin (1973) is a useful casebook of studies on a single system which gives in detail some of the methods needed to carry out work on any coastal site.

The most important studies from a management viewpoint are those which relate public pressure on coastal areas to changes in stability and wildlife interest. These studies must begin with accurate mapping. Ritchie (1970) outlines the standard method used on the beaches of Sutherland. Each system is described in terms of five headings: rock structure and general physiographic setting (including the water table); materials (nature and sources of sand); processes (marine and aeolian); vegetation; and history of land use (including present use), especially common grazing. The same problems can be attacked from a different angle by studying the direct effects of different levels of public and biotic pressure on soils and vegetation, especially the critical limits of trampling for various types of turf and the effects of

vegetation types on visitor use and animal grazing. Simple techniques for studying access pressure are given in another handbook in this series, Footpaths (Agate, 1983).

Copies of records made at nature reserves or sites of special scientific interest should be sent to the Biological Records Centre, or the nearest Marine Biological Station.

MARINE CONSERVATION SOCIETY

Underwater Conservation Year 1977 marked the start of several surveys initiated by the British Sub Aqua Club. From this developed the Underwater Conservation Programme, which led to the formation of the Marine Conservation Society. This is a charitable organisation involved in underwater research, education and interpretation to the public. They organise a large number of projects for both underwater and shore-based volunteers. Their address is given on page 102.

BEACH BIRD SURVEY

The Royal Society for the Protection of Birds no longer do a national beach bird survey, but some regions and local groups undertake surveys of particular areas. Some regions of the RSPB also maintain lists of volunteers who can be called out in an emergency to assist with the rescue of oiled sea birds. Contact your local regional office of the RSPB for further information.

The Coastal Code

The coast is heavily used for recreation and other purposes, often with little awareness on the part of the public or even land managers of the need for conservation and safety. The following points are basic.

Conservation

a   Many coastal habitats are fragile and easily damaged. Avoid unnecessary trampling and machine and vehicle access. The beach, not the dunes, is the place to play and dig.

b   The coast is the home of seals, seabirds, waders and wildfowl. Stay clear of breeding sites to avoid frightening the parents and exposing the young to predators. Keep dogs under control.

c   If you spearfish, keep away from other water users and do not fish in areas of special conservation interest. If you dig bait, collect it from a wide area rather than causing severe damage in one spot. Always backfill holes and replace stones in the position you found them.

d   Detergents, paints, solvents and fuel are poisonous to marine life. Don't dump them overboard. The wash from fast power boats can destroy salt marsh banks and nests in estuaries, so limit your speed near shore.

e   Take notes and photographs, not specimens. Many marine organisms are scarce or slow growing and can easily be depleted. Do not pull up seaweed unless there is a special reason. Plants of shingle banks and sand dunes are important for stabilising the soil and should not be damaged. If you are leading an educational group, demonstrate material without removing it. Never take repetitive samples from the same locality without expert advice.

Safety

If you see anybody in trouble or find anything suspicious dial 999 and ask for the coastguard. Be ready to give a full description of the place and nature of the emergency. The times of high tides are available from the coastguard, local newspapers and tide tables.

a   Never swim without first obtaining advice from local people or the coastguard. Never swim on an ebb tide. Never swim after drinking alcohol.

b   Never play with air beds, rubber rings or small inflatable craft on an ebb tide. Always ask someone on shore to keep an eye on you. Always wear old clothes, not just a swim suit. If you are unable to get back to land, cover the head with clothing and curl into a ball to reduce heat loss and dehydration.

c   Never walk along a beach on an incoming tide – you may be cut off by the sea. Cliffs are often undercut and unstable. Do not approach the cliff edge or sit directly at its foot.

d   Power boats are dangerous inshore. Keep well out to avoid bathers. If you operate a yacht or boat, fill in a card (available free from the coastguard, yacht clubs, harbour masters and marinas) which gives details of the type of craft, safety equipment and operating area. Send it to the local coastguard rescue headquarters. Also, always tell someone reliable where you are going and when you expect to be back.

e   Take away litter and bottles. Do not build fires on pebbles, since these can heat up and explode. It is best to build fires below the high water mark so that any debris is swept clean by the tides.

f   Never touch any suspicious objects washed ashore or found in dunes and marshes. It may be explosive. Report it to the local coastguard.

Conservation and Amenity Organisations

Biological Records Centre
Monks Wood Experimental Station, Abbots Ripton, Cambridgeshire PE17 2LS

Botanical Society of the British Isles
c/o Department of Botany, British Museum (Natural History), Cromwell Rd, London SW7

British Ecological Society
Burlington House, Piccadilly, London W1V OLQ

British Herpetological Society
c/o The Zoological Society of London, Regents Park London NW1 4RY

British Trust for Conservation Volunteers
Head Office: 36 St Mary's Street, Wallingford, Oxon OX10 OEU   0491 39766

London: The London Ecology Centre, 80 York Way, London N1 9AG   01 278 4293

South: Hatchlands, East Clandon, Guildford, Surrey GU4 7RT   0483 223294

South West: Old Estate Yard, Newton St Loe, Bath, Avon BA2 9BR   02217 2856

East Anglia: Animal House, Bayfordbury Estate, Hertford SG13 8LD   0992 53067

East Midlands: Conservation Training Centre, Old Village School, Chestnut Grove, Burton Joyce, Nottingham NG14 5D2   0602 313316

West Midlands: Conservation Centre, Firsby Road, Quinton, Birmingham B32 2QT   021 426 5588

Yorkshire & Humberside: Conservation Training Centre, Balby Road, Doncaster DN4 ORH   0302 859522

North West: 40 Cannon Street, Preston, Lancashire PR1 3NT   0772 50286

North East: Springwell Conservation Centre, Springwell Road, Wrekenton, Gateshead, Tyne and Wear NE9 7AD   091 4820111

Wales: Forest Farm, Forest Farm Road, Whitchurch, Cardiff CF4 7JH   0222 626660

Northern Ireland: Conservation Volunteers, The Pavilion, Cherryvale Park, Ravenshill Rd, Belfast BT6 OBZ   0232 645169

British Trust for Ornithology
Beech Grove, Tring, Hertfordshire HP23 5NR   044 282 3461

Cement and Concrete Association
Wexham Springs, Wexham, Slough SL3 6PL

Civic Trust
17 Carlton House Terrace, London SW1Y 5AW   01 930 0914

Council for Environmental Conservation (CoEnCo)
Zoological Gardens, Regents Park, London NW1   01 722 7111

Council for Environmental Education
School of Education, University of Reading London Road, Reading RG1 5AQ   0734 875324

Council for National Parks
4 Hobart Place, London SW1W OHY   01 235 0901

Council for the Protection of Rural England
4 Hobart Place, London SW1W OHY   01 235 9481

Council for the Protection of Rural Wales
31 High Street, Welshpool, Powys SY21 7JP   0938 2525

Country Landowners Association
16 Belgrave Square, London SW1X 8PQ   01 235 0511

Countryside Commission
John Dower House, Crescent Place, Cheltenham, Gloucestershire GL50 3RA   0242 521381

Countryside Commission for Scotland
Battleby, Redgorton, Perthshire PH1 3EW   0738 27921

Dartington Institute
Shinners Bridge, Dartington, Totnes, Devon PQ9 6JE   0803 862271

Farming and Wildlife Advisory Group
The Lodge, Sandy, Bedfordshire SG19 2DL   0767 80551

Field Studies Council
62 Wilson Street, London EC2A 2BU   01 247 4651

Forestry Commission
231 Corstorphine Road, Edinburgh EH12 7AT   031 334 0303

Friends of the Earth
377 City Road, London EC1V 1NA   01 837 0731

The Game Conservancy
Burgate Manor, Fordingbridge, Hampshire SP6 1EF   0425 52381

Geological Society of London
Burlington House, Piccadilly London W1V OJU

Institute of Terrestrial Ecology
68 Hills Road, Cambridge CB2 1LA   0223 69745

Landscape Institute
    12 Carlton House Terrace, London SW1Y 5AH
    01 839 4044

Mammal Society of the British Isles
    (Business Office), 141 Newmarket Road,
    Cambridge CB5 8HA   0223 351870

Marine Conservation Society
    4 Gloucester Road, Ross-on-Wye,
    Herefordshire HR9 5BU   0989 66017

National Farmers Union
    Agriculture House, 25–31 Knightsbridge,
    London SW1X 7NJ   01 235 5077

National Farmers Union of Scotland
    17 Grosvenor Crescent, Edinburgh EH12 5EN
    031 337 4333

National Federation of Young Farmers' Clubs
    YFC Centre, National Agricultural Centre,
    Kenilworth CV8 2LG   0203 56131

The National Trust
    36 Queen Anne's Gate, London SW1H 9AS
    01 222 9251

National Trust for Scotland
    5 Charlotte Square, Edinburgh EH2 4DU
    031 225 5922

Nature Conservancy Council
    Northminster House, Peterborough PE1 1UA
    0733 40345

The Open Spaces Society
    25a Bell Street, Henley on Thames,
    Oxon RG9 2BA 0491 573535

The Ramblers' Association
    1/5 Wandsworth Road, London SW8 2LJ
    01 582 6826

Royal Society for Nature Conservation
    The Green, Nettleham, Lincoln LN2 2NR
    0522 752326

Royal Society for the Protection of Birds
    The Lodge, Sandy, Bedfordshire SG19 2DL
    0767 80551

Scottish Conservation Projects Trust
    Balallan House, 24 Allan Park,
    Stirling FK8 2QG 0786 79697

Scottish Landowners Federation
    18 Abercromby Place, Edinburgh EH3 6TY
    031 556 4466

Scottish Wildlife Trust
    25 Johnston Terrace, Edinburgh EH1 2NH
    031 226 4602

Tree Council
    Agriculture House, Knightsbridge,
    London SW1X 7NJ 01 235 8854

Woodland Trust
    Autumn Park, Dysart Road, Grantham,
    Lincs NG31 6LL 0476 74297

World Wildlife Fund
    Panda House, 11–13 Ockford Road, Godalming,
    Surrey GU7 1QU   048 68 20551

Bibliography

The literature on coastal management and conservation is vast. The following list includes works cited in the text as well as a few others of general interest.

Aaron, J R (1954)
The Use of Forest Produce in Sea and River Defence in England and Wales. HMSO. Forestry Commission Forest Record No. 29.

Adriani, M J and Terwindt, J H J (1974)
Sand Stabilization and Dune Building. Government Printing Office, The Hague, Netherlands. Rijkswaterstaat Communications No. 19. Details on fencing, planting and sowing dunes.

Agate, E (1986)
Fencing. British Trust for Conservation Volunteers Practical Conservation Handbook.

Allen, S E (1964)
'Chemical Aspects of Heather Burning' *Journal of Applied Ecology* 1:347–367.

Bacon, J C (1975)
A Report on the Stabilisation and Prevention of Dune Erosion on National Trust Properties in Northumberland 1971–1974. National Trust. Duplicated.

Boorman, L A (1977)
'Sand-dunes'. In Barnes, R S K (ed). *The Coastline.* John Wiley and Sons. Ecology, physiology and management of dunes.

Boorman, L A and Fuller, R M (1977)
'The Spread and Development of *Rhododendron ponticum* L. on Dunes at Winterton, Norfolk, in Comparison with Invasion by *Hippophae rhamnoides* L. at Saltfleetby, Lincolnshire'. *Biological Conservation.* 12:83–94.

Brown, Andrew C H (1974)
The Construction and Design of Signs in the Countryside. Countryside Commission for Scotland.

Carey, A E and Oliver, F W (1918)
Tidal Lands. Blackie and Son. Classic on older techniques of coastal protection.

Charlton, J F L (1970)
'Fertilisation of Dune Grass'. In North Berwick Study Group (1970) qv.

Colquhoun, R S (1970)
'Pendine, Carmarthen'. In North Berwick Study Group (1970) qv.

Countryside Commission (1969)
Nature Conservation at the Coast. HMSO. Special Study Report, Volume Two, containing the report of the Nature Conservancy. Concise description of coastal habitats and conservation problems.

Countryside Commission for Scotland (1977)
Highland Beach Management Project: First Interim Report January–September 1977. CCS. Duplicated. Report by Dr W T Brand, Project Officer.

Countryside Commission for Scotland (1978)
Highland Beach Management Project: Second Interim Report October 1977–October 1978. CCS. Duplicated.

Countryside Commission for Scotland (1982)
Four Dune Grasses Information Sheet Plants 2.7.1 *Sand Fencing* Information Sheet Plants 5.2.5 *Sand Stabilisation by Spraying* Information Sheet Plants 5.2.3 *Sand Stabilisation by Thatching* Information Sheet Plants 5.2.4

Countryside Commission for Scotland (1984)
Beach Recreation Management Information Sheet Plants 5.1.2 *Engineered Protection of Beach Coastlines.* Information Sheet Plants 5.1.3

Countryside Commission for Scotland (1985)
Dune Grass Planting Information Sheet Plants 5.2.1

Doody, P (ed) (1985)
Sand Dunes and their Management. Focus on Nature Conservation No. 13. Nature Conservancy Council.

Dorset Naturalists' Trust (1974)
Marine Wildlife Conservation in Dorset. DNT. Conservation Studies No. 1.

Duffey, E (ed) (1967)
The Biotic Effects of Public Pressure on the Environment. Nature Conservancy, Natural Environment Research Council. Monks Wood Experimental Station Symposium No. 3.

Duffey, E (ed) (1967a)
'An Assessment of Dune Invertebrate Faunas in Habitats Vulnerable to Public Disturbance'. In Duffey (1967) qv.

East Lothian County Council (1970)
Dune Conservation: A Twenty Year Record of Work in East Lothian. East Lothian County Council, County Planning Department. Describes fencing, planting methods etc.

Ellis, R J (ed) (1983)
Murlough NNR Scientific Report 1982–83. The National Trust.

Fournier, F (1972)
Soil Conservation. Council of Europe. Brief treatment of dune stabilisation.

Fuller, R M (1975)
'The Culbin Shingle Bar and Its Vegetation'. *Transactions of the Botanical Society of Edinburgh*. 1975:42:293–305.

Garson, P (1985)
'Rabbit grazing and the dune slack flora of Holy Island, Lindisfarne, NNR'. In Doody (1985) qv.

Gaskin, A J (1970)
'Culbin Forest'. In North Berwick Study Group (1970) qv.

Gaudet, J J (1974)
'The Normal Role of Vegetation in Water'. In Mitchell, D S (ed), *Aquatic Vegetation and Its Use and Control*. Unesco. Paris.

Goldsmith, F B, Munton, R J C and Warren, A (1970)
'The Impact of Recreation on the Ecology and Amenity of Semi-natural Areas: Methods of Investigation Used in the Isles of Scilly'. *Biological Journal of the Linnean Society*. 2:4: December 1970:187–306.

Green, Brynmor H (1972)
'The Relevance of Seral Eutrophication and Plant Competition to the Management of Successional Communities'. *Biological Conservation*. 4:378–84. Analysis of sand dune and chalk downland dynamics.

Gresswell, R Kay (1953)
Sandy Shores in South Lancashire. Liverpool University Press. Geomorphology and coastal development.

Haas, J A and Steers, J A (1964)
'An Aid to Stabilisation of Sand Dunes: Experiments at Scolt Head Island'. *Geographical Journal*. 130:265–7. Early use of 'Unisol' latex emulsion.

Hawksworth, D L (ed) (1974)
The Changing Flora and Fauna of Britain. Academic Press. Systematics Association Special Volume No. 6.

Hepburn, I (1952)
Flowers of the Coast. Collins New Naturalist.

Hewett, D G (1970)
'The Colonization of Sand Dunes after Stabilization with Marram Grass (*Ammophila arenaria*)'. *Journal of Ecology*. 58:Nov 1970:653–68.

Hewett, D G (1973)
'Human Pressures on Soils in Coastal Areas'. *Welsh Soils Discussion Group Report*. 14:1973:50–62.

Hewett, D G (1985)
'Grazing and mowing as management tools on dunes' *Vegetatio* 62:441–447.

Hollis, G W (1931)
'Fixation of Shifting Sand'. *Journal of the Forestry Commission*. 10:23–4. Planting techniques.

Hudson, M (1967)
'The Biotic Effects of the Creation of Estuarine Barrages'. In Duffey (1967) qv.

Huxley, T (1967)
'Is Wildfowling Compatible with Conservation?'. In Duffey (1967) qv.

Jane, F W and White, D J B (1971)
'The Botany and Plant Ecology of Blakeney Point and Scolt Head Island'. In Steers, J A (ed). *Blakeney Point and Scolt Head Island*. National Trust.

Jones, W E (1974)
'Changes in the Seaweed Flora of the British Isles'. In Hawksworth (1974) qv.

Kirk, T R (1970)
'Hydraumatic Seeding'. In North Berwick Study Group (1970) qv.

Knox, A J (1974)
'The Agricultural Use of Machair'. In Ranwell (1974) qv.

Loftas, Tony (1972)
The Last Resource: Man's Exploitation of the Oceans. Penguin Pelican. Current trends and future problems in marine management.

Mason, Nicholas (1974)
Winterton Dunes National Nature Reserve, Little Tern Report, Breeding Season 1974. Nature Conservancy. Internal report.

Mather, A S and Ritchie, W (1977)
The Beaches of the Highlands and Islands of Scotland. Countryside Commission for Scotland. Summary of a series of area Beach Reports with management recommendations.

McCarthy, J (1970)
'East Lothian Dunes'. In North Berwick Study Group (1970) qv.

May, V (1985)
'The supply of sediment to sand dunes' in Doody (1985) qv.

Nash, Edward (1962)
Beach and Sand Dune Erosion Control at Cape Hatteras National Seashore: A Five Year Review (1956–1961). US Department of the Interior National Park Service. Methods of contouring, fencing and planting.

Natural Environment Research Council (1973)
Marine Wildlife Conservation. NERC. Publications Series 'B':5:January 1973. Threats to wildlife from public recreation and other coastal activities.

Nature Conservancy Council (1978)
The Natterjack Toad. NCC. Leaflet.

Nature Conservancy Council (1982)
The Conservation of Sand Dunes. NCC. Leaflet.

North Berwick Study Group (1970)
Dune Conservation 1970. East Lothian County Council. Report for the Dune Conservation Study Conference, 21–3 April 1970. Summary of practical work done on many sites in the UK.

Oosterveld, Peter (1985)
'Grazing in dune areas: the objectives of nature conservation and the aims of research for nature conservation management'. In Doody (1985) qv.

Perring, F H (1974)
'Changes in Our Native Vascular Plant Flora'. In Hawksworth (1974) qv.

Pethick, John (1984)
An Introduction to Coastal Morphology. Edward Arnold.

Phillips, C J (1975)
Review of Selected Literature on Sand Stabilisation. Department of Engineering, University of Aberdeen. Discussion of theory and practice of fencing etc. Extensive bibliography.

Pizzey, Jennifer M (1975)
'Assessment of Dune Stabilisation at Camber, Sussex, Using Air Photographs'. *Biological Conservation*. 7:1975:275–88. Case study of restoration of intensively used dune system.

Prestt, I, Cooke, A S and Corbett, K F (1974)
'British Amphibians and Reptiles'. In Hawksworth (1974) qv.

Ranwell, D S (1960)
'Newborough Warren, Anglesey II. Plant Associes and Succession Cycles of the Sand Dune and Dune Slack Vegetation'. *Journal of Ecology*. 48: February 1960: 117–41.

Ranwell, D S (1960a)
'Newborough Warren, Anglesey III. Changes in the Vegetation on Parts of the Dune System After the Loss of Rabbits by Myxomatosis'. *Journal of Ecology*. 48:June 1960: 185:95.

Ranwell, D S (1970)
'The Dune Environment'. In North Berwick Study Group (1970) qv.

Ranwell, D S (1972)
Ecology of Salt Marshes and Sand Dunes. Chapman and Hall. Outline of present state of

knowledge and suggestions for further research. Extensive bibliography.

Ranwell, D S (ed) (1972a)
The Management of Sea Buckthorn (Hippophae Rhamnoides L) on Selected Sites in Great Britain. Nature Conservancy, Coastal Ecology Research Station. Report of the Hippophae Study Group. Recommendations on uses and methods of control.

Ranwell, D S (ed) (1974)
Sand Dune Machair. Institute of Terrestrial Ecology, Natural Environment Research Council. Report of a seminar at the Coastal Ecology Research Station, Norwich. Development of machair and management response to increased pressure.

Ranwell, D S and Boar, Rosalind (1986)
Coast Dune Management Guide. Institute of Terrestrial Ecology, Natural Environment Research Council.

Ritchie, W (1970)
'Beaches of Sutherland'. In North Berwick Study Group (1970) qv.

Ritchie, W (1972)
'The Evolution of Coastal Sand Dunes'. *Scottish Geographical Magazine*. April 1972:19–35. The application of geomorphological survey techniques to problems of erosion and accretion.

Ritchie, W (1975)
'Environmental Problems Associated with a Pipeline Landfall in Coastal Dunes at Gruden Bay, Aberdeenshire, Scotland'. *Coastal Engineering*. 3:2568–79.

Roberts, E A and Venner, J P F (undated)
Braunton Burrows National Nature Reserve: Footpath Construction Trials. Nature Conservancy Council, South West Region. Duplicated.

Rothwell, Phil (1985)
'Management problems on Ainsdale Sand Dunes, NNR'. In Doody (1985) qv.

Schofield, J M (1967)
'Human Impact on the Fauna, Flora and Natural History of Gibraltar Point'. In Duffey (1967) qv.

Searle, Sidney A (1972)
Semi-permeable Windbreaks. Report of Harbour Conservancy. Duplicated.

Seaton, D (1968)
'Bornish Blow-Out: A Record of Co-operation in Overcoming Machair and Land Erosion'. *Scottish Agriculture*. Summer 1968.

Smith, Malcolm (1951) *The British Amphibians and Reptiles.* Collins New Naturalist.

Soper, Tony (1972) *The Shell Book of Beachcombing.* David and Charles. What to look for from bottles to whales.

Speight, M C D (1973) *Outdoor Recreation and Its Ecological Effects.* University College London. Discussion Papers in Conservation No. 4. Includes coastal erosion problems. Bibliography.

Steers, J A (1969) *The Sea Coast.* Collins New Naturalist. British coastal features, their development and variety.

Thomas, Gareth (1971) 'Gull Control and Reserve Management'. *Birds.* July/August 1971:246–50.

Thomas, Gareth and Richards, Penny (1977) 'Success for Tern Volunteers'. *Birds.* Spring 1977:60–1. Importance of full-time wardening of nest sites.

Trew, M J (1973) 'The Effects and Management of Trampling on Coastal Sand Dunes'. *Journal of Environmental Planning and Pollution Control.* 1:4:38–49. Amenity orientated.

Venner, J P F (1971) *The Eradication of Hippophae Rhamnoides L. from the Braunton Burrows Sand Dune System.* Senior Warden Project Report.

Warren Spring Laboratory (1972) *Oil Pollution of the Sea and Shore.* HMSO. Survey of remedies.

Watkin, E E (ed) (1973) *Ynyslas Nature Reserve Handbook.* Nature Conservancy and School of Biological Sciences, University College of Wales, Aberystwyth. Methods and examples of ecological studies on this site.

Whatmough, J (1985) 'Recreation management of sand dunes, Murlough Nature Reserve'. *Views* 3: Autumn 1985. The National Trust.

Wilcock, F A and Carter, R W G (1975) *Recreation Damage and Restoration of the Beach and Dune Environment in Northern Ireland.* School of Biological and Environmental Studies, New University of Ulster. Duplicated. Experience at Portrush, a dune system with limited sand supplies.

Wilcock, F A and Carter, R W G (undated) *An Environmental Approach to the Restoration of Badly Eroded Sand Dunes.* School of Biological and Environmental Studies, New University of Ulster. More on Portrush.

Wittering, W O (1974) *Weeding in the Forest.* HMSO. Forestry Commission Bulletin No. 68.

Yonge, C M (1949) *The Sea Shore.* Collins New Naturalist. Natural history of coastal marine life. Bibliography.

Glossary

Accretion   Process of sediment accumulation

Backdune   Dune inland of foredunes

Backshore   Shore between high water and coastal edge

Blowout   Wind-eroded area in sand surface

Community   Plants and/or animals living together under characteristic, recognisable conditions

Dominant winds   Winds of greatest effect on maritime accretion or erosion

Dune   Hill or ridge of wind-blown sand

Ecology   Study of how living things relate to their environment or surroundings

Ecosystem   The totality in which any living organism finds itself

Ecotone   Area between zones which may in itself constitute a zone with its own communities

Embryo dune   Small, often ephemeral sand mound on the backshore, which in a prograding system may develop into a new foredune

Fixed dune   Dune with a surface stabilised by vegetation

Foredune   Dune which lies nearest the sea

Foreshore   Shore between high and low water

Frontshore system   Dune system, usually prograding, which projects seaward from the main shoreline

Grey dune   Well-vegetated fixed dune with mosses, lichens, grasses and herbs

Habitat   The recognisable area or type of environment in which an organism normally lives

Hindshore System   Dune system which extends inland from the shoreline

Intertidal   Between high and low tide lines; legally, between high water mark spring tides and low water mean ordinary tides

Leach   The process by which percolating water removes nutrients from the soil

Littoral   Of or existing on a shore; intertidal

Machair   Maritime sand plain, typically calcareous (as found in northwest Scotland)

Marine   Of or pertaining to the sea

Maritime   Pertaining to the shore; legally, above high water mark spring tides

Mobile dune   Dune with an open plant community or bare of vegetation which tends to erode or move downwind

Natural succession   The process by which one community of organisms gives way to another in an orderly series from colonisers to climax

Neap tide   Tide of least range

Offset   Shoot that develops at the base of a plant which can root to form a new plant

Pan   In a salt marsh, a sunken area having poor drainage and highly saline soil

Prevailing winds   Winds of greatest frequency, often but not always the dominant winds

Prograding   Developing along or into open water

Rhizome   Fleshy root-ball from which roots and side shoots develop

Salt marsh   Intertidal area having characteristic vegetation adapated to saline soils and to periodic submergence in sea water

Slack   Area within dune system where the surface is at or near the ground water level

Spring tide   Tide of greatest range

Strandline   High tide line where debris collects

Sublittoral   Below the tides; legally, below low water mark mean ordinary tides

Thatching   Covering of brushwood laid down to protect dune grasses and help trap sand

Tiller (v)   To send forth shoots from the base; typically of grass which is mown or grazed

Water table   Level below which the soil is waterlogged

Yellow dune   Incompletely vegetated dune with bare sand exposed between plant stems

Zonation   The occurrence of communities in distinct geographical areas or zones

Index